Tacit Knowledge in Professional Practice

Researcher and Practitioner Perspectives

Tacit Knowledge in Professional Practice

Researcher and Practitioner Perspectives

Edited by

Robert J. Sternberg
Yale University

Joseph A. Horvath
Consulting Group, IBM Global Services

LEA
LAWRENCE ERLBAUM ASSOCIATES, PUBLISHERS
1999 Mahwah, New Jersey London

Lawrence Erlbaum Associates, Inc., Publishers
10 Industrial Avenue
Mahwah, NJ 07430

Cover design by Kathryn Houghtaling Lacey

Library of Congress Cataloging-in-Publication Data

Tacit knowledge in professional practice : researcher and practitioner perspectives / edited by Robert J. Sternberg and Joseph A. Horvath.
p. cm.
Includes bibliographical references and indexes.
ISBN 0-8058-2435-9 (cloth: alk. paper) — ISBN 0-8058-2436-7 (pbk. : alk. paper).
1. Tacit knowledge. 2. Cognition. 3. Professions. 4. Interdisciplinary approach to knowledge. I. Sternberg, Robert J. II. Horvath, Joseph A.
BF317.5.T33 1998
305.5'53—dc21 98-33524
CIP

Books published by Lawrence Erlbaum Associates are printed on acid-free paper, and their bindings are chosen for strength and durability.

Printed in the United States of America
10 9 8 7 6 5 4 3 2 1

This volume is dedicated to the memory of
Colonel Jeff McNally of the United States Army
—Commander, colleague, contributor, friend.
May he rest in peace.

Contents

Preface

TACIT KNOWLEDGE IN THE PROFESSIONS

Joseph A. Horvath
Consulting Group, IBM Global Services

> *We do not receive wisdom, we must discover it for ourselves, after a journey through the wilderness, which no one else can make for us, which no one can spare us, for our wisdom is the point of view from which we come at last to regard the world.*
>
> —*Marcel Proust*

People know more than they can tell. Personal knowledge is so thoroughly grounded in experience that it cannot be expressed in its fullness. In the last 30 years, the term *tacit knowledge* has come to stand for this type of human knowledge—knowledge that is bound up in the activity and effort that produced it.

The study of tacit knowledge has spanned several disciplines in the social sciences, and its provenance in an earlier, natural philosophy is extensive. Polanyi's (1973) philosophical treatise on personal knowledge, with its distinction between "focal knowledge" and "knowledge of subsidiaries," laid a theoretical foundation. Laboratory studies by Reber (see Reber, 1989) showed that knowledge of complex environmental patterns may be acquired without intention or awareness. Sternberg's investigations of tacit knowledge in the workplace—and his development of measurement instruments—helped to move tacit-knowledge research out of laboratory and into the lexicon of applied social science (see Sternberg, Wagner, Williams, & Horvath, 1995).

Although not explicitly framed in terms of tacit knowledge, Argyris' studies of defensive reasoning established the reality and consequences of unspoken knowledge within organizations (Argyris, 1990). Nelson and Winter's evolutionary theory of economic growth (Nelson & Winter, 1982) incorporated Polanyi's work on tacit knowledge into a knowledge-based theory of the firm. Working in the same tradition, Kogut and Zander (1992) showed how tacit knowledge—embedded in work routines and the ways in which labor is divided—affects the diffusion of innovation within firms and the appropriation of those innovations by competitors. Recently, tacit knowledge has become a hot topic among those interested in the new grounds of business competition. Following Drucker (1994), a great deal of work has focused on knowledge and learning as sources of competitive advantage. By studying a range of technology-intensive businesses, Leonard-Barton (1995) showed how the knowledge embedded in people, tools, and practices can develop within and sustain businesses. Nonaka and Takeuchi (1995) offered a model of organizational knowledge creation in which the socialization of individual, tacit knowledge drives a virtuous cycle of continuous innovation. A different approach was taken by Edvinsson and Malone (1997), who developed novel constructs and measures for evaluating the hidden intellectual capital of organizations. Finally, Davenport and Prusak (1998) took a pragmatic approach to the foregoing, asking how firms can work effectively with knowledge—to create an environment in which knowledge can flourish and yet be brought effectively to bear on key decisions.

PREMISES OF THE EDITED VOLUME

If much of the value-adding knowledge that resides within organizations is tacit, then new and powerful applications in the area of knowledge management and professions education are likely to require a deeper understanding of tacit knowledge as a psychological and social phenomenon. For example, can we identify patterns in the early job experiences of expert professionals? If so, we may be able to develop more effective proxies for those experiences and so move professionals more rapidly along the path to expertise. Can we identify subtypes of tacit knowledge, and, if so, can these subtypes be used to optimize or tune our approaches to knowledge management? Can we measure tacit knowledge, and, if so, can we adapt measurement approaches to the valuation of an organization's knowledge? If we are to advance on solutions to problems of knowledge elicitation, transfer, and measurement, then we need to get beyond the "hand waving" that characterizes most current discussions of tacit knowledge. That is, we must know more about tacit knowledge than that it is critical and ineffable. We need a more differentiated understanding of the broad range of phenomena that have come to be grouped under the umbrella term tacit knowledge.

To this end, the present volume is composed of chapters that, together, examine tacit knowledge across a range of professional and quasi-professional disciplines. Chapters address the tacit dimension of competent practice in law, management, medicine, military leadership, teaching, and sales. The hope, of course, is that by examining tacit knowledge in multiple contexts, we may begin to converge on a domain-independent model of its operation.

In addition, the present volume brings together both research voices and practitioner voices on the subject of tacit knowledge in the professions. Each section of the edited volume is composed of two chapters—one written by a distinguished practioner of the discipline in question, and one written by an established researcher who has studied the tacit aspects of competence in the discipline. As the chapters reflect, research contributors bring precision in the way in which concepts are operationalized—as well as a body of evidence based on programmatic study. Practitioners, for their part, bring a fresh and pragmatic perspective on the phenomena of "knowing more than we can tell." As the chapters reflect, they have stories to tell about how and why tacit knowledge is important to the development of professional competence.

This edited volume begins with a chapter by Marchant and Robinson that shows that tacit knowledge is central to effective legal practice, even in the prototypically codified domain of tax law. According to Marchant and Robinson, the essence of legal reasoning is "seeing through" the ambiguity inherent in legal rules by using previously decided cases to build an analogy. Such analogies (e.g., between decided cases and present cases) form the basis of all persuasive legal arguments. Chapter 2, by Spaeth, shows how poorly the statutory definition of legal competence (the "model rules") specifies the actual knowledge and skill requirements of legal practice. By repeatedly invoking a "reasonableness" standard, the model rules beg the question of how they are themselves to be applied and, in so doing, throw lawyers back on analogy, to prior examples of legal conduct deemed "reasonable."

In their chapter on tacit knowledge in military leadership (chap. 3), Horvath et al. focus on the stories that military officers tell about their experiences. The authors have found these stories useful in their research, both as a favored way of representing knowledge for transfer and as a point of leverage in efforts to measure tacit knowledge and validate its relationship to performance. The following chapter by Ulmer (chap. 4) highlights several of the difficulties inherent in such work. He argues persuasively that the Army has a "fundamental criterion problem" in that the evaluation of ultimate effectiveness is impossible outside the war zone. In recollecting people and events from his own distinguished career, he makes clear that the knowledge and judgment of the finest military leaders is quite difficult to disentangle from the character traits that predisposed them to listen and learn in the first place.

Chapter 5 by Patel, Arocha, and Kaufman, on medical knowledge examines, in some depth, the cognitive processes thought to underlie diagnostic expertise. Based on extensive research, the authors argue that tacit and explicit knowledge are separate in their underlying mechanism, but that the utilization of tacit knowledge depends critically on "well-formed biomedical knowledge structures." Novices reason deliberately from biomedical knowledge and, over time, become sensitive to the patterns of evidence and outcomes that tend to recur in their experience. In this way, reasoning processes become tuned to particular situations and, eventually, can operate outside of focal attention (i.e., tacitly). The following chapter, by Cimino (chap. 6), takes the reader into the examining room to show clearly how novice (i.e., student), intermediate (i.e., resident), and expert (i.e., attending) physicians might typically differ on the benchmark task of diagnosing the causes of chest pain. Notably, Cimino shows how the diagnostic reasoning of the novice is, at once, less focused than that of the intermediate and expert, yet more biased toward the confirmation of early hypotheses.

In his chapter on management (chap. 7), Argyris argues, deductively, that tacit knowledge is the primary basis for both effective managerial action and its deterioration. Drawing on decades of prior work, the author equates skill with "low requirement for deliberative thought" and, in so doing, shows how the very skill that makes managers effective under an existing "theory of action" can prevent them, and the organizations they serve, from learning effectively from their experience. Chapter 8, by Hatsopoulos and Hatsopoulos, presents an interesting marriage of scientific writing and executive recollection. The thesis around which the chapter is organized states that managers employ "dual processes" corresponding roughly to logic and intuition. The argument, supported by anecdotes from the long and distinguished career of the first author, is that managers are faced with the need to decide quickly and in the absence of complete information. As such, they must use intuition (based on accumulated tacit knowledge) to operate in advance of their own, logical, and explicit reasoning processes.

The most ambitious chapter (chap. 9), from a methodological perspective, is that of Wagner, Sujan, Sujan, Rashotte, and Sternberg, who report on a program of research investigating the nature and consequences of tacit knowledge in the sales profession. Using a measurement approach based on the identification of professional rules of thumb, Wagner et al. relate individual differences in measured tacit knowledge to indices of sales performance, and to conventional measures of verbal ability (a frequently used proxy for general mental ability). Readers will find relief from the rigors of this chapter in the one that follows, by Gregory. Drawing on a lifetime of (highly successful) salesmanship, the author reflects on the experiences and challenges that figured in his own professional development.

The final section of the edited volume, on education, begins with chapter 11 by Torff, which takes a perspective on the topic of tacit knowledge that is somewhat different from the other chapters, varied as they are. Drawing on a broad range of work in the constructivist tradition of social sciences, the author examines the tacit conceptions (or preconceptions) that teachers in training bring to their work. Following a careful exegesis of "folk pedagogy" and its consequences in the classroom, the author presents a program for moving teachers—and their students—beyond its limitations. The final substantive chapter in the volume, by Minstrell, is somewhat of a hybrid. Like the chapter by Cimino, it is authored by a practitioner whose practice has been informed by a study of cognitive educational theory. This final chapter addresses both the tacit knowledge of the professional (the teacher) and the tacit knowledge of the client (the student) whose preconceptions about the subject matter must be inferred and addressed if true learning is to occur.

We are grateful to Sai Durvasula for assistance with the preparation of this volume. Our contribution to the volume as editors and authors was supported by Contract MDA 903-92-K from the U.S. Army Research Institute.

REFERENCES

Argyris, C. (1990). *Overcoming organizational defenses*. Needham, MA: Allyn & Bacon.

Davenport, T., & Prusak, L. (1998). *Working knowledge: How organizations manage what they know*. Boston, MA: Harvard Business School Press.

Drucker, P. (1994). *The new realities*. New York: HarperBusiness.

Edvinsson, L., & Malone, M. (1997). *Intellectual capital*. New York: HarperBusiness.

Kogut, B., & Zander, U. (1992). Knowledge of the firm, combinative capabilities, and the replication of technology. *Organization Science*, *3*, 383–397.

Leonard-Barton, D. (1995). *Wellsprings of knowledge*. Boston, MA: Harvard Business School Press.

Nelson, R., & Winter, S. (1982). *An evolutionary theory of economic change*. Cambridge, MA: Harvard University Press.

Nonaka, I., & Takeuchi, H. (1995). *The knowledge creating company*. New York: Oxford University Press.

Polanyi, M. (1973). *Personal knowledge*. London: Routledge & Kegan Paul.

Reber, A. (1989). Implicit learning and tacit knowledge. *Journal of Experimental Psychology: General*, 118, 219–235.

Sternberg, R., Wagner, R., Williams, W., & Horvath, J. (1995). Testing common sense. *American Psychologist*, *50*(11), 901–912.

PART ONE

LAW

CHAPTER ONE

Is Knowing the Tax Code All It Takes to Be a Tax Expert? On the Development of Legal Expertise

Garry Marchant
University of Connecticut

John Robinson
University of Texas at Austin

Is a legal expert someone who knows the law? Knowing the law would seem to be a good starting point, but clearly, when choosing a lawyer, we look for much more than this. After all, clients want a lawyer who can win for them, but winning involves much more than knowing the law. One cannot rely on rules alone, because in the law rules such as statutes and regulations are insufficiently well defined, and thus the legal expert must resort to other sources of legal authority—primarily previously decided authorities to elaborate and explain the application of the law. This is not undesirable, because the law must be fluid and adaptive, bending as social and political circumstances demand.

As Judge Spaeth points out in the companion chapter to this one (chap. 2), no matter how codified a particular area of the law becomes, understanding and analyzing the legal principles relevant to a particular client's situation remains dependent on tacit knowledge acquired through experience and observation. This dependence on tacit knowledge is true, even though the profession tries to minimize its role. There are courses at law schools on trial advocacy, legal research, and legal reasoning. These courses ultimately fall short, because there is no agreement even among the most experienced practitioners as to the single best way to analyze a problem or develop a legal argument. And so, in the end, the legal profession, like most other professions, relies on the ad hoc nature of experience to guide junior members of the profession in the development of their expertise and competence as legal practitioners.

Legal expertise is then defined as the ability gained from experience to understand and apply the rules, statutes, and legal principles to a novel problem by using previously decided authorities to build a legal argument. The lawyer must be able to determine the critical factors from the facts and issues presented by the client. Then they must build an argument, with the strongest possible support for the client. To win, the argument should be based on all available authority that supports the client's point of view and counters an opposition's point of view, without giving the opponent any opening to counter the original argument. Knowing the law is only a small part of this process; the expert lawyer must also be able to rank available precedent as to strength and appropriateness and identify and counter an opponent's arguments. Legal reasoning is thus by nature dependent on the creative use of analogy to weave arguments that apply a favorable legal principle to a new and often diverse set of circumstances.

The legal environment makes it difficult to develop these skills and knowledge. First, only a small percentage of the legal arguments prepared by lawyers ever makes it to court. The courtroom is the only objective arbiter of legal argument, and the only place where the strength of an argument is tested, its weaknesses and strengths identified, and the outcome observed. But, of course, clients would prefer disputes be resolved without resorting to the court, so often disputes are negotiated and settlements are made. Such resolution may occur partly to avoid the cost of further conflict or based on the strength of the relative arguments of the opposing counsel. Lawyers must therefore rely not on objective outcome feedback, but on peer review, for much of their practical education. Additionally, the adversarial nature of the legal system focuses lawyers on winning for their client—on being an advocate. Although this may seem like a desirable systemic attribute, playing the role of an advocate focuses practitioners' thinking on supporting their client and thus may distract them from considering alternative points of view and possibilities. Thus, the adversarial process may act to limit them to the range of possibilities in developing legal arguments. Perhaps the outstanding lawyer is the one who looks beyond the authority that supports his or her client's point of view and, in doing so, discovers authorities that enrich and enhance his or her argument in ways unanticipated by the opposition.

The tacit nature of legal expertise has significant implications for the education of legal professionals, the management of a legal practice, and the quality of legal services. One of the key elements of legal expertise is the ability to look at a sequence of authorities and identify the principle the court has in mind based on their opinions. Legal education must focus on the development of inductive skills rather than deductive skills. Evidence suggests that using authorities to allow for the induction of principles is effective particularly when the authorities are atypical rather than typical exemplars. Also, in managing a legal practice, one of the most critical decisions a partner makes is which case to give to which associate, and associates are painfully aware of the resulting opportunities to learn and develop their expertise as a result. Because learning cannot occur frequently from feedback, peer review is used as a mechanism both for ensuring quality and as the means for mentoring and guiding the inexperienced lawyer.

IS A LEGAL EXPERT ONE WHO KNOWS THE LAW?

In legal settings, rules such as statutes and regulations are often ambiguous or indeterminate in their application to fact situations (Hart, 1961). This characteristic open texture of legal rules is useful, because legal rules must be fluid and adaptive so that they may survive for many years. In order to apply a rule to a specific situation, a lawyer must use a previous decided case. Lawyers have no choice but to rely on analogy to forge their position and interpretations. Legal rules are not typically well defined, nor are there intermediate rules that define the elements of these legal rules well enough so that a lawyer can determine the use of a general rule in a specific fact situation (Ashley, 1988). Even in highly codified areas such as taxation, the expert must resort to tax court authorities and IRS rulings to interpret and apply the code. Knowing the details of the tax code is insufficient to solve client problems; the legal expert must interpret how the code applies for a given fact situation by looking at how it and other similar or related provisions have been interpreted.

For example, Internal Revenue Code (IRC) Section 1033 allows nonrecognition of gains on certain involuntary conversions if the proceeds of the conversion are reinvested in "similar" property. To determine the scope of what constitutes "similar" property, the tax expert might look at court opinions that decide authorities under the auspices of IRC Section 1031, which allows deferral of gains and losses when property is exchanged for "like kind" property. An analogy between these two statutes is possible, because both statutes allow deferral if property is replaced with equivalent property. Thus, even the diverse and highly codified area of tax law abounds with potential applications of analogy. It is the area of taxation to which we confine the following discussion and draw examples, because it is the ideal extreme case, so codified and practiced in such diverse settings by lawyers and nonlawyers alike that to the person on the street it is the area of the law least likely to depend on tacit knowledge. Yet, as we show, an effective tax practice is very much dependent on tacit knowledge for analysis, judgment, and the development of legal expertise.

Legal Reasoning and Analysis in the Tax Domain

The legal task environment, and particularly the area of taxation, is rule based. Statutes are fixed by legislative enactment, but their application is an open question based on an understanding of the language used in the statute. Thus, there are two types of tax authorities that may be brought to bear in legal reasoning:

1. Tax statutes.
2. Interpretations and applications of the statutes in Treasury Regulations, court decisions, and IRS rulings.

The analysis of these authorities leads to the interpretation of the statutes and the selection of an appropriate tax treatment. The method of analysis and reasoning is an iterative procedure (see Fig. 1.1), in which the practi-

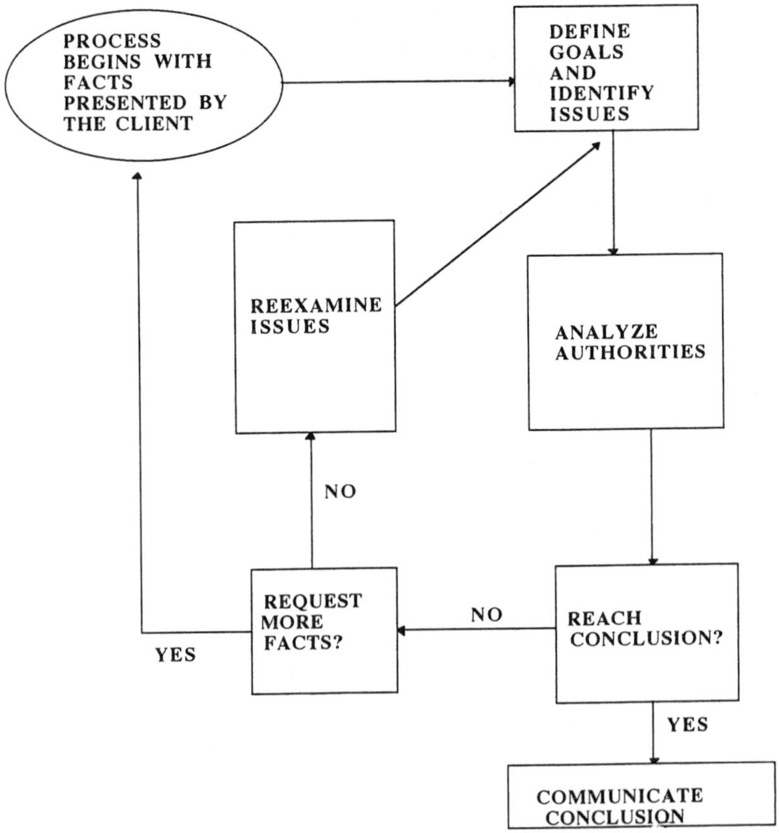

FIG. 1.1. The process of legal reasoning.

tioner identifies the goal or objective, evaluates the available authorities, and returns to request more facts or identify new issues before reaching any conclusions (Marchant et al., 1989).

The legal reasoning process comprises four steps (Buchanan & Headrick, 1970). In the first step, the practitioner must develop and evaluate the goal of the analysis based on the information provided by the client. The second step involves the use of other instances to identify the relevant facts in the client's story and to rank the importance of the issues. The third step is the selection of the appropriate treatment from the set of statutes and authorities that can be applied to a fact scenario. Finally, the fourth step involves the use of analogy: When, as is frequently the case, a situation with identical facts cannot be found, an analogy to either the facts or the treatment is used (Buchanan & Headrick, 1970; Gardner, 1987; Levi, 1949; MacCormick, 1978). Thus, legal reasoning is dependent on the use of analogy, because analogy is the basis for comparing and evaluating authorities and thereby interpreting and applying the statutes. Two general strategies can be identified in the tax domain that utilize these four basic steps of legal reasoning. These strategies—compliance and planning—define the parameters of the cognitive processes inherent in legal reasoning in the tax domain.

The Compliance Strategy. The first strategy, compliance, emphasizes the interpretation of both facts and the relevant law for the benefit of the client (Buchanan & Headrick, 1970), and consists of the following basic steps:

1. Specify an objective.
2. Identify relevant facts.
3. Search for authorities that apply a rule that leads to the desired consequences, given the identified facts.
4. Evaluate and compare the facts and legal issues in these authorities. Test the facts against the given application of the rule.
5. Accept, reject, or modify the application of the rule.

This process is appropriate in the compliance setting, where the transactions are already completed (Black, 1981).

Consider the following example of a compliance problem, which illustrates the inductive framework of legal reasoning in the tax domain. Suppose that the practitioner is presented with a client who has made support payments to a spouse before the issuance of a divorce decree. Depending on his or her expertise, the practitioner may draw on his or her knowledge of the tax laws to identify the relevant issue as the deductibility of the payments as alimony under IRC Section 71. However, because some payments preceded the issuance of the divorce decree, the practitioner may have found it necessary to consult the tax authorities to ascertain if all of the payments qualified for deduction. As the practitioner analyzed the authorities, he or she may have also found it necessary to inquire about additional facts, such as whether any written agreement existed prior to the issuance of the divorce decree and whether the client was living apart from his spouse. All of this information is sufficient to establish an immediate goal of generating an opinion as to the proper tax treatment of alimony paid before a divorce decree has been issued.

The facts and the practitioner's knowledge may not provide the practitioner with enough information for the specific type of situation to be identified and an opinion proposed. The practitioner's knowledge and the facts provided by the client form a basis for the practitioner's mental representation of the current problem. This knowledge representation forms a mental model of the problem, which the practitioner uses to move toward a solution. Mental models are made up of bundles of knowledge organized into sets of associated knowledge categories at various levels of abstraction. These categories form expectations about the client's scenario based on the assumed relationships between categories. These expectations can be overridden by specific information, but otherwise they provide the best guess as to the probable solution to the problem (Minsky, 1975). The categories that represent the practitioner's current mental model might include the general-level category "divorce and alimony," a midlevel category relating to "separation agreements," and the active goal of "determining the deductibility of the payments." No specific level information has been identified yet, and so none is included in the mental model of the current legal problem. This representation is a subset of the legal professional's domain-specific knowledge. Domain-specific knowledge of the legal professional would include basic concepts, procedural skills, and contextual attributes (Anderson, Marchant, & Robinson, 1989), and forms a critical component of the professional's expertise (Chiesi, Spilich, & Voss, 1979).

For the purpose of this example, assume that there are four possible specific categories that might lead to a solution: oral agreement, written agreement, retroactive decree, and no agreement. In this case, the practitioner's preferred interpretation of the facts is that a written agreement exists, because the client may then deduct the payments. But this cannot be confirmed, given the current state of the practitioner's knowledge. This current state is identified by two conditions. The first condition is that there are predecree support payments, and the second condition is that no solution can be confirmed. These conditions combined lead the practitioner to request more information about the agreement from the client. For the purpose of illustration, assume that the situation is relatively unambiguous and that the proper tax treatment is straightforward once the type of agreement is identified. The client might indicate, in response to the request for more information, that the agreement was oral and that no written document existed prior to the issuance of the divorce decree. This response results in additional input from the client that gives the specific category of *oral agreement,* the support necessary for its inclusion in the practitioner's mental model of the problem. Because this specific category is goal relevant, the lawyer's mental model now moves toward problem resolution.

The inclusion of the goal-relevant category, oral agreement, prompts the revision of the current mental model based on the new knowledge represented by the features of that category. The combination of this knowledge with the goal of generating an opinion about the proper tax treatment of the alimony leads to the generation of the response that alimony is not deductible. The combination of the generated response and the goal-relevant category also leads to the production of expectations about future outcomes, such as that the response will lead to higher taxes or will lower the risk of an audit by the IRS. These expectations could also be revised, based on observed future events, such as an IRS audit. This process allows professionals to learn and revise their rules and beliefs on the basis of outcomes.

The Planning Strategy. The second basic research strategy, emphasizing planning and risk assessment, concerns the recommending of actions that satisfy the client's goals while avoiding unfavorable consequences (Buchanan & Headrick, 1970). The three stages of the planning strategy are:

1. Identify possible actions for client.
2. Match facts and generalizations from authorities with the possible fact scenarios generated in the first stage, and determine potential risk.
3. Predict the likelihood of success for possible fact scenarios, and rank order alternatives.

This strategy varies from compliance in that the facts are controllable over some range of alternatives. These alternatives meet a broad set of objectives, including business objectives as well as a favorable legal outcome. The planning strategy corresponds to the tax planning process, which is described by Black (1981) as "an open fact situation where tax practitioners assess alternative tax strategies for structuring contemplated events" (p. 301).

Consider the following example of an open fact tax research problem. Suppose that the practitioner is approached by a client who intends to incorporate his or her existing business by contributing the assets of the business to a new corporation in exchange for stock. Depending on his or her expertise, the practitioner may suggest the issuance of debt in addition to the stock or, alternatively, the election of Subchapter S status. The practitioner recognizes the potential of double taxation of the business's profits and assumes that the client wishes to avoid it. The principal advantage of debt is that the payment of interest to the client would be deductible by the corporation, whereas dividend payments are not. A Subchapter S election more or less avoids the corporate tax.

In terms of cognitive processes, the appropriate knowledge is retrieved based on the scenario presented by the client. The client-provided scenario leads the practitioner to identify as the relevant goal the maximization of after-tax income within the corporate form. This generated goal then directs, within the practitioner's mental model, the search for goal-relevant knowledge and the generation of plausible alternatives. Based on the goal of maximizing after-tax income, the tax expert will retrieve the various knowledge categories related to incorporation. The expectations related to these categories will provide a basis for judgments as to taxability, depending on the alternative scenarios for incorporating a business. This set of expectations for incorporating a business includes a number of plausible alternatives, including Subchapter S election and the use of debt in the capital structure. Once a goal-satisfying alternative is found, the practitioner's mental model will generate expectations, based on the identified alternative, that will form the tax advice to the client.

Assume that a Subchapter S election is the strongest goal-relevant alternative and forms the basis of the tax practitioner's mental model used to generate expected consequences of incorporation. The use of the Subchapter S election category allows the practitioner to conclude that this alternative minimizes taxes and thus meets the goal of maximizing after-tax income of the business. The practitioner will then use the current mental model, based on his or her knowledge of a Subchapter S election and the goal of maximizing the after-tax income of the business, to generate a set of expectations as to the taxability of this corporate form and the constraints imposed by using this election. This planning scenario is communicated to the client as the best alternative given the provided information.

The tax practitioner's current knowledge could be modified if additional information were provided by the client. Suppose that the client indicated that he or she wished to issue a second class of stock to relatives. This additional information would necessitate a revision of the practitioner's mental model, because one of the constraints in electing Subchapter S is that the corporation have only one class of stock [IRC Section 1361(b)]. The practitioner will search at a more detailed level to ascertain under what circumstances a Subchapter S election is consistent with the existence of two classes of stock. Relevant authorities and cases are identified, so that the mental model may be revised to fit the new goal. The appropriate authority is selected through a process of rule competition. Rule competition is a process by which knowledge is filtered, so that only the knowledge that best fits the client's scenario is added to the mental model of the problem.

The authorities selected are determined by their relative strength, based in great part on how often they have been used in the past, and by the degree to which they match the authority to the client's scenario. The selection of an appropriate authority requires the comparison and evaluation of existing authorities with the presented or prospective facts. In the situation where no authority is specifically on point, the practitioner must resort to analogy to reach a conclusion. In the legal domain this is by far the most frequent occurrence, and so the institutionalization of analogy in legal reasoning as the rule of *stare decisis*.

Analogy and the Analysis of Legal Authorities

One of the essential components of legal reasoning is the comparison of the facts and issues in legal authorities, such as previously adjudicated cases with prospective or actual fact situations. This comparison is particularly important where the application of the law is ambiguous, because it will lead to the use of analogy to generate a solution to the current problem based on legal authorities. As Einhorn and Hogarth (1982) pointed out, analogies provide a model of a problem, thereby directing attention to a specific set of features. Analogical reasoning is a comparison of the structure of complex systems. An analogy exists when the relationships of two systems, from different domains, are the same, even though the objects of the systems are different (Gentner, 1982). For example, consider the scientific analogy used to explain atomic theory. To explain the structure of the atom and the relationship of electrons to the nucleus of the atom, physicists made an analogy to the structure of the solar system with the planets rotating around the sun. Sternberg (1977) argued that we "reason analogically whenever we make a decision about something new in our experience by drawing a parallel to something old" (p. 353). Sternberg simply highlighted the practical relevance of analogical reasoning in our everyday experience. The use of analogical reasoning can be seen in the interpretation of metaphor, the construction of new scientific models, the making of predictions and diagnoses, and in any situation that requires a novel problem solution (Gick & Holyoak, 1983). Legal reasoning is such a situation when the application of the statutes is unclear.

The usefulness of an analogy depends on recognizing the "significant similarity" (Holland, Holyoak, Nisbett, & Thagard, 1986, p. 287) between the source of the analogy, such as a previously adjudicated case, and the problem requiring solution. Holland et al. indicated that often the role of analogy is to make situations that appear unrelated seem more similar by a process of selectively abstracting from the appropriate elements contained in the source of the analogy. As an example, consider the goals of the radiation and military problems used by Gick and Holyoak (1983). For the military problem the goal is "capture fortress with army," and for the radiation problem the goal is "destroy tumor with ray." Both of these goals are abstracted to "overcome target with force." This abstraction maps the similarities in the relations of the two analogs, and reduces their differences.

Consider a more ambiguous version of the alimony example discussed earlier. Suppose the client responds to the tax professional's request for more information by indicating that, although no "written agreement" exists, an agreement was made on videotape. Whether the videotape will qualify as a "written agreement" under IRC Section 71 is uncertain. The specific category "written agreements" has no goal-relevant information and, therefore, no solution is possible. To arrive at a solution requires the modification of the rule about the validity of agreements contained in the current mental model. In legal reasoning, comparing and evaluating decided cases through the use of analogy is the primary means for the modification of rules during problem solving.

In this case, the practitioner might attempt to analogize the treatment of a videotape agreement under the tax law to the treatment accorded a videotape contract under the statute of frauds. This analogy would lead to the generation of the rule that a videotaped agreement may be evidence of an agreement, and, thus, the alimony may be deductible. As before, this solution would also lead to the generation of expectations about its implications for the client, which could be revised on litigation of the case. In addition, a new rule has been developed and associated in the practitioner's memory with unwritten agreements in alimony.

Gick and Holyoak (1983) described analogical problem solving as a five-step process:

1. Representation of an analog in memory.
2. Recognition of the potential analogical relationship.
3. Initial mapping of the base analog to the target problem.
4. Extension of the mapping by constructing new knowledge about the target, and thereby completing the analogy.
5. Testing of the hypothesized solution.

Gentner (1982) described analogies as "structure mappings" where identical relations among different objects are mapped. This mapping process may, as Gick and Holyoak (1983) indicated, involve features of the analogs that are not explicit. Completing most analogies involves a search for an alternate view of the source of the analogy. This alternate view of the source is where the relations of the problem being solved are matched to the source (Schon, 1979). The propositions of both the source and the problem must be decomposable into identities and differences (Tversky, 1977; Tversky & Gati, 1978), so that the identities may be used to generate the analogy.

As Gick and Holyoak (1983) showed, an analogy may be either a success or a failure. A successful analogy has two components: identities and structure-preserving differences. A structure-preserving difference is a difference associated with an identity. For example, consider the mapping of the components of these two goals: "capture" from the military problem, and "destroy" from the radiation problem. "Capture" and "destroy" are mapped into the concept "overcome"—the identity within the two goal components. The portion of the components not contained in the concept "overcome" is the structure-preserving difference. This difference does not affect the cause–effect relations within the two analogs.

A failed mapping also has two components: structure-violating differences and indeterminate correspondence. Structure-violating differences are differences between the source of the analogy and the problem that lead to failure of the analogy when the causal links of the source of the analogy are altered. For example, if a more specific level of the military and radiation problems were analyzed, the role of the army and the rays would not correspond. A direct attack on the fortress endangers the army, but a direct attack on the tumor does not endanger the rays. This lack of role parallelism is a structure-violating difference (Gick & Holyoak, 1983). Indeterminate correspondence occurs when the propositions of the source of the analogy cannot be conclusively related to the propositions of the problem. For example, the solutions to both the military problem and the radiation problem require the assumption that the forces of the small groups of soldiers and the lower-intensity rays, when combined, are equivalent in intensity to the army as a whole and a single high-intensity ray. This assumption is not explicitly stated in either of the problems. Indeterminate correspondence occurs when this type of assumption cannot be made—the analogy is incomplete and fails.

To illustrate this analogical process in the legal setting, consider two such seemingly disparate tax laws as IRC Section 267 (Losses, Expenses, and Interest With Respect to Transactions Between Related Parties) and IRC Section 1091 (Deferral of Losses Associated With "Wash Sales"). A goal of Section 267 is to "disallow losses on sales between related parties." A goal of Section 1091 is to "disallow losses where a purchase is closely associated with a purchase of substantially identical securities." Both of these goals can be abstracted to "defer recognition until a bona fide disposition occurs." Thus, although these two code sections differ in many respects, a decided court case regarding one of these code sections may be useful in resolving an issue regarding the other.

This discussion of the use of analogy in legal reasoning has thus far ignored the adversarial nature of the legal process. Unlike other areas, where analogy is a common form of reasoning, in the legal domain the use of analogy is modified by the lawyer's role as advocate. This forces the practitioner to always consider the desired outcome of his or her client when using analogies to analyze authorities.

Analogy and the Construction of Legal Arguments

Legal reasoning ultimately is the construction of arguments to justify a legal position. These positions are frequently based on decided court cases. Arguments in support of a position are constructed by drawing analogies to prior authorities won by parties in similar situations. Authorities that suggest contrary conclusions are distinguished by pointing out dissimilarities in the underlying legal issues (Ashley, 1988). As noted earlier, this use of analogous precedent in the construction of legal argument is formalized in common law by the principle of *stare decisis,* in which courts follow previously decided authorities in resolving current similar disputes.

Given the adversarial nature of the legal process, when constructing a legal argument the advocate must decide which features of an authority are important in determining the outcome, and what relationship those features have to features in the problem situation. To justify a favorable outcome, the advocate compares the problem to a prior case that resulted in an outcome that, given the current situation, the client would find desirable. In addition, the advocate distinguishes the problem from prior authorities with unfavorable outcomes and argues that the decision should not be made in the same way as those authorities. To strengthen the argument against the use of particular prior authorities as precedent, the advocate uses counterexamples that are similar to the unfavorable authorities but have favorable outcomes. Thus, the important characteristics of a case for use as precedent in constructing a legal argument are the similarities and differences of the case with the problem situation and the outcome of the case (Ashley, 1988).

The critical factors in constructing a legal argument are the identification and application of authorities whose combination of similarities, differences, and outcomes provide the most persuasive argument. Analogical reasoning integrates knowledge from authorities and applies that knowledge to a new situation. To make an analogy, one first represents the current problem and associated knowledge in a mental model. This model is used to direct a search for an analogous case. Correspondences between selected elements of the analogous case and the problem are built, and a position is established (Novick, 1988). However, the number of possible correspondences is immense, so mechanisms are required to help the practitioner identify the more worthwhile correspondences and ignore the highly improbable ones. Holyoak and Thagard (1989) suggested that three factors are used to govern the analogical process: structural consistency, semantic similarity, and pragmatic centrality. These factors act as constraints on the process by limiting the number of potential correspondences considered.

Structural consistency restricts analogies to situations with a high degree of similarity between the source of the analogy and the problem. This constraint pushes the analogical process toward an emphasis on surface similarity. Semantic similarity focuses the analogical process on abstracting from the source of the analogy and the problem those relations that they both share. This constraint widens the range of possible sources of the analogy by allowing analogies based on similar relations, rather than just identical relations as imposed by the structural consistency constraint. Pragmatic centrality, the final constraint, emphasizes the importance of explicit and implicit knowledge about the purpose for which the analogy is being constructed. Pragmatic considerations encourage analogies that are initially assumed to hold or are considered so significant that they must be found because they are essentially to the purpose for which the analogy is being constructed.

In constructing an argument based on analogy, considerations of pragmatic centrality would be expected to dominate other factors. For instance, Kunda (1987) showed that motivation to attain a particular outcome for an argument will bias the assessment of similarity. However, Holyoak and Thagard (1989) argued that although pragmatic considerations will guide the analogical reasoning process, these considerations cannot override the constraint on forming an analogy imposed by the similarity of the object and relations of the source of the analogy to the problem. Thus, although pragmatic considerations may act to induce analogical reasoning, the use of the analogy is constrained by structural consistency and semantic similarity. The interaction of semantic similarity and pragmatic centrality are particularly important in the legal setting because of the adversarial nature of the process.

In a series of experiments, Marchant, Robinson, Anderson, and Schadewald (1991, 1993) examined the use of analogy to build an effective argument in tax law. In the earlier study, both experts and novices were placed in two conditions. In one condition there was no available source for the analogy to a given problem, and in the second condition there was an available source for the analogy to a given problem. The number of subjects using the source of the analogy to solve the presented problem was measured in each condition. This study found that experts had a distinct advantage over novices in using knowledge from a previously decided case. However, experts with a great deal of experience saw their performance decline, apparently because they had proceduralized the rule in this situation and did not look any further. The tax environment may reward the use of efficient but ineffective strategies that satisfy the client because the client is rarely audited. This lack of feedback perpetuates a strategy that is inappropriate, but successful because it meets the client demand for minimal tax. These results are consistent with Frensch and Sternberg (1989), and suggest that even in the legal environment, proceduralization may occur that blinds the expert to the different or unusual circumstances that might occur.

In Marchant et al. (1993), pragmatic centrality was manipulated by giving subjects either a source for the analogy consistent with the client's desired outcome or a source inconsistent with the client's desired outcome. Tax experts displayed a greater rate of transfer than did novices. Pragmatic considerations significantly affected what information was transferred. Experts who were more sensitized to client needs engaged in a very different process than did novices who were less influenced by pragmatic concerns than by overall validity of argument. Many of the differences between experts and novices in tax practice can be attributed to differing strategies used to support desired outcomes rather than differences in knowledge representations. For example, the results of this study indicate that experts were using a justification strategy focused on arguing for the outcome their client desired, whereas novices used a validation strategy searching for analogies that provided the strongest argument, whether or not they supported the client's desired outcome.

More recently, Krawczyk, Marchant, and Robinson (1996) examined tax experts' ability to select the appropriate legal authorities. In this study, experts were asked to select from potential sources of an analogy in solving a tax problem. These potential sources differed in the degree to which they were similar to the tax problems, both on the surface and structurally. A second experiment also manipulated whether the outcome of the potential sources did or did not match the client's desired outcome for the tax problem. Krawczyk et al. found that experts, in selecting authorities, focus almost exclusively on surface similarity, even when there is an authority with a high degree of structural consistency. In selecting an authority, the semantic similarity dominates the process; in the mapping of analogs to make the argument, the structural consistency is dominant. This counterbalances the selection stage. In all instances, this behavior is moderated but not overridden by pragmatic considerations. These studies all suggest that the source of legal expertise is not which legal rule to apply, but rather the subtle melding of semantic similarity, structural consistency, and pragmatic considerations to generate the precedent that makes the strongest argument.

The Impact of the Legal Environment on the Development of Legal Expertise

The legal environment provides only limited opportunities for getting feedback on an argument. This is because many arguments will never reach court, which is the final arbiter of the success or failure of a legal argument. This is particularly true in the tax context, where arguments are rarely inspected through an audit. Without feedback, lawyers must often rely on peer review, which is a subjective form of feedback. Courtrooms are great opportunities for learning the strengths and weaknesses of an argument and how an opponent uses those strengths and weaknesses. Without feedback about process and outcome, learning is very difficult. Thus, the experiences a novice lawyer has in court are quite important, because there may be few such opportunities.

The other difficulty of the legal environment is its adversarial nature, which focuses lawyers on their role as advocates and thus narrows their flexibility and the range of possible precedents they examine. This bias may lead to similarity judgments that are stretched beyond reasonableness because of the need to justify an argument. Narrowing of focus means that lawyers may find the authorities that support the desired position, but they may not be suitably familiar with all the other related authorities that may be the source of their opponent's argument or their opponent's counter to their argument. Being focused to this extent in this context means that the lawyer may be surprised, and no lawyer wants to be surprised in the courtroom. The opportunity to learn and develop the skills of an expert lawyer is impeded by this framing of a lawyer's thinking as a combatant in the quest to win.

Instructional Strategies for the Development of Legal Expertise

Two different strategies may be used to teach tax law: by cases, and by rules. Law schools have almost exclusively adopted the case-based approach, but schools of accounting have, in preparing tax practitioners, adopted a more rule-based approach. Anderson, Marchant, and Robinson (1989) examined the impact of these two strategies, as well as a hybrid "examples" strategy, on student performance. They found that both the cases strategy and the examples strategy outperformed the rules strategy. In addition, performance in the case and examples conditions was even more enhanced if the authorities used in instruction were atypical rather than typical exemplars. Atypical exemplars that show how an underlying principle can be stretched are more informative of the nature of the principle than is the standard case. In a second study by Anderson, Marchant, Robinson, and Schadewald (1990), it was again found that a case strategy was the superior strategy, particularly when the instructional case was used to illustrate a principle that was inconsistent with existing knowledge. Preexisting knowledge had a strong impact on the performance of these students. This result also suggests the importance of understanding how a sense for the variability of legal principles applied across contexts interacts with specific authorities used to facilitate performance.

DISCUSSION

Knowing the detail of the law is not enough to make a legal expert. The skills of a legal expert have more to do with identifying, prioritizing, and utilizing analogies based on previously decided authorities to build an argument that at once supports strongly a clients position and blocks any possible counter-argument. Developing this tacit knowledge is the key to legal competence and to success as a lawyer, yet it can only be gained through experience and engagement in the adversarial process. Much of what is learned in law school is the language and principles of practice that are the necessary starting point for a lawyer. But in order to develop competence, the lawyer—to be successful—must use the lessons of experience, the knowledge gained from mentors, and observation of the legal system in action.

What is the characteristic structure of tacit knowledge? In legal reasoning, the tacit knowledge is not structured around the formal rules of the law but rather around the experiences of applying authorities to problems. The tacit knowledge of a lawyer is structured around the identification of key facts and the search for appropriate precedent using search mechanisms based on similarity, consistency, and pragmatic considerations. How does a lawyer know which facts are critical, out of all the facts recounted by a client? Once the key facts are found, then the lawyer must search for authorities similar enough to the problem to be supported as acceptable precedent and at the same time supportive of the position desired by the client. Throughout this process, the lawyer must keep uppermost in his or her thoughts the potential actions of the adversary.

How is tacit knowledge related to the intention to learn and awareness of having learned? Many lawyers will recount how they learned more from one afternoon in the back of the courtroom than they did in an entire semester of law school. Yet, when asked what they learned, they cannot describe it satisfactorily. The use of moot courts by law schools is recognition of the value of experience and feedback. On the other hand, within a law firm there are few opportunities for objective feedback other than peer review. Peer review has two functions within the firm. One is as a quality control mechanism designed to protect the firm and ensure consistency of service to clients. The second function is as a formalization of the mentoring relationship between senior expert lawyers and their junior associates. Yet there has been no evaluation of the benefit to novices of this type of mentoring relationship. Additionally, partners are not rewarded for how well they transfer what they know to novices. Indeed, in many professional services organizations such as law firms, the incentive is for individuals to not share what they know and thus further protect their economic value to the organization. The haphazard nature of this process makes it even more difficult for the novice lawyer to acquire the tacit knowledge so necessary for the development of expertise. Associates understand the limitations of the environment, and struggle in their early years of practice to work with the partners who are the better mentors. They also try to be given the assignments that will afford them the best opportunity for learning with a minimal risk of serious failure.

What are the implications for professional education, and particularly of structuring the job experience? Both for educators of lawyers and for managers of law firms, there are many implications. Firms must balance quality concerns with providing valuable learning experiences. Evidence suggests that unusual or atypical situations may provide a greater learning opportunity for the lawyer than will standard situations. Firms are trying to use technology to leverage expertise through expert systems and shared databases, but they must clearly consider how this technology interacts with the tacit knowledge that defines legal competence. Much of the technological change may, in fact, be reducing rather than increasing effectiveness. For example, a number of firms have started using computer-based analysis systems for finding and analyzing prior authorities and rulings. They have found much resistance among practitioners who feel confined by the one-page screen and prefer their old method of using multiple volumes of authorities, which they may have open all at once. Increasingly, there is the use of internships and other practice-based experiences in the time students are at law school. Is this enough? The rate of derailment and outplacement for high-potential associates at the top law firms might suggest no. Perhaps there should be a return to the legal apprenticeship of old. In this system, mentoring is formalized and performance of the mentor is directly measured by the success of his or her apprentices. Additionally, students learn in a practice context, developing their tacit knowledge in a somewhat more deliberate manner.

REFERENCES

Anderson, U., Marchant, G., & Robinson, J. (1989). Instructional strategies and the development of tax expertise. *The Journal of the American Taxation Association, 10,* 7–23.

Anderson, U., Marchant, G., Robinson, J., & Schadewald, M. (1990). Selection of instructional strategies in the presence of prior related knowledge. *Issues in Accounting Education, 5,* 41–58.

Ashley, K. (1988). Arguing by analogy in law: A case-based model. In D. Helman (Ed.), *Analogical reasoning: Perspectives of artificial intelligence, cognitive science and philosophy* (pp. 205–224). Dordrecht, The Netherlands: Kluwer.

Black, R. L. (1981). The problem with tax problems. *The Tax Executive, 18,* 299–313.

Buchanan, B. G., & Headrick, T. G. (1970). Some speculations about artificial intelligence and legal reasoning. *Stanford Law Review, 42,* 40–62.

Chiesi, M. L., Spilich, G. J., & Voss, J. F. (1979). Acquisition of domain-related information in relation to high and low domain knowledge. *Journal of Verbal Learning and Verbal Behavior, 18,* 257–273.

Einhorn, H. J., & Hogarth, R. M. (1982). Prediction, diagnosis and causal thinking in forecasting. *Journal of Forecasting, 3,* 23–36.

Frensch, P. A., & Sternberg, R. A. (1989). Expertise and intelligent thinking: When is it worse to know better? In R. Sternberg (Ed.), *Advances in the psychology of human intelligence* (Vol. 5, pp. 157–188). Hillsdale, NJ: Lawrence Erlbaum Associates.

Gardner, A. L. (1987). *An artificial intelligence approach to legal reasoning*. Cambridge, MA: MIT Press.

Gentner, D. (1982). Are scientific analogies metaphors? In D. S. Miall (Ed.), *Metaphor: Problems and perspectives* (pp. 106–132). Brighton, England: Harvester.

Gick, M. L., & Holyoak, K. J. (1983). Schema induction and analogical transfer. *Cognitive Psychology, 14,* 1–38.

Hart, H. L. A. (1961). *The concept of law*. Oxford, England: Clarendon.

Holland, J. H., Holyoak, K. J., Nisbett, R. E., & Thagard, P. R. (1986). *Induction: Processes of inference, learning and discovery*. Cambridge, MA: MIT Press.

Holyoak, K. J., & Thagard, P. R. (1989). Analogical mapping by constraint satisfaction. *Cognitive Science, 13,* 295–355.

Krawczyk, K., Marchant, G., & Robinson, J. (1996). *The selection of authority in legal argument: Semantic similarity, pragmatic centrality and analogy*. Unpublished manuscript, School of Business Administration, North Carolina State University.

Kunda, Z. (1987). Motivation and inference: Self-serving generation and evaluation of causal theories. *Journal of Personality and Social Psychology, 53,* 636–647.

Levi, E. H. (1949). *An introduction to legal reasoning*. Chicago: University of Chicago Press.

MacCormick, N. (1978). *Legal reasoning and legal theory*. Oxford, England: Clarendon.

Marchant, G., Robinson, J., Anderson, U., & Schadewald, M. (1989). A cognitive model of tax problem solving. *Advances in Taxation, 2,* 1–20.

Marchant, G., Robinson, J., Anderson, U., & Schadewald, M. (1991). Analogical transfer and expertise in legal reasoning. *Organizational Behavior and Human Decision Processes, 48,* 272–290.

Marchant, G., Robinson, J., Anderson, U., & Schadewald, M. (1993). The use of analogy in legal argument: Problem similarity, precedent and expertise. *Organizational Behavior and Human Decision Processes, 55,* 95–119.

Minsky, M. (1975). A framework for representing knowledge. In P. H. Winston (Ed.), *The psychology of computer vision* (pp. 211–277). New York: McGraw-Hill.

Novick, L. R. (1988). Analogical transfer, problem similarity and expertise. *Journal of Experimental Psychology: Learning, Memory & Cognition, 14,* 510–520.

Schon, D. A. (1979). Generative metaphor: A perspective on problem-setting in social policy. In A. Ortony (Ed.), *Metaphor and thought* (pp. 254–283). Cambridge, England: Cambridge University Press.

Sternberg, R. J. (1977). Component processes in analogical reasoning. *Psychological Review, 84,* 353–378.

Tversky, A. (1977). Features of similarity. *Psychological Review, 84,* 327–352.

Tversky, A., & Gati, I. (1978). Studies of similarity. In E. Rosch & B. B. Lloyd (Eds.), *Cognition and categorization* (pp. 79–98). Hillsdale, NJ: Lawrence Erlbaum Associates.

CHAPTER TWO

What a Lawyer Needs to Learn

Edmund B. Spaeth, Jr.
Pepper Hamilton LLP, Philadelphia

The editors of this book have explained their two goals. The primary goal is "to explore the tacit aspects of competence in a number of different disciplines." By "tacit aspects" they mean "knowledge and skills that guide behavior but are not readily available to introspection." "Much of the knowledge that people use to succeed on the job," they stated, "is acquired implicitly—without intention to learn or awareness of having learned." The secondary goal is "to relate tacit aspects of competence to the problem of developing (or developing into) the effective practitioner." The authors of chapter 1 and I discuss these matters in the context of the legal profession. In chapter 1, Marchant and Robinson addressed the relevant current research in psychology; in this chapter, I examine the acquisition of tacit knowledge from the perspective of a practitioner.

My discussion starts with an examination of the legal profession's definition of "competence," as stated in the profession's official rules of conduct. As I proceed, however, the focus of my inquiry becomes not sharper but fuzzier.

At first it seems that the legal profession regards competence as a skill that is self-consciously, not tacitly, acquired. As we look further at the rules of conduct, however, it becomes apparent that the profession recognizes that an essential element of a competent practitioner's knowledge is knowing how to form a wide variety of "reasonable" judgments.

Before proceeding to consider to what extent the ability to do this is acquired self-consciously, and to what extent it creeps up on one unnoticed, our inquiry hits a speed bump. At certain critical junctures, the rules of conduct permit or require a lawyer to exercise judgment, but the rules provide no guidelines of reasonableness or otherwise. In addition, it turns out, even when a lawyer is required to act reasonably, the profession (as regards some important aspects of practice) has been unable to agree on a standard of reasonableness. Thus, it won't do to ask only what the tacit aspects of legal competence are; with no agreement on what is reasonable, there can be no definition of what is competent (beyond the minimal definition that a competent lawyer is one who knows enough to avoid being disciplined or held liable for malpractice).

The problem is that lawyers cannot agree on which of their several roles is the most important. Confronted with a choice of roles, different lawyers will act differently. Accordingly, later in this chapter we broaden our inquiry to consider generally the sorts of tacit knowledge a lawyer needs to acquire, without limiting ourselves only to the "competent" practitioner. At the end of the chapter, we consider what I think is the most difficult question, the answer to which continues to elude me: How does a lawyer decide what is reasonable? Stated differently: How does it happen that one lawyer decides to practice in a way that another lawyer rejects? To what extent is the lawyer's decision the result of knowledge acquired, in the editors' words, "implicitly—without intention to learn or awareness of having learned"?

THE LEGAL PROFESSION'S OFFICIAL DEFINITION OF COMPETENCE: SOME PRELIMINARY OBSERVATIONS

We begin with the legal profession's official definition of *competence*, as stated in the American Bar Association's Model Rules of Professional Conduct, promulgated in 1983 and since then adopted by most state courts. Model Rule 1.1 provides: "A lawyer shall provide competent representation to a client. Competent representation requires the legal knowledge, skill, thoroughness and preparation reasonably necessary for the representation." Before we examine this definition in detail, a few preliminary observations are in order.

What about the newly admitted lawyer, or the lawyer asked to undertake a representation in a field of law in which he or she has had no experience (the general practitioner, say, asked to represent someone charged with a violation of the securities or antitrust statutes)? *Can* such a lawyer have "the legal knowledge . . . reasonably necessary for the representation"?

One might suppose that the answer to this question is obvious: No. But that would be a blow to lawyers—and there are a lot of them—who don't want to be told that they should not take on every possible new client. To mollify such lawyers, the Comment to Model Rule 1.1 states:

> A newly admitted lawyer can be as competent as a practitioner with long experience. Some important legal skills, such as the analysis of precedent, the evaluation of evidence and legal drafting, are required in all legal problems. Perhaps the most fundamental legal skill consists of determining what kind of legal problems a situation may involve, a skill that necessarily transcends any particular specialized knowledge. A lawyer can provide adequate representation in a wholly novel field through necessary study. Competent representation can also be provided through the association of a lawyer of established competence in the field in question.

This is a fudge, to be blunt. A lawyer who doesn't know the field will not be competent to analyze precedent, evaluate evidence, or draft documents; because the lawyer won't know what to look for, the critical precedent won't be understood, the critical piece of evidence will remain undisturbed in the files, and the terms of the document won't anticipate all that they should. Nor can a client, except rarely, await the lawyer's "necessary study" to become competent in a field "wholly novel" to the lawyer.

Most lawyers, alerted by malpractice actions against other lawyers, recognize this reality and therefore follow the suggestion in the Comment that they enable themselves to provide competent representation by associating with "a lawyer of established competence in the field in question." That, of course, is what young lawyers hope to do when, after graduating from law school, they go to work for a law firm. But it is also what seasoned practitioners do when asked to handle a matter in a field about which they know little or nothing.

A different problem of competence arises when a lawyer is asked to undertake a representation in a field in which he or she is competent but within limits that the lawyer fears will interfere with his or her ability to do a good job. Model Rule 1.2(a) provides that "[a] lawyer shall abide by a client's decisions concerning the objectives of representation. . . ." The Comment to the rule states:

> A clear distinction between objectives and means sometimes cannot be drawn, and in many cases the client–lawyer relationship partakes of a joint undertaking. In questions of means, the lawyer should assume responsibility for technical and legal tactical issues, but should defer to the client regarding such questions as the expense to be incurred. . . .

Suppose the client refuses to pay the expense of an expert witness who the lawyer believes is essential. Some lawyers will proceed with the representation, against their better judgment that, without the expert, the client's objectives will probably not be realized. Other lawyers will decline the representation, partly out of professional pride ("I won't do it if I can't do a good job"), but also to avoid being blamed later by the client for the bad result the lawyer expects will ensue ("You didn't explain to me that the expert was all that important").

The reason for making these preliminary observations is to clear the field of discussion. The problems encountered by the inexperienced lawyer or the nonspecialist, and by the lawyer under constraints that the lawyer regards as unwise, are real problems, but they are tangential to our inquiry. From here on, let us assume that the lawyer we are discussing is "a lawyer of established competence in the field in question," free to represent the client by spending what it takes to do a good job. What sort of "tacit knowledge" does such a lawyer need to acquire?

DO LAWYERS SELF-CONSCIOUSLY LEARN HOW TO BE COMPETENT?

It is not apparent from Model Rule 1.1 that the legal profession recognizes that there are *any* tacit aspects of the knowledge one must acquire to become "a lawyer of established competence in the field in question." As noted, the rule defines competence as "requir[ing] the legal knowledge, skill, thoroughness and preparation reasonably necessary for the representation," and the Comment to the rule suggests that competence can be acquired ("adequate representation" can be provided), even in "a wholly novel field . . . through necessary study." Thus, the rule may be understood to exclude as an element of competence any "tacit" knowledge; that is (to refer again to the editors' definition), to exclude knowledge "acquired implicitly—without intention to learn or awareness of having learned."

When Model Rule 1.1 is read in context, however, it becomes apparent that the legal profession doesn't really consider competence to be a bookish skill that can be learned by the "thorough study" of such subjects as "the analysis of precedent" and "the evaluation of evidence." Indeed, carefully read, Model Rule 1.1 itself acknowledges that an essential element of competence is knowledge that cannot be acquired only from the books. Thus, the rule defines the elements of competence as "the legal knowledge, skill, thoroughness and preparation *reasonably necessary* to the representation" (emphasis added). One doesn't learn how to act "reasonably" by staying in the library.

This suggestion that competence has a judgmental element is confirmed by examination of other Model Rules, which contain many references to a lawyer's obligation to act reasonably. To cite some of the more striking of these references: Model Rule 1.3 requires "reasonable diligence and promptness." Model Rule 1.4 requires that a client be "reasonably informed" and matters explained "to the extent reasonably necessary." Model Rule 1.6 permits certain disclosures of confidential information "to the extent the lawyer believes reasonably necessary" to achieve specified results. Model Rule 1.7 forbids conflicts of interest unless, among other requirements, "the lawyer reasonably believes" that representing one client will not adversely affect others. Model Rule 3.2 requires "reasonable efforts" to expedite litigation, and Model Rule 3.3 mandates "reasonable remedial measures" against false evidence; also, under Model Rule 3.3, a lawyer may refuse to offer evidence that the lawyer "reasonably believes" is false. Model Rule 4.3 requires a lawyer, when dealing with an unrepresented person, to make "reasonable efforts" to correct any misunderstanding of the lawyer's role. Model Rules 5.1 and 5.3 require "reasonable efforts" to ensure that the lawyers in a firm and the nonlawyer assistants comply with their professional obligations. And so on go the rules.

This variety of requirements to act reasonably reflects the legal profession's conception of competence. Most lawyers, if asked to define competence, would probably say that an essential element of competence is sound judgment. Although "sound judgment" is not mentioned anywhere in the Model Rules, that only reflects the drafters' choice of words. A lawyer who exercises sound judgment will surely have acted "reasonably." Moreover, under Model Rule 1.1, a lawyer who fails to exercise sound judgment will be incompetent, because such a lawyer will have failed to provide "the legal knowledge, skill, thoroughness and preparation reasonably necessary for the representation." Thus, it is fair to conclude that the Model Rules and the legal profession do recognize tacit knowledge as an essential element of competence. One can acquire the ability to exercise reasonable, or sound, judgment only from experiencing the difficulties of practice. To be sure, some of the lessons of experience are self-consciously learned; others, however, are learned unconsciously, or "tacitly."

DO LAWYERS' RULES OF CONDUCT PROVIDE, AND DO LAWYERS AGREE, ON HOW THE COMPETENT LAWYER SHOULD PRACTICE?

Before we try to sort out the lessons of experience, we need to examine one further aspect of the Model Rules. At two critical junctures the rules offer a lawyer a choice of courses of action, with no guidelines, either by way of an admonition to make a "reasonable" choice or otherwise. The first of these junctures occurs when a lawyer must decide whether to reveal confidential information; the second, when a lawyer must decide how to counsel a client.

Model Rule 1.6, entitled "Confidentiality of Information," provides generally that "[a] lawyer shall not reveal [confidential] information," but there are some exceptions to this general rule. One of the exceptions is that a lawyer "may reveal" confidential information "to prevent the client from committing a criminal act that the lawyer believes is likely to result in imminent death or substantial bodily harm." Note that the rule does not say that the lawyer "shall reveal" such information; and the Comment to the rule expressly states that "[a] lawyer's decision not to [reveal] does not violate" the rule.

The Comment identifies "factors" to be considered in deciding whether to reveal confidential information: "the nature of the lawyer's relationship with the client and with those who might be injured by the client, the lawyer's own involvement in the transaction and factors that might extenuate the conduct in question"; also, "where practical, the lawyer should seek to persuade the client to take suitable action." These observations, however, cannot be characterized as guidelines; they are too Delphic. For example: If the lawyer's "relationship with the client" is close (what does that mean?), does that factor weigh against disclosure? If the lawyer's relationship with "those who might be injured" is close, does that factor weigh in favor of disclosure? Given that the only injury the lawyer may try to prevent by revealing confidential information is a criminal act likely to result in imminent death or substantial bodily harm, what difference does it make whether the lawyer's relationship to those who might be injured is closer than or not so close as the lawyer's relationship with the client? The Comment answers none of these questions, or other similar questions, but instead leaves the lawyer at sea.

Model Rule 2.1 provides that "in rendering advice [to a client], a lawyer may refer not only to law but to other considerations such as moral, economic, social and political factors, that may be relevant to the client's situation." Again, note the wording: "may refer," not "shall." Also again, the rule provides no guidelines. In fact, the Comment to Model Rule 2.1 reminds one of those investment brochures that say that the market may go up, but then again, it may not. According to the Comment: "Although a lawyer is not a moral advisor as such, moral and ethical considerations impinge upon most legal questions and may decisively influence how the law will be applied." So, does a lawyer counsel on moral and ethical considerations, or not?

At this point, we are brought up short. It seemed that we were moving, smoothly enough, toward the conclusion that, to be competent, a lawyer has somehow to acquire, among other abilities, the ability to exercise reasonable, or sound, judgment. With this conclusion established, we could then proceed to examine how a lawyer acquires that ability, in the expectation that the acquisition would involve both conscious and unconscious, or tacit, learning. But Model Rules 1.6 and 2.1 do not impose a standard of "reasonableness"—they make disclosure or counseling optional. How, then, is a lawyer to decide whether to disclose confidential information or not; to decide whether, when rendering legal advice, to refer to moral considerations or not? Stated differently: How is a lawyer to know whether the choice made is a competent or incompetent choice?

These are deeply troubling questions. Almost by instinct, rooted in legal tradition, lawyers will not disclose a client's confidence; and they do not regard themselves as their clients' moral counselors but rather as legal technicians engaged to accomplish objectives that the law permits but that cannot be accomplished without a lawyer's assistance. To instruct lawyers, as Model Rules 1.6 and 2.1 do, that in some situations they may act against these instincts is unsettling: "If I may, should I? Is the lawyer's traditional role as a technician who keeps confidences somehow, or sometimes, unworthy? Should I aspire to more? What kind of lawyer do I—should I—aspire to be?"

The reason these questions are unsettling is that the legal profession has been unable to agree on which of several roles a lawyer should play. There is agreement that lawyers do play different roles, but there is no agreement on which of these is the most important.

The Preamble to the Model Rules states: "A lawyer is a representative of clients, an officer of the legal system and a public citizen having special responsibility for the quality of justice." Although the Preamble states that these roles are "usually harmonious," it goes on to acknowledge both that "in the nature of law practice, however, conflicting responsibilities are encountered," and that the resolution, or attempted resolution, of these conflicting responsibilities lies at the heart of the practice of law: "Virtually all difficult ethical problems arise from conflict between a lawyer's responsibilities to clients, to the legal system and to the lawyer's own interest in remaining an upright person."

An illustration may be helpful. Suppose a client is determined, for economic reasons and against the lawyer's advice, to engage in illegal dumping of toxic waste, or to withhold reporting that use of the client's pharmaceutical product may produce adverse side effects. This information is confidential, because the lawyer has acquired it in the course of advising the client. Should the lawyer (should a lawyer who is competent) nevertheless—after notice to the client to give it one last chance—disclose the information to the authorities and thereby prevent the client's contemplated crimes?

This question has racked, and continues to rack, the legal profession, with the result that the rules of professional conduct differ widely. Model Rule 1.6, as we have seen, makes disclosure optional, if but only if the contemplated crime "is likely to result in imminent death or substantial bodily harm." Many jurisdictions have rejected this formulation. Some do not require that the crime threaten "imminent" death or harm. Some do not limit the threatened harm to physical harm, but instead permit disclosure to prevent substantial financial injury. Some require disclosure to prevent death or substantial bodily harm and permit it to prevent not just a "crime" but a "fraud," which would encompass financial harm. Some do not require but permit disclosure to prevent any sort of crime. And so on and on, to the point where current editions of rules of professional conduct have elaborate tables or similar compilations enabling practitioners to compare the rules of different jurisdictions.

The reason for this diversity is that the profession can't agree on which role a lawyer should play when the obligations incident to the different roles are in conflict. A lawyer who gives priority to his or her role as a representative of clients, bound to keep their confidences, will not notify the law enforcement authorities to prevent the client's contemplated crimes. A lawyer who gives priority to his or her obligation to the legal system—the obligation of "an officer of the court," as it is often put—will notify the authorities. Those who approve Model Rule 1.6 give a very high, almost absolute, priority to the lawyer's role as representative of clients: Better that an innocent person be injured than a client's confidence betrayed. Those who permit, or even require, disclosure in circumstances in which Model Rule 1.6 forbids disclosure give higher priority to the lawyer's role as one who has special responsibilities for the quality of the legal system.

It is not pertinent to our discussion to debate the merits of these different rankings. What is pertinent to note is that the legal profession has studiously evaded the issue. Except for those formulations that require disclosure in certain situations, the lawyer is left at sea: "In these situations you may not disclose confidential information; in these other situations [however differently these other situations may be defined] you may disclose, but also, you may choose not to. Suit yourself, according to which of your roles you think should prevail."

The Model Rules, not surprisingly, do not admit to their evasion. Rather, they try to paper it over. Thus, the Preamble to the Model Rules, after acknowledging that "virtually all difficult ethical problems" arise when a lawyer must choose among conflicting responsibilities, assures us:

> The Rules of Professional Conduct prescribe terms for resolving such conflicts. Within the framework of these Rules many difficult issues of professional responsibility can arise. Such issues must be resolved through the exercise of sensitive professional and moral judgment guided by the basic principles underlying these Rules.

In reflecting on this passage, one must choose between derision and outrage. What "terms"? What "basic principles"? To suggest that the Comment to Model Rule 1.6, which has been quoted previously, offers guidance is insulting, and nothing any more enlightening appears anywhere else in the rules.

The consequences of the legal profession's failure (more accurately, its inability) to decide which of a lawyer's roles should prevail are especially striking in the field of litigation. Several provisions of the Model Rules enjoin lawyers to act reasonably when conducting litigation: no "frivolous," only "good faith," arguments—Model Rule 3.1; "reasonable efforts to expedite litigation"—Model Rule 3.2; "reasonable remedial measures" against false testimony—Model Rule 3.3; and "fairness" to the opposing party and counsel—Model Rule 3.4. Lawyers who give priority to their roles as officers of the court and counselors to their clients interpret these rules one way; "zealous advocates," as they usually describe themselves—lawyers who consider their highest duty to attempt to achieve their client's objectives—interpret these rules in another way.

This difference in practice is especially striking in the pretrial stage of litigation, which is mostly conducted outside the immediate supervision of a judge. The tactics of the zealous advocates are often described as "hardball," "scorched earth," and "take no prisoners." These metaphors are appropriately violent. During interminable depositions, lawyers shout and curse at each other and witnesses. In response to discovery requests, documents are produced in jumbled disarray, on paper hard to read and hard to copy. Motions are served in numbers and at times calculated to cause the other party the greatest possible inconvenience and expense: "Paper them to death!"

Are these the tactics of the competent lawyer? This question, more than any other, reveals the fracture in the legal profession's conception of itself. Many lawyers answer that the hardball players are not only not competent but a disgrace to the profession. These lawyers believe, and practice their belief, that they can vigorously and effectively represent their clients without engaging in conduct that they regard as uncivil, unreasonable, and not in good faith. To this response, the hardball players reply that civility is a mark of timidity, a snobbish gentility—in any event, evidence of an unwillingness to fight, really fight, for one's client.

There is no covering up this difference, nor is there any prospect of one view prevailing over the other. Some of the most well-known and wealthy practitioners are hardballers; many clients seek them out, and pay them handsomely, for the very reason that they do play hardball. This being so, these hardballers can afford to brush aside the disdain of those who regard them as bullies and sharp practitioners.

This is not to say that there are no limits. Sometimes a zealous advocate becomes so intemperate that an outraged judge imposes sanctions that hurt—perhaps even entering judgment against the lawyer's client. The point is that the legal profession's rules of conduct are so variously interpreted and so loosely enforced that one cannot define with any precision an accepted standard of practice. One can speak in negative terms: A competent lawyer will not fail to interview essential witnesses, or to look up the most recent interpretations of a controlling statute, and so on. But beyond agreeing on such minimum standards of performance, some lawyers will consider that competent representation of a client requires conduct that other lawyers will disdain.

The fact is, both the hardballers and their more civil colleagues have a point. Sometimes civility does mask timidity or reflect a too-ready acceptance of things as they are; for many years the organized bar, as represented by the American Bar Association, was a self-satisfied guild, inhospitable to women and minorities, and oblivious to the injustice of the prevailing order. But also, sometimes the hardballers aren't courageous fighters for justice—they are simply greedy bullies.

It is important not to overstate the point. Lawyers are not at odds about *everything*. Granted, a standard of "reasonable conduct" is very general, but at least for many of the situations a lawyer encounters it is workable enough and, in applying it, lawyers will reach pretty much the same result. For example, a lawyer should have little difficulty complying with the requirement of Model Rule 1.5 that "[a] lawyer's fee shall be reasonable." The rule contains a useful list of "factors to be considered in determining the reasonableness of a fee," such as the time and labor required and the fee customarily charged in the locality for similar legal services. But even without this list, the nature of fee setting is so similar to other monetary transactions that determining whether a fee is reasonable should present no particular difficulty. And so it is with many of the other situations requiring reasonableness. Whether clients have been "reasonably informed" (Model Rule 1.4) so that they may intelligently decide what course of action to follow; whether a potential conflict of interest is "reasonably" likely to have an adverse effect on the client–lawyer relationship (Model Rule 1.7)—these situations and many of the others referred to in the Model Rules should present no insoluble difficulty.

The fact remains that, with respect to many of the decisions that a lawyer must make in the course of practice, there is no agreement about the proper way to proceed. Thus, the innocent-sounding question of "What sort of knowledge does the competent lawyer need to acquire?" has led us into a dark wood. What we are really searching for, it turns out, is the identity of the sort of knowledge that a lawyer needs to acquire to practice as a competent lawyer, within the rules of professional conduct, *and* within the lawyer's own conception of how a lawyer should practice.

WHAT SORT OF KNOWLEDGE DOES A LAWYER ACQUIRE ON THE WAY TO LEARNING HOW TO PRACTICE?

With this broadening of our inquiry, let us try to identify the sorts of tacit knowledge a lawyer acquires on the way to developing a personal conception of how to practice. Because the practice of law is the application of abstract principles to particular situations involving individuals whose interests and philosophies are often very different, we may proceed by first asking how a lawyer learns the legal principles relevant to the client's situation, and next asking how a lawyer learns to apply those principles in a way that, if possible, will achieve the client's objective while honoring the lawyer's conception of how law should be practiced.

It might seem that very little, if any, tacit knowledge would be involved in learning the principles of law relevant, say, to preparing a will for a client or defending a claim that a client has violated the antitrust laws. To be sure, the principles may vary enormously in degree of complexity, and the legal materials in which they are embedded (statutes, regulations, decisions by courts and administrative agencies, etc.) may be few or voluminous, clear or obscure. But there they are—in the books. So, look them up. Learn them, in other words, not tacitly but self-consciously. The depth of different lawyers' understanding will not vary according to their tacit knowledge but instead according to which lawyer has studied hardest—has most thoroughly searched out and mastered the relevant legal materials.

This view of the matter so often seems accurate that it is easy to accept it as accurate. Judges, for example, regularly observe that one lawyer's brief has overlooked a case or a bit of legislative history that the other lawyer's brief discusses. Law firms regularly measure an associate's performance by how thoroughly the associate has stated the relevant legal principles and authorities interpreting those principles. Furthermore, there is nothing "tacit" about learning how to do legal research. It used to be a matter of knowing how to use certain written indices; now it involves knowing how to manipulate data stored in computers. "Legal research" is a specific course taught in every law school, and every careful law firm routinely trains its personnel in the latest technological improvements.

In fact, however, understanding the legal principles relevant to a particular client's situation does involve tacit knowledge. Sometimes (if not often), the outcome of the matter will be decided based on whether a lawyer has acquired that tacit knowledge.

An anecdote illustrates this point. An associate had prepared an appellate brief. It was a good brief, stating the applicable legal principles correctly, and citing and accurately stating the principal decisions interpreting those principles. As often happens in a large law firm, the senior partner who would argue the case had generally supervised the preparation of the brief but had not written it or done the research on which it was based. In preparing for oral argument, however, the partner read and reread the decisions cited in the brief—and the case took on a different shape. Not much different, but different. One decision in particular seemed to the partner to distill the principal point to be made. Accordingly, this decision was made the focus of the oral argument, and it became the focus of the appellate court's subsequent decision in favor of the client.

Another illustration: A lawsuit almost always presents many issues. Every one of the issues may have some merit in the sense of being supported by some legal authority. In preparing a brief, an associate will often argue all of the issues, only to find that the senior who will argue the case has revised the brief to eliminate all but two or three—perhaps all but one—of the issues.

In both illustrations, the different ways of proceeding are attributable to the senior lawyer's greater degree of tacit knowledge. The senior has learned, by ways unnoticed at the time, to gauge the relative weight of the applicable legal principles more accurately than can the junior.

If asked to reflect on how this happened, the senior may give a variety of explanations. "Watching other lawyers" will often be one; "I learned the hard way," is frequently another. Such explanations, however, are incomplete. One doesn't suddenly say to oneself, "*Now* I know how to choose from the relevant authorities which is the most persuasive!" That knowledge isn't attributable to an identifiable event, whether listening to another lawyer's effective argument or brooding over losing a case. Rather, it grows on one, only partly sensed, until one day one hangs one's hat on a specific case, eliminates every issue but one, at first with apprehension and then with growing confidence.

In handling a case, of course, a lawyer does not proceed in so segmented a way as the previous illustrations may suggest. That is, a lawyer does not first ask, "What are the legal principles applicable to this matter?" and then, "How shall I apply them?" The lawyer must first decide what "the matter" *is,* because only then can the applicable legal principles be identified, and deciding what the matter is involves skills different from legal research and analysis. These skills may generally be described as the skills a lawyer needs to acquire to be able to learn the facts of the case.

Here, too, there would seem to be little call for tacit knowledge. After all, the facts are out there, somewhere. The lawyer's job is to know—to learn—how to find them, personally or with the help of others. The impression that tacit knowledge has little to do with knowing how to get the facts seems often confirmed by practice; some lawyers negotiate better deals or get better verdicts because they simply know more about the facts of the case; they've dug deeper and looked further than has opposing counsel. Again, however, tacit knowledge may be decisive. Without quite knowing how they learned to do it, some lawyers are able to get more out of examining documents and interviewing potential witnesses than other lawyers can.

Lawyers know this, and so courses on interviewing are offered to law students participating in clinical programs and to practicing lawyers in continuing legal education programs. Nevertheless, an element of tacit knowledge persists. Like finding the law, finding the facts is a skill that lawyers can, and do, self-consciously learn; but they also acquire the skill unconsciously. They get better, and know they have, without quite realizing how it happened. Practice, of course, is one reason, as with playing tennis: One gets better just by continuing to try to hit the ball. Another reason is that the ability to empathize—to see the situation through the eyes of the person being interviewed, to sense whether something is being held back, and why—develops with experience, without its expansion quite being recognized. The greater the variety of persons interviewed and the greater the variety of the facts sought, the more skillful the lawyer will become in learning the facts of a case.

As we proceed further, beyond the lawyer's legal analysis and discovery of the facts, the balance between self-conscious and tacit learning gradually changes, with the relative importance of tacit learning becoming greater. An experienced lawyer, for example, will prepare and present a case very differently than will an inexperienced lawyer. The selection and preparation of the witnesses, the order in which their testimony is presented, the choice of issues to be emphasized, the cross-examination of the opponent's witnesses—these and many other aspects of the case will be handled differently. Also, no matter how thorough the pretrial preparation, a trial is a fluid event, with surprising changes of direction. A witness, for example, blurts out an unanticipated, and damaging, response. Experienced counsel will be more resourceful in coping with, or exploiting, such an event than will inexperienced counsel. And this is equally true of a transactional practice: Lawyers attempting to close a merger agreement may encounter events even more difficult to predict than in litigation.

Most lawyers would probably disagree with very little of what I've said so far. Nevertheless, they would be uncomfortable with the entire subject of "tacit" knowledge. The practice of law is a highly competitive enterprise, and successful competitors try to leave as little as possible to chance. Learning something "tacitly" sounds like acquiring it by chance—learning it or not according to the experiences you happen to have, or miss having. Thus, even in fields of practice where tacit knowledge is most apparent, lawyers try to minimize its role. That is why elaborate courses in trial advocacy are offered and well attended, in which the participants' every move, from the beginning to the end of a trial problem, is videotaped and criticized again and again: "Don't do it that way; do it this way." There is no tacit learning here. Mentoring programs are another example. Recognizing that a junior lawyer may unconsciously learn from a senior's conduct, many law firms try to make the learning self-conscious by pairing the junior with a senior, with the express instruction that the senior is to provide an example for the junior's emulation.

In the end, however, the attempt to minimize the role of tacit learning runs into a wall. If the legal profession were agreed on the ideal lawyer, then, perhaps, lawyers could self-consciously learn how to become such a lawyer. But as we saw from our survey of the profession's rules of conduct, there is no such agreement. Lawyers can, and do, self-consciously learn a great deal about how to try a case or negotiate a deal. But there are a great many different ways to perform such tasks competently, within the rules. In the end, the lawyer must choose among these ways. And that is where tacit knowledge becomes decisive.

As I remarked at the beginning, just what this tacit knowledge is—how it determines a lawyer's choice of role—is a question I have been unable to answer. Why is it that some lawyers will practice hardball, whereas others won't; will disclose an intended crime, whereas others won't; will not hesitate to counsel a client that a contemplated course of action, although legal, is reprehensible, whereas others will hold their tongues; will in many other situations interpret their professional obligations differently than do other lawyers? Plainly, each lawyer is practicing in accordance with an individual conception of how one should practice. But where did the conception come from? It didn't come from the legal profession's rules of conduct, nor from any consensus outside the rules.

WHAT DO LAWYERS NEED TO LEARN TO PRACTICE IN ACCORDANCE WITH BOTH THEIR PROFESSION'S RULES OF CONDUCT AND THE DEMANDS OF THEIR OWN CONSCIENCES?

However accurate this analysis may be, it seems fair to say that it reflects the legal profession's current state of moral crisis. Whether this crisis is more severe than it has been in the past is a matter on which opinions differ, but it is, in any event, severe. There is much talk—by the bench, the bar, the academy, and in the popular press—about "the demise of professionalism" and "the loss of professional values." Illustrative, although somewhat extreme (but only by a little bit), are the reflections of the dean of a leading law school on "the lost lawyer," and on whether, as a dean, he can in good conscience continue to train students for law practice. And it is true that many graduates of law school become disenchanted with the practice, having come to believe that to be successful as lawyers they must practice by rules that are discordant with their personal code of conduct.

Speaking in general terms, it may be said that the reaction of the legal profession to this state of affairs has been to concentrate its attention on the law schools. Thus, a great deal of thought has been given to how legal ethics—or "professional responsibility"—should be taught to law students, to the end that when they practice they will do so as "professionals" and not as ruffians and hired guns. As another effort, the American Bar Association has issued a major report urging that the law schools do a better job teaching their students the skills they will need to practice effectively; graduates should come better prepared, it is said, to do what lawyers do.

To venture an expression of my own view: These efforts are useful, but superficial. Without question, we can teach legal ethics more effectively; in many law schools it is still looked down on by the faculties as a "soft" subject, not susceptible of rigorous analysis or productive research. And, although there will always be tension between teaching scholarship and teaching specific skills, law schools can, without losing intellectual rigor or damping down innovative thinking, do a better job preparing their students for the real world. In my view, however, better teaching is unlikely to equip law students with the sound judgment that a lawyer, to be competent, must have.

Oliver Wendell Holmes, in one of his letters to Frederick Pollock, observed: "We learn how to behave as lawyers, soldiers, merchants, or what not by being them. Life, not the parson, teaches conduct." Proponents of clinical legal education appreciate the force of Holmes' observation; they know that experience produces a degree of understanding that cannot be gained only from studying the cases. But law school lasts only 3 years; with all the cases that must be studied, there is simply not enough time for clinical education to provide students with enough experience to enable them to be competent practitioners.

In any case, Holmes' observation doesn't help solve the legal profession's moral crisis. I agree that a lawyer's workplace—whether the lawyer practices alone, in a firm, in a corporate legal department, or in a government agency—"teaches conduct." But what does that mean? Does it teach good conduct or bad? Too often, the answer is "Bad."

This has led some to suggest that the profession should concentrate its efforts not on the law schools but on lawyers' workplaces. And indeed, many law firms are self-consciously adopting policies to inculcate the standards by which the firm expects its partners and associates to practice. To cite an illustrative example: A law firm that has decided that the "professional" (the "good") lawyer should engage in *pro bono* work may make its lawyers' compensation dependent on evidence that they have devoted a given number of hours to such work. Another example: A law firm may create internal procedures for the regular review of how its lawyers practice to determine whether they are adhering to the firm's standards.

Such firms, however, have been able to achieve what the legal profession has not achieved: A definition of a lawyer's proper role, which is to say, a decision on which of a lawyer's several roles is the most important and should therefore prevail when the roles conflict. The firms' lawyers, in other words, have reconciled the definition of the competent lawyer, as contained in the profession's formal rules of conduct, with the demands of their personal consciences.

And at this point I should like to refer the reader back to chapter 1, because although there are aspects of tacit and also self-conscious learning distinctive to the legal profession (some of which I have tried to identify), in the end, I suggest, we must look further, if we are to decide what a lawyer needs to learn. Lawyers define, or fail to define, a personal conception of how to practice law the way others define, or fail to define, a personal conception of how they should go about their activities—in medicine, business, politics, teaching, or whatever. Thus, we must ask not what lawyers need to learn, tacitly or otherwise, to be successful practitioners, but what does anyone need to learn to be able to adapt to the turmoil of life and to the constraints imposed on us, whether those constraints include the ambiguous conceptions underlying the legal profession's rules of conduct or the perhaps clearer rules of another activity.

PART TWO

MILITARY COMMAND

CHAPTER THREE

Experience, Knowledge, and Military Leadership

Joseph A. Horvath
Yale University

George B. Forsythe
United States Military Academy

Richard C. Bullis
Patrick J. Sweeney
United States Military Academy

Wendy M. Williams
Yale University

Jeffrey A. McNally
John M. Wattendorf
United States Military Academy

Robert J. Sternberg
Yale University

Just back from several weeks of high-intensity simulated combat in the California desert, Bill, a young lieutenant in the field artillery, described a particularly challenging leadership problem that he had faced the previous week while fighting the OPFOR—the closest thing to a real enemy that an officer faces during peacetime.[1] That problem was dealing with a boss who was reluctant to listen to his subordinate leaders.

> My battery commander[2] doesn't listen to his NCOs and officers. At the National Training Center (NTC), he made us dig individual positions every time we

[1]The OPFOR is the opposing force against which Army units train in high-fidelity, simulated combat at the National Training Center.

[2]An Army captain with between 5 and 7 years of commissioned service and responsibility for approximately 130 soldiers.

> stopped, even in the offense, which often slowed our progress. The other batteries didn't dig in as much as we did, and the observer-controllers told us we dug in entirely too much. I think the battery commander was going by the book, but it was really a problem for us because our sections were understrength, and this requirement was unrealistic for the fast-paced mission we were on. Digging in so much really burned us out and morale suffered. So I went to my commander individually to ask about his policy. He shared his reasoning with me, but I still wasn't sure that he appreciated the impact it was having on the soldiers' morale and on our ability to accomplish the mission. So I decided to use METT-T [a framework for assessing a tactical situation, the initial step in military planning] to structure the reasons for my counterargument. I've found that the persuasiveness of my arguments with the boss increases if I can demonstrate how his directive adversely impacts on the unit's mission accomplishment. Using METT-T works.

Jane, a transportation company commander, sat in the hot Georgia sun during a break in the day's mission, and talked about how much she had learned in her first 6 months of command. She spoke of her initial urge to micromanage her unit—to be a hands-on leader just as she had been as a young lieutenant—and of how she came to realize the ineffectiveness of this approach:

> When I first took command there were a lot of things I wanted to fix in the company. Even though I told myself I wasn't going to micromanage as a commander, I ended up doing it. I quickly became overwhelmed; I couldn't do it all. Finally, I realized that I had been micromanaging. I learned to spot check, to trust my subordinate leaders, and to give them some leeway. For example, to spot check, I'd go around the company area and see what was going on—get a general impression. If I found a problem, I'd go find the responsible leader and point out what I had found. I'd let him solve the problem; I tried to avoid telling him how to solve it. If I found a big problem, I'd have the subordinate research it and come back to me with alternative solutions. This gets him involved and gives ownership for the problem. Once I decide on a final solution, I let the subordinate leader implement it. I've found that getting subordinate leaders involved gives them ownership and responsibility for the problem; it also promotes their development and increases their commitment.

Mark,[3] an infantry battalion commander, shared his thoughts on battalion-level leadership as he bumped along a dusty trail in his vehicle en route to inspect training (the ride to the training site was his only free moment the entire day). He told two stories that together spoke volumes about the

[3]An Army lieutenant colonel with approximately 17 years of service as an officer and responsibility for approximately 500 soldiers.

challenges of battalion command—planning, protecting the organization, and caring for soldiers:

> When I took over battalion command, I knew I had to plan at least a year out. I was concerned about planning in advance so my soldiers could have predictability in their lives. I provided my soldiers and their families with a copy of the 6-month training schedule so they could make plans, and I followed the schedule because I wanted my soldiers to trust me. I think they really appreciated this because it showed I cared about their welfare. Furthermore, I made a point of stressing planning during training meetings with my commander and his staff. One time, I publicly challenged my boss and his staff for changing the training plan at the last moment just before a major field exercise. I pointed out that the change violated training doctrine and set a poor example for our subordinate leaders. After the meeting, my commander came to my office and let me have it. He said I was correct, but my approach alienated him and his staff. I learned that in a public forum, I should speak directly to the point of contention and avoid evaluative statements about the boss and his staff. This saves the boss embarrassment and preserves my relationship with him, which is essential for the success of my battalion.

These stories illustrate the structure and substance of practical knowledge for military leadership. They reflect the personal lessons of experience derived from the school of hard knocks, not textbook knowledge taught in the classroom. They are the lessons of the battlefield, the motor pool, the rifle range, and the command post. Military leadership knowledge is embedded in these stories. In a sense, the stories *are* the knowledge. In fact, Bill, Jane, and Mark had to be helped to uncover the lessons in their stories. Although they told their stories with ease and flair, verbalizing the specific lessons seemed to them unnatural and unnecessary.

Army officers' knowledge about leadership is goal directed and action oriented; it is about when and how to exercise direct and indirect influence in order to accomplish the mission. Much of the knowledge in these stories supports the Army's formal leadership doctrine—how to plan ahead, take care of your soldiers, and develop your subordinates. Other pieces of advice supplement the doctrine—how to deal with the boss and protect the unit. The stories also appear to reflect the developmental challenges the officers faced as they assumed leadership positions of increasingly greater scope and responsibility, and were faced with novel problems.

Overview

These stories and many others were generated by practicing military leaders as part of a 6-year program of research on practical knowledge for military leadership. Our joint team of researchers from Yale University and the United

States Military Academy has been studying what Army officers learn about leadership from their on-the-job experiences. Our aim is to identify this knowledge, construct instruments to measure it, and explore its relationship to leadership effectiveness, with the ultimate aim of helping the Army to better develop the hidden knowledge assets that reside in its highly skilled and committed officer corps.

This chapter offers a summary of our work to date on tacit knowledge within the U.S. Army. Following a brief overview of the officer professional development system in the Army (with a specific emphasis on leadership development), we explore the concept of practical knowledge for military leadership. Next, we discuss where this concept fits into the literature on leadership and professional cognition. We then present a summary of our research, including our initial findings. Finally, we discuss the implications of our work for officer education and development.

LEADERSHIP AND PROFESSIONAL DEVELOPMENT IN THE ARMY

The Army's official view of leadership is presented in three documents: Field Manual 22-100, Military Leadership (Headquarters, Department of the Army, 1990); Field Manual 22-103, Leadership and Command at Senior Levels (Headquarters, Department of the Army, 1987b); and Department of the Army Pamphlet 600-80, Executive Leadership (Headquarters, Department of the Army, 1987a) that address leadership at different organizational levels: junior (leadership of units up to and including battalion), intermediate, and executive. *Leadership* is defined in these documents as an interpersonal influence process in which direct and indirect means are used to get others to accomplish the organization's goals. Influence is achieved by providing purpose, direction, and motivation. The definition suggests that leadership is more than headship; the ability to influence is not based solely on formal authority or position power. The term *other* is used in this definition (rather than the term *subordinate*) because a leader may have to exercise influence beyond the organization's boundaries in order to accomplish the mission. Army doctrine assumes that leadership processes are qualitatively different at various levels in the military hierarchy; hence, different doctrinal manuals are employed at the different levels.

The Army's doctrine further implies that leadership and management are overlapping concepts. The Army uses the term *leader* to refer to all incumbents in supervisory positions within military organizations. Thus, the term *leader* provides a role label in the military context in the same way that the term *manager* provides a role label in civilian organizations. Leadership and management are processes used to fulfill role expectations, and both are necessary for an incumbent to meet his or her supervisory role requirements.

Army doctrine addresses the issue of leader knowledge much more thoroughly than does the civilian research literature, specifying broad categories of knowledge relevant to leadership (Headquarters, Department of the Army, 1990). These "things a leader must know" include standards, oneself, human nature, one's job, and one's unit. Army doctrine also specifies nine leadership competencies—things leaders must be able to do. The nine competencies were developed in the 1970s through a wide-ranging study of military officers at all command levels. The nine competencies include: communications, supervision, teaching and counseling, decision making, soldier-team development, technical and tactical proficiency, planning, use of available systems, and professional ethics (Headquarters, Department of the Army, 1990). The nine competencies and their descriptions provide a framework for specifying what leaders need to be able to do in order to be effective and successful. Other Army field manuals contain important practical knowledge, at a more detailed level, about the combat environment and the human response to it, and about how to motivate, counsel, and train soldiers.

The U.S. Army has one of the most comprehensive systems of professional development of any organization or profession in the world. According to Army doctrine, leader development occurs through three complementary processes: institutional training, self-development, and operational assignments (learning on the job). On-the-job experiences provide opportunities for officers to learn how to apply leadership knowledge codified in doctrine and taught in the Army school system. On-the-job experiences also provide a context for acquiring new knowledge about leadership—knowledge for which acquisition is not well supported by doctrine or through formal training. Thus, Army leadership doctrine acknowledges the importance of experiential learning in the acquisition of leadership knowledge. Similar trends have been identified in the civilian sector, where experience is regarded as an important feature of executive development (McCall, Lombardo, & Morrison, 1988). During their careers, officers cycle between operational assignments and attendance at professional schools; formal professional education is integrated throughout a career so that officers are prepared to meet professional demands and learn from experience as they advance in the organization.

The hierarchical nature of military organizations makes the study of professional expertise particularly challenging. In the military, expertise required of leaders changes as a function of organizational level. Although captains, lieutenant colonels, and generals are all members of the same profession, the nature of their work calls for very different kinds of expertise, and hence different sorts of job knowledge. Over the years, the Army's professional development system has evolved to meet this reality. For example, formal education and training and frequent job rotations are used to provide officers with requisite experiences for the development of level-specific expertise.

TACIT KNOWLEDGE FOR MILITARY LEADERSHIP

What do leaders know about leading? Surprisingly, this question has been largely ignored by leadership researchers. Less than a single page of *Stogdill's Handbook on Leadership* (Bass, 1990) addressed what leaders know. Other published reviews (Hollander, 1985; Yukl, 1989) and our own search of the literature (Horvath, Williams, et al., 1994) support the conclusion that leadership knowledge has not been studied explicitly or systematically. In other domains, however, knowledge derived from experience, and its relationship to competent performance, has been studied extensively.

In exploring practical knowledge for military leadership, we turned to the work of Robert Sternberg and colleagues, who have examined tacit knowledge and intelligent behavior in such settings as research psychology, sales, primary education, and business management (Sternberg, Wagner, Williams, & Horvath, 1995; Sternberg, Wagner, & Okagaki, 1993; Wagner & Sternberg, 1985). One of our goals was to explore the applicability of the tacit knowledge framework to professional education, in order both to increase our understanding of the tacit component of professional expertise in the military and to develop methods that facilitate the acquisition and application of tacit knowledge in a professional-practice setting.

Our use of the tacit-knowledge construct derives most directly from Sternberg's triarchic theory of human intelligence (Sternberg, 1988).[4] According to Sternberg, tacit knowledge is a key to intelligent behavior in practical settings; it is the practical know-how that one needs in order to succeed. As we conceive of it, tacit knowledge is a natural concept (Smith & Medin, 1981) that refers to a type of knowledge that has been shown in previous research to be useful in predicting performance in real-world endeavors (Wagner & Sternberg, 1985). By *natural concept,* we mean that it is held together by the resemblance of tacit-knowledge items to one another and not by a set of singly necessary and jointly sufficient features. Because tacit knowledge is a natural concept, we should not expect judgments about what is and is not tacit to be "all or none." Instead, judgments should be based on a particular item's degree of resemblance to other exemplars of the concept.

---

[4]The term *tacit knowledge* has roots in works on the philosophy of science (Polanyi, 1966), ecological psychology (Neisser, 1976), and organizational behavior (Schön, 1983). The adaptation of the term to account for individual differences in practical intelligence reflects an intellectual debt to all of these sources.

Tacit knowledge has three characteristic features: It is intimately related to action, it is relevant to the attainment of goals that people value, and it is acquired with little help from others. Furthermore, tacit knowledge is often not available to conscious introspection; it is knowledge that people may not know they have or may find difficult to articulate. Knowledge with these properties is called *tacit* because it often must be inferred from actions and statements. In Sternberg's framework, tacit knowledge is both the product of more general knowledge-acquisition abilities and an important predictor of competent performance in practical contexts (Sternberg et al., 1993). On the other hand, tacit knowledge is not synonymous with knowledge acquired in informal settings, nor is it a proxy for general intelligence. Finally, tacit knowledge is important to but not sufficient for effective performance. In our work, we have been interested in tacit knowledge about military leadership—knowledge about the exercise of influence in an organizational context.

A complementary way of thinking about the tacit-knowledge construct is as a cognitive phenomena defined in terms of the learning processes that produce it and the memory systems that encode it. According to this conceptualization, tacit knowledge is knowledge that is acquired through personal experience rather than received from others (i.e., through instruction). As such, tacit knowledge is encoded originally in episodic rather than semantic memory,[5] although over time it may become stored as generalized knowledge through processes of compilation or reflection. Tacit knowledge may be employed in performance situations either directly (through the influence of stored cases on behavior) or indirectly (through the application of generalized knowledge derived from personal experiences). In summary, tacit knowledge may be defined in terms of either its characteristic features or in terms of the mental processes and structures that produce knowledge with these features.

An extensive program of empirical research has shown that tacit knowledge can be measured, that it increases with experience, and that scores on tacit-knowledge measures provide a significant and independent increment in prediction (beyond that provided by general intelligence, or "IQ") for certain indexes of professional success. Research has also shown that different aspects of tacit knowledge are correlated among themselves, and that tacit knowledge can be conveyed through case-based instruction (Sternberg & Wagner, 1993; Wagner, 1987; Wagner, Rashotte, & Sternberg, cited in Sternberg, Wagner, & Okagaki, 1993; Wagner & Sternberg, 1985).

Questions about what it takes to be competent and to perform intelligently in the real world of professional practice have been addressed by researchers

[5]According to Tulving (1972), episodic memory is memory for specific, personally experienced events, such as stories, cases, or situations. Semantic memory, on the other hand, is memory for general, impersonal knowledge that transcends specific episodes.

before. Studies of expertise (e.g., Chi, Feltovich, & Glaser, 1981; Forsythe & Barber, 1992; Norman, 1990; Patel & Groen, 1992; Schmidt, 1990) and reflective practice (e.g., Cervero, 1988; Schön, 1987) have explored the nature of expertise and the effects of experience on its development. Our approach extends this earlier work in a number of ways. First, we have sought to identify a subset of expert knowledge—tacit knowledge—that critically supports competent performance in professional endeavors (in our case, military leadership). Second, we have sought to disentangle knowledge about leadership from other features of military expertise; we seek the "soft" knowledge that is relevant to effective professional performance but that is often attributed solely to the dispositions or traits of the leader. By extension, the tacit-knowledge framework may hold promise for identifying similar features of expert performance in other professional domains (e.g., working with patients and clients, or working in professional teams).

IDENTIFYING THE LESSONS OF EXPERIENCE

We began our exploration of practical knowledge for military leadership by going to the source—leaders of units in the active-duty Army (Forsythe et al., 1995; Horvath, Forsythe, et al., 1994). It was during these interviews that we met Bill, Jane, Mark, and many others. In all, we interviewed 81 Army officers at their work sites during the summer of 1993. These officers were identified by their senior commanders and were drawn from each of three organizational levels (platoon, company, and battalion). The sample represented officers from all basic specialty categories (e.g., infantry, armor, artillery, engineers, aviation, signal, supply, transportation, and maintenance). Nine percent of the officers in our sample were female, a proportion that is comparable to that in the population of U.S. Army officers.

During the interviews, we asked the officers to relate a story about a job-related experience from which they had learned something about leadership at their current organizational level. We made it clear that we were interested in specific examples of informal knowledge about leadership acquired in their current job. That is, we were *not* interested in leadership doctrine or theory expressed in books or taught in classes, nor were we interested in purely technical knowledge (e.g., military tactics, supply and maintenance procedures). By asking for stories, we were able to get subjects talking about their concrete experiences instead of abstract leadership concepts. We also encouraged subjects to express, in their own words, the leadership lessons learned in the specific situations that they described. After each interview, we prepared a written summary, seeking to capture each story and its associated lessons about leadership in words that were as close as possible to the subject's own. In all, the interviews produced 81 written summaries, each containing a number of specific stories and associated lessons.

As a first step in our analysis of the data, we identified the tacit knowledge contained in the interview summaries. Two members of the research team served as raters in the preliminary stages of this process. They independently read each summary, and identified the knowledge that qualified as tacit knowledge for military leadership according to our stated criteria. Next, the two raters performed a preliminary coding of the identified tacit knowledge contained within each story. This coding expressed each piece of identified knowledge as a mapping between a set of antecedent conditions ("IF" statements), a set of consequent actions ("THEN" statements), and a brief explanation ("BECAUSE" statement). We also used other logical operators ("AND," "OR," and "ELSE") to indicate conjunctive relationships, disjunctive relationships, and complex procedures, respectively. In all, we identified a final set of 174 coded knowledge items that together represented the tacit knowledge contained in the interview data.

We believe that the procedural formalisms (in terms of which we codified tacit knowledge) are best thought of as markers or "pointers" to complex, predominately implicit mental representations that are not directly available to conscious introspection. Because we cannot identify these implicit knowledge structures directly, we must content ourselves with examining the traces that these knowledge structures leave in the stories that our subjects told. Hence, the knowledge items that we constructed are not, strictly speaking, the tacit knowledge of the domain, but rather the best available representation of how that tacit knowledge is deployed in solving actual problems.

Finally, we grouped the tacit-knowledge items into categories in order to identify the general themes in our leaders' stories. Members of an expert panel independently sorted the items into categories of their own devising. Each individual performed three sorts—one for each of the three organizational levels. No constraints were placed on the size and number of sort categories; individuals were free to use whatever inclusion rules they wished as long as no categories overlapped. We then cluster-analyzed the results of the independent sortings in order to uncover natural groupings of tacit knowledge in the data set (Hartigan, 1975). The resulting, hierarchically organized clusters were printed in the form of tree diagrams, which the members of the expert panel then interpreted. High-level subclusters in the tree diagrams were labeled based on the content of the included items. These subclusters were then taken to represent content-based categories of tacit knowledge.

What did we learn about tacit knowledge from the stories our leaders shared with us? First, we learned that tacit knowledge for leadership exists and that, as we expected, it is embedded in the stories that leaders tell about their experiences. Although their espoused theories sound more or less alike, the stories that leaders tell are quite varied and provide a better window onto their leadership practice. This finding replicates previous tacit-knowledge research and is consistent with studies of managerial learning (McCall et al., 1988). Our findings further suggest that the content of military leadership tacit knowledge varies by organizational level. In general, the tacit-knowledge content for a particular level reflects the salient developmental challenges that leaders face when they approach that level. We also learned about the functions of tacit knowledge—it appears to both instantiate Army leadership doctrine (i.e., make it more applicable in specific situations) and augment or fill gaps in doctrine by providing knowledge through direct experience. In what follows, we provide a summary of our interview findings for each of the leadership levels we investigated.

Platoon Level

Platoon leaders (such as Bill, whose story we told earlier) have very limited experience in Army leadership—typically 1 to 3 years. Nevertheless, they are responsible for supervising soldiers (approximately 25 to 45 in number) with much longer time in service. They also exercise direct leadership through face-to-face interactions with their subordinates, and they must do so without much in the way of formal position power. Not surprisingly, the tacit knowledge about leadership at the platoon level reflects these challenges. The picture that emerges from the tacit knowledge for platoon leaders is that of men and women trying to get a foothold in their organizations. Many of the stories contained tacit knowledge about motivating subordinates. Motivating relatively more experienced subordinates in direct encounters without much formal authority also raises issues of personal credibility for platoon leaders. Similarly, credibility must be established with the boss if platoon leaders are to protect their limited autonomy. Not surprisingly, our platoon leaders talked about how they established credibility with their subordinates and their boss. Indeed, Bill's story was about establishing credibility with his company commander. But establishing credibility and authority over others with greater experience can be stressful. Hence, tacit knowledge about managing the self was relatively more frequent at this level than at higher levels (company and battalion). Finally, we were surprised that platoon leaders had few stories about developing subordinates—an important Army leadership competency. This result may reflect a limited capacity to develop subordinates due, in part, to the fact that platoon leaders have fewer resources, less discretion, and limited experience—all necessary preconditions for developing others.

Company Level

What is the typical experience of company commanders? They have more experience than platoon leaders, having themselves served as platoon leaders, completed officers' advanced training, and often held positions on a battalion-level staff. They have considerably more position power—they exercise the authority to administer nonjudicial punishment (e.g., reduce rank or withhold pay) and they decide how missions will be accomplished. Furthermore, they lead larger groups (typically 120 to 200 soldiers); hence, they have less direct contact with their subordinates. Again, the tacit knowledge about leadership at the company level reflects this organizational reality.

In general, the company commanders we interviewed appeared to be caught between the interpersonal requirements of direct leadership and the emerging need to take an institutional perspective to fulfill their responsibilities. Their increased discretion is reflected in the emergence of tacit knowledge about directing and supervising others—note Mary's story about micromanaging and developing her subordinates. By contrast, stories about establishing oneself did not appear, either because company commanders have already mastered these lessons or because the aura of command takes care of credibility issues. Finally, the company commander's role requires the incumbent to consider the needs of subordinates and simultaneously coordinate with higher headquarters. Hence, we found in the stories of our company commanders tacit knowledge about cooperating with others and balancing mission accomplishments against the needs of subordinates.

Battalion Level

Finally, what is the typical experience of battalion commanders? First, battalion commanders have considerable experience in the Army, having served from 16 to 20 years as officers. Second, their selection for command, the result of a highly competitive process, is a public recognition of their past success. Third, they enjoy considerable power and discretion in discharging the legal authority of command. Finally, the size of the groups they lead (typically 500 to 700 soldiers) makes it impossible to lead through direct, face-to-face encounters. Consequently, their influence is more often indirect than is the influence of leaders at lower levels.

The tacit knowledge we obtained from battalion commanders suggests that system-level thinking is a key developmental challenge at this level. Tacit knowledge for protecting the organization and managing organizational change was unique to our battalion commanders' stories. We also found that the composition of tacit knowledge about communicating differed from that obtained at the lower levels. That is, battalion commanders had learned to use indirect methods and systems of communication, whereas the tacit knowledge of leaders at lower levels concerned the exercise of leadership in face-to-face encounters. Finally, tacit knowledge about dealing with poor performers was unique to this level, a finding we attribute to the authority and discretion regarding personnel matters that is vested in battalion commanders.

Overall, the findings from the interview study encouraged us to continue our exploration of tacit knowledge for military leadership. The knowledge we obtained was relevant to professional practice in the Army and, as best we could determine, had been acquired through on-the-job experience with little direct support from others. The stories we heard during the interviews helped us to understand how our subjects' knowledge is applied to practice, and allowed us to develop procedural formalisms for representing that knowledge. Although our technique was subject to the general limitations of retrospective methods, it did provide a theoretically sound approach to identifying knowledge about military leadership that normally is not subject to introspection and articulation.

That professionals learn valuable lessons from experience is a conventional assertion—witness the rise in problem-based, contextualized learning in professional education. However, some lessons of experience are particularly important to competent performance, and the knowledge that we identified seemed to be of this type. It reflected both the challenges facing practitioners and the limitations of formal knowledge as a guide to meeting these challenges. These insights will help guide future efforts to understand the nature of professional expertise and to structure programs to facilitate its development.

There are several limitations to the generalizability of our findings from this interview study. First, the military is unique as a profession in that professional membership is tied to organizational membership. Thus, professional competence includes organizational (leadership) as well as a technical (battlefield operating systems) knowledge. During the interviews, we intentionally tried to disentangle leadership knowledge from technical knowledge. However, given the unique features of military organizations (e.g., salience of rank/status differences), it is not clear to what degree some of the tacit knowledge that we obtained might apply to other types of professional organizations. We also relied on battalion and brigade commanders to provide a representative sample of officers at each level, and so were unable to assess the extent to which the officers in our sample represent a range of leadership effectiveness. It may be that less effective leaders were underrepresented in our sample.

We turn now to a description of the next phase of our research program, in which we attempted to address these and other limitations of the interview study as well as to explore further the tacit knowledge construct as it pertains to military leadership.

VALIDATING THE LESSONS OF EXPERIENCE

The interview study left us with a number of unanswered questions. For example, how do we know that the lessons learned by our 81 subjects constitute good advice about military leadership? Does endorsement of this advice differentiate leaders in terms of their experience? In this section, we describe the methods used to answer these questions and to explore the tacit knowledge obtained in our interview study. Our aim was to identify items that were most promising for construction of tacit-knowledge assessment instruments (Forsythe et al., 1996; Horvath et al., 1996). To do this, we presented the 174 tacit-knowledge items obtained in the interview study, reformatted into a Tacit Knowledge Survey (explained later in this chapter), to a large sample of Army officers enrolled in military education courses. Each respondent in the sample represented one of three organizational levels (platoon, company, and battalion) and one of two degrees of leadership experience (experienced and novice). We reasoned that the most promising items for purposes of future development would be those that best discriminated between experienced and novice leaders (i.e., those on which experienced and less experienced leaders differed in their ratings).

Army officers enrolled in various military educational programs of the U.S. Army Training and Doctrine Command (TRADOC) participated in this study. The TRADOC schools conduct continuing professional education for Army personnel at schools around the country. During their careers, Army officers cycle between operational assignments and enrollment in TRADOC schools. We selected TRADOC schools as a source of subjects for two reasons. First, the courses offered by these schools provide a ready pool of active-duty officers at all the levels under consideration in our study. Second, by sampling students enrolled in various courses (with courses targeted to officers at different career stages), we were able to stratify the sample according to the degree of leadership experience possessed by subjects at each level under study. Officers designated as *novices* completed Tacit Knowledge Surveys for the next level of command (the focus of the course in which they were enrolled), whereas officers designated as *experienced* completed Tacit Knowledge Surveys for the level of command they had just completed. By administering to these subjects a survey asking them for ratings of tacit-knowledge items, we hoped to explore the relationship between leadership experience and ratings of tacit knowledge at a given level.

We collected the tacit-knowledge survey data through the mail from officers enrolled in 13 different courses at nine separate locations. At each course and location, we obtained random samples of officer students; a member of the research team conducted the sampling using class rosters provided by points of contact at the schools. Packets containing the Tacit Knowledge Survey appropriate to level and degree of experience were mailed to points of contact who distributed them to the students in the sample. Each packet contained a cover letter explaining the purpose of the study and asking for support from the selected officers. Completed packets were returned to the points of contact, who bundled the materials and shipped them to members of the research team at Yale. We obtained by these means a remarkably high response rate of 79%.

Data obtained from this sample provide information about the relationship between endorsements or judgments of tacit-knowledge items and degree of leadership experience. With this sample, we hoped to learn if ratings of tacit-knowledge items distinguished or discriminated between experienced and novice leaders at a given level. Items that discriminate based on experience would be of clear value in constructing valid instruments for measuring tacit-knowledge. Given our definition of tacit knowledge as knowledge grounded in personal experience, discriminating items would support the construct validity of our instruments quite directly.

We used the 174 tacit knowledge items obtained from the interview study to develop Tacit Knowledge Surveys (TKS). The development process involved two phases: recoding the items, and constructing measurement scales. We began by recoding the tacit-knowledge items obtained from the interview study (originally expressed as a complex mapping of antecedent conditions onto consequent actions) into briefer, more comprehensible form. We derived a recoding algorithm for reducing the items to their essential elements and applied this algorithm to each of the 174 items. The algorithm employed basic operations such as the condensation, abstraction, and deletion of nonessential information from the tacit-knowledge items. The rewritten items were routed to military members of the research team, who made additional revisions in order to increase the comprehensibility of the items for a military audience and in order to preserve the intention of the interviewees who provided the knowledge. The complete set of rewritten items was divided by level—battalion, company, and platoon—and used to construct three forms of the Tacit Knowledge Survey.

In the scale construction phase, we first identified the dimensions on which subjects were to rate the tacit-knowledge items. Dimensions reflected our interest in determining if each item represented good advice about military leadership that might not be common knowledge. The final TKS contained four 7-point rating scales, which were used to elicit judgments about each item of tacit knowledge. A detailed discussion of the scales and their development is provided in Horvath et al. (1996).

We analyzed the data for the TRADOC sample in three stages. First, we computed summary statistics (means and standard deviations) for the TKS rating scales by leadership level. Second, we derived intercorrelations among the rating scales for the TKS by leadership level. Correlation coefficients were computed on the question means in order to remove the effects of within-subject response dependencies. A principal components analysis of the intercorrelation matrix for each leadership level yielded only one component with an eigenvalue greater than or equal to 1, and we interpreted this to indicate a general factor of "quality." We decided to use the goodness scale in subsequent analyses rather than form a composite variable because the correlation between the goodness and concept scales was near unity, and, of the four scales, these two permitted relatively straightforward inferences about the respondents' leadership knowledge.[6] Finally, we conducted a series of discriminant analyses on the goodness ratings in order to identify the most promising tacit-knowledge items in the data set. In the data set, cases were subjects, discriminating variables were goodness ratings on the tacit-knowledge items in the TKS, and groups were the two levels of experience (experienced vs. novice). Discriminant analyses allowed us to assess the discriminating power of the combined set of tacit-knowledge items, and to rank items relative to one another on an index of discriminating power.

What did we learn from this study about the lessons of experience, and how will what we have learned help us to develop valid assessment instruments? First, we identified items obtained from the interview study that appear to discriminate between experienced and novice military leaders at each of three command levels. Because the theory suggests that tacit knowledge is domain-specific knowledge acquired through experience, we now have greater confidence that our corpus of items contains a sample of the content domain for military leadership. Following Messick's (1995) unified approach to validity, these results support the content aspect of validity and may eventually help us to link the items to the underlying construct of tacit knowledge for military leadership.

A detailed analysis of each tacit-knowledge item using the TRADOC data set offered additional insights into the content domain. For some of the highly discriminating items, high goodness ratings were characteristic of experienced leaders, whereas, for other items, endorsement of the item was more characteristic of novice leaders. Apparently, some of the items obtained in the earlier study might have *seemed* to be good advice to the incumbent leaders being interviewed, but may actually have reflected a naive approach to leadership. For example, several items of tacit knowledge for platoon leaders obtained from the interview study related to passing on orders from above and on managing the boss. The TRADOC data suggest that advice about when *not* to pass on orders from above as one's own (i.e., as though one agreed fully with them) is characteristic of novice platoon leaders, but that advice about how to confront the boss who issues an unpopular directive is characteristic of experienced leaders. Although both items appear plausible on the surface, the advice about not passing on orders as one's own may be naive or ineffective. Hence, the information gleaned from the TRADOC sample for each item will guide our development of scenarios and response alternatives in the assessment phase of the project.

Most important, we subjected the tacit-knowledge framework to a rigorous content validation before test construction in an effort to specify a priori the

---

[6]By contrast, the "known" and "often" scales do not support straightforward inferences about the respondents' leadership knowledge; they only tell us what the respondents believe other leaders know about leadership.

knowledge associated with competent practice in our domain of interest. Although there may be no objectively correct knowledge about military leadership, this procedure has moved us closer to specifying content that appears to differentiate experienced from novice leaders and that appears to be associated with relatively more effective performance. Therefore, we have set the stage for further construct and criterion validation of our assessment instruments.

As in past tacit-knowledge research, we must still rely on an expert profile for test scoring.[7] Nevertheless, the procedure we followed in the validation study provides a basis for test construction and for understanding and interpreting the expert profile that we will generate for scoring purposes. In addition, the content validation procedures have helped us to identify those tacit-knowledge items (and associated situations) that are most promising for the development of experienced-based professional training programs. We are presently engaged in designing three tacit-knowledge assessment instruments, one for each leadership level. Our plan is to develop an expert scoring profile for the instruments and to gather evidence bearing on their construct validity from a large sample of Army officers.

IMPLICATION FOR OFFICER DEVELOPMENT, EDUCATION, AND TRAINING

Although our research is not yet complete, we believe the tacit knowledge for military leadership project has, to date, yielded several important findings about the nature of leadership knowledge, and that these findings have implications for leader development. In addition, our work offers a rigorous test of Sternberg's tacit-knowledge framework—an influential approach to understanding and developing professional expertise. In the final section of this chapter, we offer our current thinking on these topics.

Practicing military leaders believe that certain aspects of leadership are simply "known." They are not explicitly taught, and thus are not readily available to conscious introspection or verbalization. Indeed, many of the officers whom we interviewed had difficulty verbalizing the lessons in their experience when asked to do so directly. "Tell us what you've learned about leadership from your experience as a company commander" often resulted in a comment such as, "I don't know, it's hard to put into words." As we probed for specific knowledge, we often heard platitudes or maxims such as "Know your job, set the example, and take care of your soldiers." But when we asked them to tell us stories about situations in which they felt

---

[7]Tacit-knowledge tests are scored by comparing a subject's pattern of responses to that obtained from a group of nominated experts.

they learned something about leadership, we discovered within them a rich and complex body of knowledge about leadership. This knowledge was grounded in the context of practice. It operationalized or supplemented the doctrinal guidelines, and it represented the developmental challenges that officers face as they advance in their careers. Some of this knowledge appears to differentiate officers based on their experience, suggesting that it is learned over time through experience in real-world settings. In sum, our work to date confirms that there is something to the construct of tacit knowledge. It appears to be a privileged type of job knowledge, one that is strongly associated with the development of professional expertise.

What are the implications of our work for leadership education and training? At this point, we don't foresee developing materials that will "teach" the tacit knowledge. Indeed, we found the task of "unpacking" the tacit knowledge from the stories to be very unsatisfying. The reformatted tacit-knowledge items, which we used in the content validation study, lacked the richness of the knowledge embodied in the stories themselves. As mentioned earlier, the items per se are not the tacit knowledge but instead are simply markers for the complex mental representations presumed to underlie intelligent problem solving. Knowing the items is *not* the same as knowing military leadership. Thus, teaching the tacit knowledge directly does not seem to us a reasonable solution.

Instead, we are focusing our attention on workplace situations that set the stage for experiential learning and that thus figure critically in the professional development of Army officers. The keys to education, knowledge management, and training lie, we believe, more in the contexts and the processes of learning than in the knowledge itself. Our data offer important insights into the kinds of on-the-job experiences that are important for learning about leadership, and we intend to pursue these implications in future work. Our plan is to develop materials that will assist leaders in anticipating and exploiting the relevant learning opportunities for themselves and their subordinates as these opportunities occur naturally in the workplace. This approach offers the additional advantage of extending our understanding of how tacit knowledge is acquired.

ACKNOWLEDGMENTS

Work on this chapter was supported by Contract MDA903-92-K from the U.S. Army Research Institute. This chapter does not represent the position or policies of the government, and no official endorsement should be inferred. The authors wish to thank Trueman Tremble, Jr., for helpful comments on the work.

REFERENCES

Bass, B. M. (1990). *Bass and Stogdill's handbook of leadership: Theory, research, and managerial applications.* New York: Free Press.

Cervero, R. M. (1988). *Effective continuing education for professionals.* San Francisco: Jossey-Bass.

Chi, M. T. H., Feltovich, P. J., & Glaser, R. (1981). Categorization and representation of physics problems by experts and novices. *Cognitive Science, 5,* 121–152.

Forsythe, G. B., & Barber, H. F. (1992, April). *Military strategic thinking: Expert–novice differences in the structure and content of cognitive representations.* Paper presented at the Annual Meeting of the American Educational Research Association, San Francisco.

Forsythe, G. B., Horvath, J. A., Sweeney, P. J., Bullis, R. C., Williams, W. M., & Sternberg, R. J. (1996, April). *Content validation of tacit knowledge for military leadership.* Paper presented at the Annual Meeting of the American Educational Research Association, New York.

Forsythe, G. B., Horvath, J. A., Sweeney, P. J., McNally, J. A., Wattendorf, J. M., Williams, W. M., & Sternberg, R. J. (1995, April). *Tacit knowledge for military leadership.* Paper presented at the Annual Meeting of the American Educational Research Association, San Francisco.

Harris, I. B. (1993). New expectations for professional competence. In L. Curry & J. Wergin (Eds.), *Educating professionals.* San Francisco: Jossey-Bass.

Hartigan, J. A. (1975). *Clustering algorithms.* New York: Wiley.

Headquarters, Department of the Army. (1987a). *Executive leadership* (Pamphlet 600-80). Washington, DC: U.S. Government Printing Office.

Headquarters, Department of the Army. (1987b). *Leadership and command at senior levels* (FM-22-103). Washington, DC: U.S. Government Printing Office.

Headquarters, Department of the Army. (1990). *Military leadership* (FM-22-100). Washington, DC: U.S. Government Printing Office.

Hollander, E. P. (1985). Leadership and power. In G. Lindzey & E. Aronson (Eds.), *Handbook of social psychology.* New York: Random House.

Horvath, J. A., Forsythe, G. B., Sweeney, P. J., McNally, J. A., Wattendorf, J., Williams, W. M., & Sternberg, R. J. (1994). *Tacit knowledge in military leadership: Evidence from officer interviews* (Technical Report). Alexandria, VA: U.S. Army Research Institute for the Behavioral and Social Sciences.

Horvath, J. A., Sternberg, R. A., Forsythe, G. B., Sweeney, P. J., Bullis, R. C., Williams, W. M., & Dennis, M. (1996). *Tacit knowledge in military leadership: Supporting instrument development* (Technical Report). Alexandria, VA: U.S. Army Research Institute for the Behavioral and Social Sciences.

Horvath, J. A., Williams, W. M., Forsythe, G. B., Sweeney, P. J., Sternberg, R. J., McNally, J. A., & Wattendorf, J. (1994). *Tacit knowledge in military leadership: A review of the literature* (Technical Report). Alexandria, VA: U.S. Army Research Institute for the Behavioral and Social Sciences.

McCall, M. W., Lombardo, M. M., & Morrison, A. M. (1988). *The lessons of experience: How successful executives develop on the job.* New York: Lexington.

Messick, S. (1995). Validity of psychological assessment: Validation of inferences from persons' responses and performances as scientific inquiry into score meaning. *American Psychologist, 50*(9), 741–750.

Norman, G. R. (1990, April). *The role of prior processing episodes.* Paper presented at the Annual Meeting of the American Educational Research Association, Boston.

Patel, V., & Groen, G. J. (1992, April). *Cognitive frameworks for clinical reasoning: Application for training and practice.* Paper presented at the Annual Meeting of the American Educational Research Association, San Francisco.

Polanyi, M. (1973). *Personal knowledge.* London, England: Routledge & Kegan Paul.

Schmidt, H. G. (1990, April). *The intermediate effect.* Paper presented at the Annual Meeting of the American Educational Research Association, Boston.

Schön, D. A. (1987). *Educating the reflective practitioner: Toward a new design for teaching and learning in the professions.* San Francisco: Jossey-Bass.

Smith, E. E., & Medin, D. L. (1981). *Concepts and categories.* Cambridge, MA: Harvard University Press.

Sternberg, R. J. (1988). *The triarchic mind: A new theory of human intelligence.* New York: Penguin.

Sternberg, R. J., & Wagner, R. K. (1993). The g-ocentric view of intelligence and job performance is wrong. *Current Directions in Psychological Science, 2,* 1–4.

Sternberg, R. J., Wagner, R. K., & Okagaki, L. (1993). Practical intelligence: The nature and role of knowledge in work and school. In H. W. Reese & J. M. Puckett (Eds.), *Mechanisms of everyday cognition* (pp. 205–227). Hillsdale, NJ: Lawrence Erlbaum Associates.

Sternberg, R. J., Wagner, R. K., Williams, W. M., & Horvath, J. A. (1995). Testing common sense. *American Psychologist, 50*(11), 912–927.

Tulving, E. (1972). Episodic and semantic memory. In E. Tulving & W. Donaldson (Eds.), *Organization of memory.* New York: Academic.

Wagner, R. K. (1987). Tacit knowledge in everyday intelligent behavior. *Journal of Personality and Social Psychology, 52,* 1236–1247.

Wagner, R. K., & Sternberg, R. J. (1985). Practical intelligence in real-world pursuits: The role of tacit knowledge. *Journal of Personality and Social Psychology, 48,* 436–458.

Yukl, G. (1989). Managerial leadership: A review of theory and research. *Journal of Management, 15,* 251–289.

CHAPTER FOUR

Military Learnings: A Practitioner's Perspective

Walter F. Ulmer, Jr.
Former President and CEO, Center for Creative Leadership

At the headquarters of the Center for Creative Leadership in Greensboro, North Carolina, on a sunny Monday morning in July 1985, the staff was gathered to meet the incoming president. There was anxiety in the air. Part of it, quite understandably, came from my entering their world from a different domain. Neither academician nor management consultant, I had spent the last 37 years in the U.S. Army—4 as a cadet at West Point and 33 as an officer.

In the search for a new president and CEO, several representatives from the Center had visited Fort Hood, Texas, my final command in the Army. Fort Hood remains the largest military post in the Western world, with a daytime population of military, Department of Defense civilians, private contractors, and military families of about 80,000. There were 6,000 trucks, 2,500 armored vehicles, more helicopters than in the combined French and British armies, 5,300 sets of family housing spread around its 630 square miles, and, most important, 40,000 soldiers. Other elements at four Army posts several hundred miles away, along with a number of Army Reserve units, created a total Corps complement of about 120,000. (When I joined it, the Center had about 120 full-time staff; it has since grown to over 400. The transition in the summer of 1985 from 120,000 soldiers to 120 civilians was memorable. It was also less traumatic than one might think.)

Command of Fort Hood and III Corps was an opportunity to use all of the leadership and management experience I had gathered between 1952 and 1982. From whatever sources and processes—genetic, formal education, specific experience, or tacit learning—Fort Hood allowed application of theory on a large scale. My primary task as III Corps commander was to be prepared to move the Corps on short notice to reinforce the Northern flank of the NATO defense. Several times each year we would take contingents from the United States to participate with the German, British, and Dutch units that were our primary defense partners. When the Chief of Staff of the Army assigned me to Fort Hood, he asked that I keep an eye on leadership and climate development. Fortunately, the two missions—readiness for deployment and leader development—were not only compatible but also interdependent. We could not develop and sustain a large organization capable of executing the NATO mission unless there was a climate in which leaders could lead. As one Army pamphlet described Airland Battle doctrine, "Success will depend on having leaders at all levels who understand the commander's intent and are able and willing to act with initiative and common sense within that intent. . . ." Junior leaders—sergeants and lieutenants and captains—had to be mentally and psychologically prepared to take charge, innovate, and just do what made sense. The knowledge and insights of the more senior leaders were obviously crucial to any such doctrine of battlefield decentralization.

SOME BACKGROUND FOR CONTEXT

One advantage of an Army career is that junior leaders have direct responsibilities for the training and well-being of soldiers. In December 1953, 18 months out of West Point, we returned from the end of the Korean War to a post in Japan where I took command of my first unit. I had been a platoon leader of 30 soldiers for a few months back in the States, and then executive officer of this same company of 200 soldiers. It was an Amphibious Tractor unit equipped with 53 armored, amphibious vehicles designed to carry assault troops from a ship miles offshore onto and over the beaches. There was a wider range of competencies among soldiers and officers in 1953 than there is today. We have upped the standards. There is less toleration of bizarre behavior, with fewer "characters." Our more efficient managerial systems have squeezed out a bit of the richness. Still, there is enough human diversity and untamed vigor to make life in troop units often exciting, and rarely dull. (In fact, in 1998, a dwindling defense budget combined with increasing numbers of operational missions have produced a nearly frenetic pace.)

This experience was followed by command of two other companies, one tank company in an Infantry Division in Korea, and another in an airborne infantry regiment of the 82d Airborne Division at Fort Bragg, North Carolina. Between these companies and the assignment at Fort Hood were commands of a Cavalry Squadron, an Armor Brigade of about 4,500 soldiers, and an Armored Division of 17,000 in Germany. These and other tours, such as Commandant of Cadets at West Point during interesting times (introduction of women and a major Honor Code affair), and the extensive formal schooling in which all career officers engage, provided limitless opportunities to observe, study, and practice leading. The exact processes by which learning took place remain unclear, even after my exposure to theories of adult learning and development. Later in this chapter I do some speculating about how tacit knowledge seems to play a role in the development of competencies.

ELEMENTS OF THE MILITARY PROFESSION

Most scholars agree that the "military" meets the criteria for a "profession." There are identifiable values of worth to the larger society, an area of specialized knowledge, processes for admission and certification, and standards for acceptable practice. Distinctive rituals spawned ages ago intermix with contemporary managerial techniques and the technology of cyberspace, forming a fascinating matrix. The American armed forces, facing stresses of "rightsizing" and reconfiguration similar to that of the corporate world, have seen an already perplexing local and world environment become more so. The post–Cold War scene brought challenges across the spectrum of military operations. As the geopolitical, technological, and social waves of change sweep across the landscape, the military profession has been hard pressed to tailor doctrine and organizations in response to an expanding array of missions. We expect today's military practitioner to be armed with knowledge relevant to the lingering nuclear missile threat, drug interdiction, humanitarian relief, "peacekeeping," terrorist plots, national strategy, and the continuous surveillance of much of the earth's sea, land, and airspace.

A few significant differences exist between the military and other professions. These differences create both exploitable opportunities and bothersome obstacles for development of individual expertise. First, the military warrior credo puts accomplishment of mission above life itself. "Duty first," "I'll try, sir," and "Always Faithful" are more than regimental mottoes: Even today, they inform orientation and mold behavior. Although competence is prized and rewarded within the military, "character" remains the bedrock on which reputations are made. The military historian S. L. A. Marshall (1975/1996) commented that even the infamous Captain Queeg of *The Caine Mutiny* might have been tolerated with all his other vices had he, "under fire, proved himself somewhat better than a coward" (p. 107).[1] As military planners and theoreticians look into the world of the 21st century, acknowledging the need to master ever-more-complex technology and comprehend the intricacies of global politics, such elements as "integrity," "courage," and "loyalty" still hold center stage. In October 1997, the Army introduced a revised

[1]This is as good a summary of military values as ever written.

performance appraisal form (Officer Evaluation Report) which listed Army values as: honor, integrity, courage, loyalty, respect, selfless service, and duty.

Comparing desired traits—for all of their relevance or insignificance—between the military and other professions, there is high correlation. One finds "intelligent," "energetic," "innovative," and "committed" on most lists. "Physical courage" is prominent only on the military list. Neither Harvard Medical, Yale Divinity, nor Columbia Law require completion of a 2-mile run as entrance qualifiers, nor do they expel members from the clan for becoming overweight. This link with the physical, this notification that the battle arena requires strength of many dimensions, remains a distinguishing element of the profession. During the stresses of the Vietnam era, a period of consternation in so many ways, internal studies showed high regard for traditional military values. Leaders of all ranks lamented any lapses between ideal and operational value systems.

Second, the military profession is unique in there being but one "company." One might leave General Motors and go to Ford, or leave a professorship at MIT and move to Cal Tech; to transfer to another Army, Navy, or Air Force is impossible. Within this contained community one's reputation clings and reverberates. Also, there is no lateral entry at mid-career. All generals were second lieutenants, and all admirals were ensigns. Although there is an enormously wide variation of assignments within one's career pattern—going from helicopter cockpit one year to a long-range planning desk in the Pentagon the next—the same basic culture prevails, nourished by a strong set of values. Cultural immersion and group bonding, for better or worse, are simply more complete than in the "outside" professions. The military is also an exception in that it cannot practice its primary business except in battle. Every peacetime training exercise is but a simulation of the "real thing."

Evaluating the ultimate effectiveness of a military organization is technically impossible outside the war zone, and maybe not possible there either. Although complicated formulas have been derived to measure the state of training and the readiness of equipment, all such models remain approximations. Subsequently, the military has a fundamental criterion problem. If professional competence leads to battle-ready units, but battle-readiness measurements remain imprecise, then the pillars of individual effectiveness are less than tightly defined. Fortunately, some kind of intuitive feel plus exhaustive attempts to codify standards have resulted in an ability to sustain operational reliability. American military operations from Grenada to Panama, the Gulf, Haiti, Bosnia, and even Mogadishu have validated the basic models of training and professional development. Still, the debate properly continues on the exact description of the current and future attributes of the professional officer. The military has the interesting contemporary challenge of stimulating renewal and adaptation, questioning assumptions, and entertaining innovation, all within a tightly bounded institution whose membership take seriously their role in the nation's well-being.

COMPONENTS OF MILITARY COMPETENCE

If ever a profession highlighted the triviality of the "leader versus manager" debate, it is the military. The Department of Defense, even after the budget decimation of recent years, remains larger than the top 5 of the Fortune 100 companies in annual expenditures, and larger than the top 15 combined in total people. It manages global personnel, materiel acquisition, research and development, and fiscal systems of astounding size and complexity. Still, the ancient call to the soldier-in-arms for heroic leadership permeates the institution.

Competence is ultimately defined by the standards of acceptable practice. In the broadest sense, leaders within all organizations perform three basic tasks: *operate* the in-place systems (perform the day-to-day business), *build and sustain* the institution (select and train future leaders, invest in long-term research and development, create the appropriate climate, and nourish the positive culture and values of the institution), and *interface* with entities and publics outside their domain (coordinating with local or federal agencies, generating public support for their crusades, cooperating with suppliers and clients). The more senior the position, the more similarity there is between the military and corporate worlds in the performance of these general tasks.

The American and European military professions have invested enormous resources attempting to identify the underlying competencies essential for success. Not surprisingly, most of this effort has been on *operating* competencies; few historians have explored the skills involved in *building* military organizations, or in *interfacing* with outside entities. Even less effort has been devoted to dissecting the associated learning processes. Among the many thoughtful listings of competencies and values, a few are particularly cogent. First, these Army "Principles of Leadership":

1. Know yourself and seek self-improvement.
2. Be technically and tactically proficient.
3. Seek responsibility and take responsibility for your actions.
4. Make sound and timely decisions.
5. Set the example.
6. Know your soldiers and look out for their welfare.
7. Keep your soldiers informed.
8. Develop a sense of responsibility in your subordinates.
9. Ensure that the task is understood, supervised, and accomplished.

10. Train your soldiers as a team.
11. Employ your unit in accordance with its capabilities.

I see ageless wisdom in these 11 statements that have been around for decades. The challenge, of course, is in translating them into routine behaviors. A neat capturing of soldierly virtues was produced by Colonel D. M. Malone (1983). His *Competence, Candor, Commitment, and Courage* caught on as shorthand for Army ideal characteristics of leaders (see Malone, 1983).

Another set of desired attributes of senior leaders, developed with some reference to the military context, was outlined by Marshal Sashkin. Sashkin isolated three "personal capabilities" as central to competence in "strategic leadership": cognitive capacity, self-efficacy (explained as belief in oneself as an effective agent of change), and power motive (described as recognition of the essentiality of power and influence in accomplishing organizational goals). These are not far from the "three pillars of generalship" noted in the 1930s by J. F. C. Fuller (1937) in his *Generalship: Its Diseases and Their Cure*: courage, creative intelligence, and physical fitness. Some research has downplayed the role of high intelligence, but I would reject any such thesis. Leaders who make inept decisions soon lose the trust of their subordinates. During periods of battlefield stress, I have found it wonderfully comforting to have bright people beside and above me.

My own list comes mostly from personal experience, modified a bit by the literature of history and behavioral science. Recognizing that *behaviors,* and not *characteristics* or *traits,* are what matters, we might start with what could be called the "leadership hygiene factors." They are essential, yet, by themselves, do not guarantee success: intellectual acuity, technical competence, organizational commitment, high energy, integrity, physical and moral courage, and communications skills. Building on these essentials, two particular aspects of personality and their attendant behaviors seem to account for most of the difference among individuals in sustained leadership effectiveness: receptivity to new ideas, and mode of decision making (ability to include others appropriately in the process). Of course, the key question is how these traits or behaviors are—or are not—assimilated.

Individuals who have developed what might be called the "essential hygiene factors" and have sustained a receptivity to new ideas and an inclusive decision-making style appear to have some common instincts. They seem to process inputs from both the cognitive and emotional realms simultaneously. Furthermore, they balance tactical, strategic, and interpersonal issues, even under stress. Their mental reserves are not easily overtaxed. They do not compartmentalize the segments of their intellectual work—their information processing is in the multiplex mode and surely nonlinear.

Grant and Lee both possessed these capacities. Each responded to both strategic and personal considerations in the same breath, Grant probably even more so than Lee. Joshua Chamberlain, the Bowdoin College professor turned soldier par excellence, exemplified at the battle of Little Round Top in 1863 an amalgam of heroic, strategic, and interpersonal sensitivities. This mixture of talent and learned behavior defies clear measurement, yet produces near unanimity among observers regarding its presence. Many aspects of the knowledge and behaviors attributable to such highly regarded professionals are detectable in their early years. As lieutenants they rarely blunder except in the area of basic skills not yet mastered. Second mistakes are uncommon. Some officers very high on traditional scales of intelligence are notable for their effectiveness. Others of high intelligence are notably unimpressive. However, I have observed few of very modest conventional intelligence who had assimilated enough "street smarts" to become highly effective at senior levels.

LEARNING WITHIN THE PROFESSION

Army officers have considerably more formal education than do their counterparts in the corporate world. Over 85% of Army generals have a Master's or higher degree. Army officers average 2 years in formal schooling during their first decade of service. Military schools cover the gamut of subject matter. The most senior curricula include national strategy, international politics, and management of complex systems. Current "doctrine" in warfighting, in management techniques, in "operations other than war," and in leadership are included in schools appropriate to the experience level of the students. For some officers, this mandatory education is augmented by attendance at graduate programs in civilian institutions. Most career officers serve at least one tour of 2 to 4 years as a member of a school faculty. (Service on faculties in the 1930s was seen as the critical assignment in developing the Pattons, Marshalls, and Eisenhowers for their World War II responsibilities.)

Most adult learning takes place on the job, not in the classroom. Furthermore, research in a variety of environments indicates that "failure" at executive levels in organizations is rarely attributable to lack of technical knowledge. Army War College explorations of differences between highly effective senior officers and those of undistinguished reputations led to a focus on sensitivity to context, resiliency, and integrity as major discriminators. Similar results were reported from a more formidable 6-year study of corporate executives done by CCL. That study, producing a book entitled *The Lessons of Experience* (see McCall et al., 1988), isolated factors that led to "derailment" or premature side-tracking on the way to career success. Technical incompetence again was not high on the list of causal factors, but being able to "mold a team," "learn from mistakes," and "follow through with commitments" were very high.

The military culture both enhances and inhibits individual and organizational learning. By "organizational learning" I mean the collective capacity of the organization to seek out and process new information and make necessary adjustments to doctrine, goals, and procedures. By "individual learning" I mean the enhancement of self-awareness that facilitates embracing new perspectives, sheds dysfunctional behaviors, and raises sensitivity to context. The mix of traditional military values with the personality characteristics of typical career officers is a powerful tonic. It sustains attention to obligations, provides the gall to attack at night over unwelcome terrain, and perpetuates a relentless can-do attitude that wins wars. In a less positive vein, one must note the combined unwholesome potential of our American penchant for prompt results, the military urge for demonstrable outcomes, and an institutional system of rewards that reinforces fixation on the present. For further discussion of the contemporary environment and its potential impact on executive learning, see Ulmer (1998). However, these mixes of values and circumstance can also be a positive stimulus for acquiring the prized critical skills of the profession.

Lieutenants will not become captains and company commanders unless they demonstrate certain proficiencies and aptitudes. High energy, commitment to the task at hand, and mental agility are universally appreciated, as is the more ambiguous package of sensitivities and behaviors from which "leadership" emerges. The lieutenant tank platoon leader, with his four tanks and 15 men, carries his background of prior indoctrination into the culture and watches the people around him. He searches for clues that will link theory to reality. The busy world of daily action provides a rich source of data if he can interpret the signals. The lieutenant learns that mastery of basic tasks of soldiering is essential if he is to gain respect from soldiers. His primary mentor, the company commander, is almost always nearby. His savvy platoon sergeant is a handy source of tips, and the lieutenant's peers are available and scrambling with the same learning curve. He has been taught the principles of leadership. If the lieutenant is in a reasonably supportive local climate, if his company commander is the coach he is supposed to be, the acquisition of the less specific skills of officership somehow become part of his person. He senses when to joke with soldiers and when not to; when to give a little slack and when to be unyielding; when to stand right on top of the action and when to leave people alone. Often this learning takes place during serious operations, when the platoon leader has responsibilities rarely given to a civilian counterpart until years later, if ever. The lieutenant may be in the jungle interdicting drug runners, in the villages of Haiti policing the police, guarding the dismantling of nuclear weapons systems in Ukraine, clearing mines along a muddy road in Bosnia, or attacking a terrrist headquarters lodged in the middle of some crowded city. Street smarts alone can take a lieutenant a long way. However, there is an additional requirement of broad mental quickness—a basic cognitive versatility needed for dealing with the complex ambiguities of the executive suite.

At middle and senior levels in the military, the culture has high potential for inhibiting individual growth and learning, thereby constraining organizational learning as well. Nontraditional, informal, and deeper learning seems particularly vulnerable to the downsides of a powerful culture. The genesis of the anti-learning virus is military discipline and its companion piece—resistance to disorder or change. The stronger the rationale for disciplined accountability, the more sacrosanct is the assumption of a knowledge hierarchy. The greater the perceived repercussions of organizational failure, the more tightly the culture avoids experimentation. Because discipline in battle remains the bedrock of functioning, the requirement for discipline and accountability remain uncontested. The real miracle may be that American military organizations are globally recognized as excellent in warfighting, yet increasingly comfortable in permitting traditional assumptions regarding authority and hierarchy to be scrutinized.

The major casualty in the learning camp is self-growth. Self-growth, particularly among adults, requires self-awareness. Self-awareness requires feedback regarding individual strengths and weaknesses. "Coaching" and "feedback" are increasingly touted as necessary elements of leading, but most often come into play when addressing specific technical skills. Although learning subtle aspects of self-development is not ingeniously and routinely stimulated by the military institution, such development does take place. It is a somewhat erratic and serendipitous process. Hearty personalities defy the pernicious downsides of the bureaucracy, and emerge not only strategically competent but also emotionally robust and philosophically bold. Military memoirs often reflect continuous learning, although few have revealed much about the learning processes. Introspective commentary is not a hallmark of military writing. This may not mean that self-awareness is totally absent, but rather that the military personality is uncomfortable with public contemplation. Whether there is a correlation between self-awareness—which seems to be essential for self-revitalization—and the ability to absorb tacit knowledge deserves some study. I see no clear relation between the two.

SPECULATION ABOUT PERSONALITIES AND LEARNING

For more than 20 years, the Center for Creative Leadership (CCL) has been collecting data on the personality characteristics of Army brigadier generals. Most of the information has come from questionnaires completed by the officers themselves. Confirming information has been derived from staff observations and by questionnaires completed by subordinates, bosses, and peers of the officers. Because the questionnaires consist primarily of standardized psychometric instruments, the results may be compared with other executive groups. As one example of such comparison, 2 of the 16 psychological types identified by the Myers-Briggs instrument (the ESTJ and ISTJ) account for over 50% of the generals' personalities. In the adult population as a whole, those two types account for less than 30%. David Campbell, Ph.D., has been the principal researcher using these data. In a 1987 address (see Campbell, 1987), he commented that the profile of the typical general officer might be labeled "the aggressive adventurer." He described that personality as "dominant, competitive, action-oriented patriotic men who are drawn naturally to physically adventuresome militaristic activities."

Dr. Campbell continued:

> Despite my few misgivings, I am impressed by most of the officers I have been working with . . . general officers that we have now are outstanding—they are bright, well-educated, experienced, responsible and well indoctrinated into democratic ways. Further, in the few ways we have to evaluate them in comparison with civilian leaders, the generals come across as more impressive. . . . As a group these officers are not only maintaining a world-class defense organization, they are also running a remarkably effective social institution. . . .

In other words, many of the practitioners have been learning to cope and lead, through one mechanism or another.

The characteristics of the typical brigadier general described by Dr. Campbell must have been molded significantly by genetics and early childhood environment. These personality types migrated naturally to the "sound of the guns." However, within their range of personalities there are notable differences in aptitudes for learning. We need further research to locate the intersections between standard personality measures and individual ability to soak up the collections of insights that make up tacit knowledge.

Most generals whom I had known when they were lieutenants had changed over the years in their world view. A conspicuous few had not. All remained committed to the values of the institution. They had all survived the tests of battle. They were capable of discussing the intricacies of the national industrial base, the integration of various systems for global satellite surveillance, or the geopolitical impact of nuclear weapons testing. Those few who had moved upward in the ranks despite being known as questionable leaders appeared to have one characteristic in common: Their youthful self-confidence had coalesced into arrogance. They spoke often and listened infrequently. Their style prevented warm contact with the rest of the world, with resultant gaps in their pictures of reality. And, in a very few but conspicuous cases, their prior street smarts had turned into a self-serving deviousness.

Typical measures of cognitive functioning might not have discriminated between these two groups of "successful" people. The area recently defined as "emotional intelligence" would account for some part of the variance. The more effective leaders had a style that could be considered "transforming" when that was called for, including presentation of a clear, attractive vision of the desired future; a work mode that provided intellectual challenge to subordinates; and attention to people as individuals. They also displayed a genuine interest in creating a better future, and were able to share recognition in accomplishments. They were not without ambition or desire for notoriety—neither Norm Schwarzkopf nor Colin Powell are shrinking violets—but those needs did not corrupt their personalities. Some number of them had dazzling charisma; however, if there is a relationship between charisma and tacit knowledge, I do not understand it.

INDIVIDUAL DIFFERENCES AND LEARNING

Prior to assuming command of an armored division, it was my good fortune to have had field command experience at company, battalion (four or five companies), and brigade (three to five battalions, five in my case) levels, and to have been an assistant division commander for 18 months as a brigadier general. Serving under Major General George Patton (the son of the WWII legend) as one of his Assistant Division Commanders was one of many opportunities to see strong personalities in action. The younger Patton, like his father, held a powerful cluster of beliefs, and was anxious for action, impatient with incompetence, and remarkably open to suggestions from his staff and subordinate commanders. Such experiences honed my knowledge of tactics, weapons, maintenance, logistics, and administration. Service in active theaters in Korea and Vietnam permitted me to see and feel how people (including myself) and machines functioned under stress. Yet, to this day, I do not know exactly how my colleagues or I devised our techniques for leading large organizations. Nor do I know how one retains enough of that priceless feel for what goes on in the depths of the organization to keep a realistic view of the second- and third-order impact of our orders and policies. Senior officers need a kind of empathetic foresight that penetrates organizational compartmentalization. It appears that this capacity comes from deep within the personality, and is quite immune to development through conventional learning.

I have a friend who is an expert woodsman. He walks through the underbrush, notices a few leaves here and a scratch on a tree fungus there, and tells me what animals have passed through recently and what they were thinking at the time. Watching one of my peers who was a first-rate division commander, I noticed that he, too, could read signs. He knew when to jump into the critique, and when to keep quiet. He knew during review and analysis sessions that if a chart showed that a certain organization reported 98% of its attack helicopter fleet operational with all systems ready—weapons, avionics, and airframes—then something was wrong. The mental processes that go into ferreting out implausible data are not mechanical; some leaders smell the inconsistencies and others do not. Standard intelligence measures do not uncover the source of the difference—it is the experienced application of some special sense. Whether or not this sense can be measured and developed is, to me, an open question. There are conventionally bright but ineffective people who cannot be made whole through the usual methods of higher education. Attendance at the Harvard Business School or similar executive programs does not seem to greatly increase the capacity for integrated, adroit thinking.

FUTURE PROFESSIONAL COMPETENCIES

The traditional paraphrasings of basic qualities seem relevant to tomorrow. Malone's *Competence, Candor, Commitment, and Courage,* and Major General J. F. C. Fuller's three pillars of generalship—courage, creative intelligence, and physical fitness—still hit the mark. The eleven "Principles of Leadership" remain useful. Still, if there is not significant learning of new competencies centered on how to apply these timeless principles, the future of a robust American military may be in doubt. Just as a confluence of forces caused the dissolution of the Soviet Union—worldwide television and the strength of the American military being two of the external elements compounding the internal pressures from a bankrupt economy—there is a watershed of events that could lead to diminished vigor within the American military profession. I mentioned these forces earlier: dwindling military budgets in the face of expanding military missions; a cohort of skilled young people less interested in military service; a variety of quasi-military missions that could diminish the ability to train and sustain units for the complexity and hostility of future battlefields; a likelihood of less differentiation between military and political subject matter, and its attending potential dilution of specific military expertise; technological advances that require both materiel and intellectual response from the military services; keen competition for the energetic and altruistic personalities that the military must attract and retain; and the expectations of both enlisted and commissioned members of the Armed Forces for a work environment that is rational, supportive, and emotionally rewarding to them and to their families. All this is occurring in an era when the hardships and dangers of routine military life are evermore distant from the dream of a comfortable lifestyle.

The keystone to a relevant, healthy profession is learning. There can be no organizational learning if individual learning is truncated. Organizational learning is simply the collective ability of the people involved to sense the external and internal realities and take requisite, innovative action. Organizational learning involves an awareness of the need to learn, a model for learning, and the creation of an environment that supports and rewards learning. Neither the civilian nor military worlds typically have all three parts: *awareness, model,* and *environment.* Defining, integrating, and implementing these three parts constitute a major challenge.

Perhaps tacit knowledge can be seen in part as the intellectual lubricant that fosters both self-awareness and contextual sensitivity. In any case, the development of more sophisticated models for learning must precede any adventure in meaningful institutional redesign. Sustainment of an efficient and effective military centers around the full development of human potential. This translates into a pressing need for better appreciation of what "knowledge" really is—and how best we acquire it.

REFERENCES

Campbell, D. (1987, August). *The psychological test profiles of brigadier generals: Warmongers or decisive warriors?* Address presented at Division 14 of The American Psychological Association Convention, New York.

Fuller, J. F. C. (1937). *Generalship: Its diseases and their cure.* London: Hutchinson.

Malone, D. M. (1983). *Small unit leadership: A commonsense approach.* Novato, CA: Presidio Press.

Marshall, S. L. A. (1996). Leaders and leadership. In R. L. Taylor & W. E. Rosenbach (Eds.), *Military leadership* (3rd ed., p. 107). Boulder, CO: Waterview Press. (Original work published 1975)

McCall, M. W., Jr., et al. (1988). *The lessons of experience: How successful executives develop on the job.* Lexington, MA: Lexington Books.

Sashkin, M. (1992). Strategic leadership competencies. In R. L. Phillips & J. G. Hunt (Eds.), *Strategic leadership: A multiorganizational-level perspective* (pp.139–160). Westport, CT: Quorum Books.

Ulmer, W. F. (1998). Military leadership in the 21st century: Another bridge too far. *Parameters, 27*(1), 4–25.

PART THREE

MEDICINE

CHAPTER FIVE

Expertise and Tacit Knowledge in Medicine

Vimla L. Patel
José F. Arocha
McGill University

David R. Kaufman
University of California, Berkeley

All nature is art, unknown to thee;
All chance, direction, which thou canst not see;
All discord, harmony not understood;
All partial evil, universal good;
And, spite of pride, in erring reason's spite,
One truth is clear; Whatever IS, is right
—Alexander Pope, *An Essay on Man*

Observers of the medical profession have often commented on the tension between the art and science of medicine. The science of medicine is viewed as emerging from the "bench" in the laboratories. Indeed, clinical medicine is built on a foundation that draws on the biomedical sciences of anatomy, biochemistry, as well as physiology and applied sciences such as pathology, radiology, and medical physics. The art of medicine has been seen as "practice at the bedside." In medical folklore, the bedside has become a metaphor for all patient care. The science of medicine in clinical practice sees the physician as correlating or applying principles in an axiomatic or deductive fashion to a patient's symptoms, yielding a precise diagnostic solution. The artistic approach involves the use of intuition, experience, and holistic perceptions in making clinical judgments and in the delivery of humane care. Traditionally, the scientific dimension is viewed as the application of explicit knowledge, and the more intuitive artistic side draws on tacit knowledge. Although there is some truth in this distinction, the actual boundaries are much harder to delineate. As research into the study of expert performance has demonstrated, there is considerable tacit knowledge that underlies scientific reasoning in medicine (Patel, Arocha, & Kaufman, 1994). Similarly, there is a wealth of inarticulate scientific knowledge that supports the seemingly intuitive judgment of the expert practitioner. The poem by Alexander Pope exemplifies this paradox, where art and science and the tacit and explicit are blurred in the service of some common underlying order. Although all may not yield to a collective good, the hope is that it will yield some common understanding.

The tension between art and science, as well as the tacit and the explicit, is not unique to medicine, but rather characterizes all disciplines where theory is applied to practice. In the medical profession, physicians sometimes speak of moving from the bench to the bedside; in other words, science in service of practice. As observers and investigators of cognitive performance in the professions, we endeavor to understand the tacit as well as the explicit dimensions of knowledge. Research into the nature of expertise has, for the most part, focused on investigations of explicit knowledge in well-constrained laboratory tasks that have some relationship with real-world tasks. However, in recent years, investigators have attempted to gain insight by studying real-world performance. This necessitates a kind of metaphoric reversal, where we now move from observations at the bedside to studies at the bench. The practice of everyday clinical medicine serves as the basis for the systematic investigation of issues in a laboratory setting.

In this chapter, we argue for the importance of domain knowledge in the acquisition of medical expertise. Domain knowledge informs practice, and practice, in turn, shapes knowledge. As explicit medical "textbook knowledge" becomes reified in the practice of medicine, the tacit dimension becomes increasingly important. Tacit knowledge, by definition, refers to the inarticulate aspects that cannot be taught explicitly and therefore are only acquired via direct experience. This raises the question of what is the nature of the experience that promotes the acquisition of tacit knowledge. This is one of the focal issues in this chapter. We outline a systematic approach to the study of medical expertise through which we attempt to understand the role that the acquisition of tacit knowledge plays in competent and expert performance. The approach is based on both laboratory and "real-world" research, and on the use of knowledge elicitation methods. These methods allow us to investigate cognitive processes underlying the performance of medical students, physicians in training, and expert clinicians.

The first section introduces definitions and distinctions pertaining to implicit and explicit knowledge, and distinguishes different stages in the development of expertise. We subsequently discuss findings from laboratory research that indicate that medical experts develop expanded, interconnected, and coherent knowledge bases, which foster the use of knowledge-based reasoning strategies. However, laboratory studies paint only part of the picture. To complete the landscape, we argue for an extension of the basic research to include investigation of how experts perform in real-world environments. Research in real-world environments necessitates a shift of emphasis from the study of cognitive processes of the single person to the study of collective decision-making processes involved in the workplace of health care practice. Although findings from the bench concerning the nature of expertise yield valuable insights into proficient and competent performance, they fall short of accounting for the behavior of experts at the bedside (Cimino, chap. 6, this volume). The acquisition of tacit knowledge takes place in real-world environments, which involve decision making under time pressure and constraining conditions, characterized by the interplay of multiple factors.

In this chapter, we discuss the information-processing constraints imposed on medical decision-making processes in combination with sociocultural and organizational constraints that influence clinical practice. We characterize a process by which tacit knowledge is acquired through clinical experience.

IMPLICIT AND EXPLICIT KNOWLEDGE

It is commonly accepted among scholars in diverse fields that there are two basic types of knowledge: knowledge that can be verbalized, such as knowledge of facts and concepts; and knowledge that cannot made verbal, such as intuition and knowledge of procedures. The former type of knowledge has received a great deal of attention in cognitive research. This research has addressed the role of domain-specific knowledge in problem solving and reasoning in diverse fields (Chi, Glaser, & Farr, 1988; Ericsson & Smith, 1991). However, after many years of investigating the effects of domain-specific knowledge, cognitive researchers have realized that informal knowledge is as important as, and sometimes more important than, formally acquired knowledge (Carraher, Carraher, & Schlieman, 1985; Sternberg, Wagner, & Okagaki, 1993; Wagner & Sternberg, 1987). Probably nowhere is the study of implicit knowledge more important than in the professions, where a large part of learning occurs in practice, after formal training has been completed.

First, it is important to clarify some basic conceptual issues and definitions regarding the concepts of knowledge and expertise. In philosophy, knowledge is defined as justified belief. However, this definition refers only to knowledge that is explicitly formulated in symbolic form. In addition, the term *knowledge* is also used to refer to nonverbal forms of information. We can think of this knowledge as phylogenetically more primitive than is symbolic knowledge, as is evident in the example that the bee knows the path that leads to the food. The bee possesses knowledge, but we cannot say that it has beliefs, much less that these are justified. In a similar vein, a child knows how to walk, but we cannot say that he or she has a justified belief about walking. The reason we make this distinction is simply to show that the term *knowledge* covers what seems to be different forms of information stored in an animal's nervous system, humans included, which involves more than can be stated verbally.

We can relate the distinction between verbal and nonverbal knowledge to the one, originally made by Ryle (1949), between "knowing that" and "knowing how"; and to the more recently made distinction by cognitive scientists (e.g., Anderson, 1983) between declarative and procedural knowledge. Declarative knowledge is characteristic of explicit, verbalizable knowledge, and procedural knowledge is exemplary of tacit or implicit knowledge. One may argue that these two forms of knowledge follow a developmental progression, at least in some forms of learning, such as cognitive skill acquisition. Anderson (1983), for instance, argued that declarative knowledge precedes procedural knowledge. There is, however, evidence that this is not always the case, suggesting that the two forms of knowledge may involve different mechanisms (Siegler, 1989). In sum, *tacit knowledge* is used to refer to knowledge that is not easily articulated, and frequently involves knowledge of how to do things. We can infer its existence only by observing behavior and determining that this sort of knowledge is a precondition for effective performance. Tacit knowledge can be identified in assumptions, biases, ways of looking at the world, and forms of behavior that take advantage of situational factors.

There is a great deal of evidence suggesting the psychological validity of tacit knowledge (Reber, 1989, 1993; Seger, 1994). The typical experimental methodology consists of providing subjects with problems whose solution requires the induction of an implicit rule or sets of rules. For instance, subjects may be asked to memorized a set of letter strings whose underlying presentation hides a "grammar" with specific set of rules, but not be told that the presentation of strings has an underlying structure. They are then compared with a control group, who are asked to learn the same stimuli presented in a randomized fashion. When the experimental and the control subjects are compared, the results show that the former perform better in the memory task than do the latter. Although the experimental subjects seem to learn the underlying rule system, they show no conscious awareness of it. Similar research has been conducted using artificial but meaningful materials as stimuli (Broadbent, Fitzgerald, & Broadbent, 1986). For instance, Wagner (1987) investigated the role of implicit knowledge in more complex, real-world situations, such as those involved in managerial performance.

The reason we have presented the notions of explicit and implicit knowledge in some detail is that we think that the key to understanding the role of implicit knowledge in expert performance lies in the relationship between formally acquired knowledge and informally acquired knowledge. We make the following claims: (a) Explicit knowledge and implicit knowledge are two separate forms of knowledge, which are effected by different mechanisms and acquired through different experiences; (b) the equivalent to these two types of knowledge in the medical domain are domain-specific knowledge, which is explicitly acquired, and practical clinical knowledge, which is partially learned through experience in hospitals and other health care settings; (c) the successful utilization of implicit knowledge rests on the acquisition of well-formed, biomedical knowledge structures; and (d) implicit knowledge is situated—that is, it becomes available in routine situations of practice. Advances in learning are often dependent on making tacit knowledge explicit and thereby amenable to conceptual change.

WHAT IS MEDICAL EXPERTISE?

Definitions of Expertise in Medicine

Usually, someone is designated as an expert based on a certain level of performance, as exemplified by Elio ratings in chess; by virtue of being certified by a professional licensing body, as in medicine, law, or engineering; on the basis of academic criteria, such as graduate degrees; or simply based on years of experience or peer evaluation (Hoffman, Shadbolt, Burton, & Klein, 1995). The concept of an expert, however, refers to an individual who surpasses competency in a domain (Klein & Hoffman, 1993; Sternberg, 1996). Although competent performers, for instance, may be able to encode relevant information and generate effective plans of action in a specific domain, they often lack the speed and the flexibility that we see in an expert. A domain expert (e.g., a medical practitioner) possesses an extensive, accessible knowledge base that is organized for use in practice and is tuned to the particular problems at hand. For instance, when solving routine cases, the expert physician makes use of immediate nonanalytic responses. Nonanalytic reasoning refers to a process where one considers a whole (such as a medical case) rather than thinking about each feature of a problem (specific findings). In these circumstances, deliberation would result in considerable inefficiency. In addition, there are diagnostic tasks in perceptual domains such as dermatology and radiology in which a significant degree of skilled performance is nonanalytic in nature, relying more on pattern recognition than deliberative reasoning (Brooks, Norman, & Allen, 1991). Also, the expert practitioner working in a complex real-world clinical setting, such as a hospital, must have a sound grasp of the organizational, social, and political contexts of practice that may affect his or her efficiency. This knowledge allows the expert to act in an adaptive way to the constraints and changes of the practical environment (Sternberg & Horvath, 1996).

In the study of medical expertise, it has been useful to distinguish different types of expertise. Patel and Groen (1991) distinguished between general and specific expertise, a distinction supported by research indicating differences between subexperts (e.g., expert physicians who solve a case outside their field of specialization) and experts in terms of reasoning strategies and organization of knowledge. General expertise corresponds to expertise that cuts across medical subdisciplines (e.g., general medicine). Specific expertise results from detailed experience within a medical subdomain, such as cardiology or endocrinology. An individual may possess both, or only generic expertise. The different levels of expertise are explained in the definitions that have been modified from Patel and Groen (1991), displayed in Table 5.1.

The medical domain is sufficiently well defined that it is possible to distinguish between generic and specific knowledge. The notion of an intermediate is a working definition, because it refers broadly to anyone who is between expert and novice. We make a distinction between two kinds of novices, because technical domains such as medicine require prior knowledge for even minimal comprehension. Thus, a beginner is defined as someone who knows at least the rudiments of diagnostic classification, such as a medical student. In contrast, a layperson possesses minimal knowledge of medicine or knowledge that can be acquired without any formal training (e.g., from popular books).

THE COGNITIVE APPROACH TO MEDICAL EXPERTISE

Research on medical expertise has been highly influenced by the cognitive, or information processing, approach. A goal of this approach has been to

TABLE 5.1
Different Levels of Expertise

Layperson	A person who has only commonsense or everyday knowledge of a domain. It is equivalent to a naive person.
Beginner	A person who has the prerequisite knowledge assumed by the domain. Here we distinguish among beginners, depending on the degree and quality of their knowledge. We have identified, for instance, early, intermediate, and advanced beginners.
Novice	A layperson or a beginner. However, the term is mostly used to refer to a beginner or to someone initiated into a domain or a discipline.
Intermediate	Anybody who is above the beginner level but below the subexpert level. As with the beginner or the novice, intermediates are represented by various degrees, depending on their level of training.
Subexpert	A person with a generic knowledge but inadequate specialized knowledge of the domain.
Expert	A person with a specialized knowledge of the domain. We also have made the distinction between medical experts in terms of the nature of their practice, as medical practitioners or medical researchers.

characterize expert performance in terms of the cognitive structures and processes used in problem solving and decision making, using carefully developed laboratory tasks (Chi, Feltovich, & Glaser, 1981; Chi et al., 1988; Lesgold et al., 1988). This research, which originated in the work of deGroot (1965) in the domain of chess, was further developed into a research paradigm within the information-processing approach to cognition, as exemplified by the seminal work of Newell and Simon (1972). The expertise paradigm expanded and replicated the work of deGroot (Chase & Simon, 1973) and spanned the range of content domains including physics (Larkin, McDermott, Simon, & Simon, 1980), sports (Starkes, Deakin, Allard, Hodges, & Hayes, 1996), music (Sloboda, 1996), and medicine (Patel et al., 1994). Edited volumes—Chi et al. (1988), Ericsson and Smith (1991), Ericsson (1996), and Hoffman (1996)—provide a good general overview of the area.

This research has focused on differences between subjects varying in levels of expertise in terms of memory, reasoning strategies, and in particular the role of domain-specific knowledge. Among the expert's characteristics uncovered by this research are the following:

1. Experts are capable of perceiving large patterns of meaningful information in their domain that novices cannot perceive.
2. They are fast at processing and at the deployment of different skills required for problem solving.
3. They have a superior short-term and long-term memory for materials (e.g., clinical findings in medicine) related to their domain of expertise, but not outside their domain.
4. They typically represent problems in their domain at deeper, more principled levels, whereas novices show a superficial level of representation.
5. They spend more time assessing the problem prior to solving it, whereas novices tend to spend more time working on the solution itself and little time in problem assessment.

The critical factor that accounts for the superiority of expert performance has been found to be in the highly interconnected knowledge bases of the expert. However, these expert characteristics should not be thought of as necessary nor sufficient, but instead as features representing a prototypical category (Sternberg & Horvath, 1996). Individual experts may differ substantially in terms of exhibiting these kinds of performance characteristics (e.g., superior memory for domain materials).

In the next section, we present an overview of research on medical expertise that addresses the roles that domain knowledge and clinical practice play in clinical reasoning. We show that expert problem solving is efficient and accurate, and that the efficiency of the reasoning process employed by the expert depends on having an extensive knowledge base.

The Role of Domain Knowledge and Clinical Practice

> The true scientific investigator completely loses sight of the utility of what he is about. Do you think that the physiologist who cuts up a dog reflects, while doing so, that he may be saving a human life? Nonsense. If he did, it would spoil him for a scientific man; and then vivisection would become a crime. (C. S. Peirce, *Collected Papers, I*)

One of the principal characteristics of experts in any domain is that they possess an extensive body of well-organized and highly differentiated knowledge. For example, an expert cardiologist can recognize very subtle differences between two medical problems that are very similar in presentation. This highly structured knowledge base enables the expert to use efficient and effective problem-solving strategies such as forward reasoning (Ericsson & Smith, 1991). *Forward reasoning* is characterized by drawing inferences from available data (e.g., a patient's symptoms) and sequentially moving toward the solution of a problem without having to explicitly test and evaluate hypotheses (e.g., medical diagnoses). This strategy results from having acquired and exercised knowledge repeatedly in particular contexts. For example, if a physician has seen the same kind of medical problem many times, then he or she is likely to recognize important cues that will lead more directly to a solution. This is in contrast to a novice physician who will have to think through the problem more explicitly and make many inferences to arrive at a correct diagnosis. Over time, the lengthy reasoning process becomes compiled into shorter, more direct chains of inferences that are stored in the physician's memory and are directly available to be retrieved when similar problems are encountered. The one potentially negative consequence of this learning process is that it is often very difficult for an expert to "unpack" a compiled chain of inferences because the underlying knowledge has become tacit. A physician, for instance, may correctly diagnose a clinical case but when asked, he or she may not be able to retrieve the explanation supporting the diagnosis (cf. Arocha & Patel, 1990).

As mentioned previously, we make a distinction between specific and generic expertise. *Specific expertise* refers to the skills and knowledge a physician has in his or her own domain. *Generic expertise* corresponds to general medical knowledge that every physician acquires through training. In one study, we asked expert physicians, in and out of their domains of expertise (experts and subexperts), to solve two cases: one complex and another one less complex (Patel, Groen, & Arocha, 1990). Experts, as well as subexperts, used forward reasoning (i.e., reasoning from clinical data to

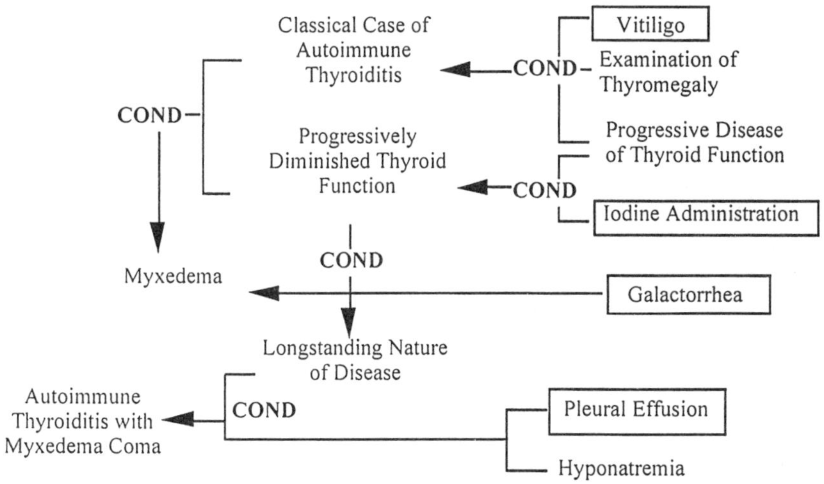

FIG. 5.1. Semantic network representation of the explanation of a clinical case in endocrinology by an expert endocrinologist. Concepts within boxes represent clinical data given in the case. The symbol **COND** indicates conditional relations; **CAU** indicates causal relations; and **RSLT** indicates result.

diagnosis) in the less complex case, making little use of causal reasoning. This pattern of reasoning is evident in an expert solving a less complex case in his or her own domain of practice, as illustrated in the diagram in Fig. 5.1. The figure presents an explanation of an endocrinology problem by an endocrinologist. The nodes (words in boxes) represent patient data in the case, whereas the rest of the terms represent the inferences made by the physician. The physician's explanation uses very few pieces of patient data to arrive at a diagnosis. With only four findings—*vitiligo, thyromegaly, progressive disease of thyroid function,* and *iodine administration*—the expert is able to generate a chain of inferences, autoimmune thyroiditis, leading to *myxedema* and then produce the final diagnosis of *autoimmune thyroiditis with myxedema coma.*

The direction of reasoning is forward except at the very end of the explanation (see bottom of the figure), where a loose end, respiratory failure, is explained causally on the basis of the hypometabolic state (slowed metabolic state) of the patient. The term *loose ends* has been used to refer to findings that are unaccounted for by the major hypothesis that is being considered. Each of the experts made a rapid and correct diagnosis. Their reasoning was characterized by one large component with forward reasoning leading to a diagnosis and a small component with backward reasoning to explain the anomalous patient cue.

How does a subexpert perform when confronted with the same problem? Joseph and Patel (1990) compared endocrinologists (experts) and cardiologists (subexperts) in solving an endocrinology problem. Similar to the experts, the subexperts made an accurate diagnosis in this less complex case. However, they required much longer periods of time to arrive at a solution. The cardiologists generated the main diagnostic component in a forward-directed reasoning pattern, but left many loose ends unexplained. Both endocrinologists and cardiologists were able to recognize relevant information.

In solving the complex case, only the experts were able to correctly diagnose the problem. Complex problem solving often requires a physician to fill in gaps in the evidence presented to them. Experts have specific expectations concerning the type of symptoms that are likely to be present in a particular medical problem. In this context, they inferred additional relevant findings not present in the clinical text. This requires superior pattern recognition capabilities driven by tacit knowledge developed through having seen many similar cases over time.

What differences would we expect if we compared expert physicians who have similar domain knowledge, but very different practical experience? Patel et al. (1990) compared clinical practitioners to medical researchers in solving the same two clinical problems. By investigating expert practitioners and researchers in the same domain of specialization, it was ensured that the domain of knowledge remained the same, although the experts' experience differed in terms of the context of their practice. Patel et al. found that the type of practical experience of the experts was associated with the use of biomedical science knowledge. Practitioners showed little tendency to use basic science in explaining the cases, whereas medical researchers showed preference for detailed, basic-scientific explanations, without developing clinical descriptions. Unlike the practitioners, who stopped accounting for the clinical problem once a diagnosis was found, the researchers engaged in considerable causal reasoning and did not successfully resolve the problem. They typically focused on the anomalous data, in their attempt to provide a coherent account of all the data, which is consistent with an investigator's task.

The explanation offered by the biomedical researcher employs propositions originating in basic biomedical science. Cues from the problem are specifically selected that provide evidence of biomedical and physiological mechanisms, rather than the clinical manifestations of the disease. There is also greater use of backward reasoning in the researchers' explanations of the patient problem. This is illustrated in Fig. 5.2, where the researcher uses the clinical cue *diseased thyroid gland* to causally generate a physiological concept thyroid hormone, which is subsequently used to explain biochemical and physiological mechanisms underlying the patient disorder. No attempt was made to generate a clinical diagnosis.

The differential use of the cues from the problem may reflect the different goals of practitioners and researchers in solving typical problems in their own

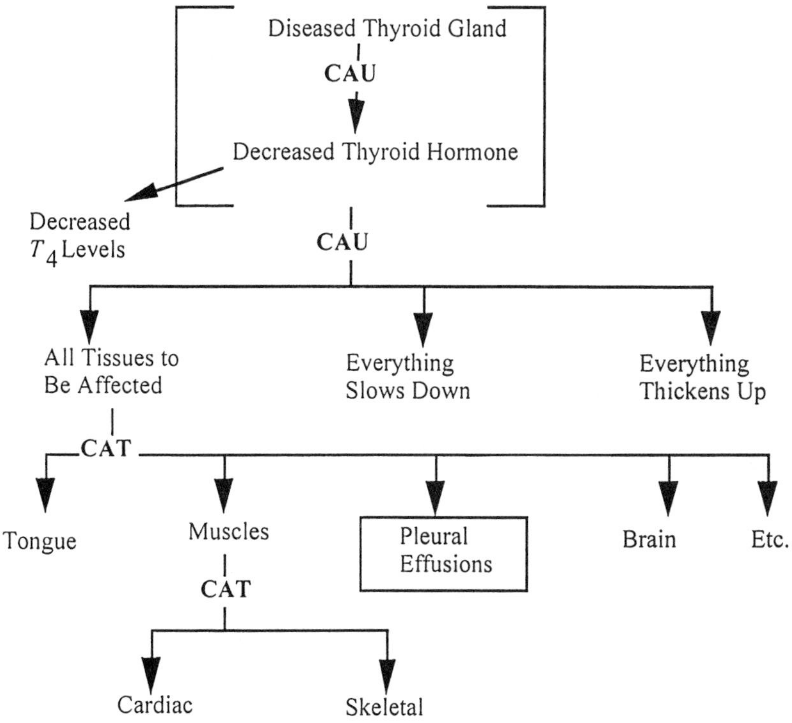

FIG. 5.2. Semantic network representation of the explanation of a clinical case in endocrinology by a researcher. The concept within a box (*pleural effusions*) represents clinical data given in the case. The symbol **COND** indicates conditional relations; **CAU** indicates causal relations; and **CAT** indicates a category.

domains. The practitioner must be able to diagnose a problem, frequently in the absence of complete data. In contrast, the researcher must describe biomedical phenomena in terms of detailed causal mechanisms. The results in this experiment can be interpreted as indicating that expert clinicians have extensive set of exemplars (clinical cases stored in long-term memory) that can be applied within their own domain of practice and can be used to generate accurate diagnoses with considerable efficiency. It is also indicated that diagnostic efficiency and nonanalytical reasoning are determined by knowledge that is particular to the practitioner's intuitive knowledge of the underlying case situation, not by the possession of conceptual domain knowledge alone. As discussed previously, physicians employ nonanalytic reasoning when solving familiar problems. In addition, there are diagnostic tasks in perceptual domains such as dermatology and radiology in which a significant degree of skilled performance is nonanalytic in nature, relying more on pattern recognition than on deliberative reasoning (Brooks et al., 1991).

DECISION MAKING IN DYNAMIC REAL-WORLD ENVIRONMENTS

We have gained a great deal of knowledge from laboratory-based studies of cognitive skills. However, the application of the theory of medical expertise has only indirectly contributed to models of learning, and has been of limited utility in developing innovative methods of instruction and assessment. In addition, theory and methods from expertise research have not been effectively exploited in order to study cognition in the workplace (Patel, Kaufman, & Magder, 1996).

Recently, we extended our research from laboratory-based tasks to complex, real-world settings (Leprohon & Patel, 1995; Patel et al., 1996). This new research was undertaken in response to a perceived need to better understand the nature of expert clinical practice and the tacit dimension of medical expertise. These investigations have been influenced by studies of newly emerging area of research, naturalistic decision making (Klein & Calderwood, 1991). This area focuses on how people make decisions in the workplace under realistic constraints. These constraints include time pressure, risk, incomplete and ambiguous information, and the need to coordinate decisions and actions within the context of a team effort. According to Orasanu and Salas (1993), team characteristics in the context of decision making include the involvement of two or more individuals, multiple sources of information, interdependence and coordination among members, adaptive management of internal resources, and defined roles and responsibilities.

Decisions in real-world environments do not represent endpoints; rather, they are a part of a decision-action cycle in which there is continuous feedback and decisions are revisited until a task has been successfully completed. In this section, we discuss two research projects that investigate decision making in naturalistic contexts. In this work, we observe two distinct phases of decision making, one in which decisions lead to immediate action and a subsequent phase in which decisions are retrospectively evaluated.

Leprohon and Patel (1995) investigated the decision-making processes used by nurses in the real emergency telephone triage. In Quebec's health care delivery system, nurses are required to respond to public emergency calls for medical help (exemplified by 911 telephone service). The study analyzed transcripts of nurse–patient caller telephone conversations of different levels of urgency and complexity, among nurses' explanations for their decisions obtained immediately after their conversations. In decision-making situations, such as emergency telephone triage, there is a sense of time urgency—decisions often have to be made in seconds and on the basis of partial and frequently unreliable or ambiguous information. In the analysis of transcripts, errors in judgment were coded as either (a) false positives, which represent interventions beyond the patient's needs (e.g., sending an ambulance in a nonemergency situation) that exact a financial cost for society; and (b) false negatives, which correspond to interventions that were insufficient to meet the patient's needs and may have compromised the patient's health. In a high-urgency situation, an ambulance is dispatched immediately with an accompanying physician. In a situation of moderate urgency, an ambulance is sent with only paramedics, to arrive within 20 minutes. In a low-urgency situation, the patient may be given advice or a referral to a nearby clinic.

Leprohon and Patel (1995) observed three patterns of decision making that reflected the perceived urgency of and ambiguity of the situations. The first pattern corresponds to immediate response behavior evoked in situations of high urgency. In these circumstances, decisions are made rapidly and actions are triggered by symptoms in a forward-directed fashion. The nurses in this study responded with perfect accuracy in these situations. The second pattern involves limited problem solving in situations of moderate urgency with moderately complex cases. These circumstances resulted in the highest percentage of decision errors (mostly false positives). The third pattern involves deliberate problem solving and planning, and is normally elicited in response to low-urgency situations. In these circumstances, a nurse will evaluate the whole situation and explore possible solutions, such as identifying the basic needs of a patient and referring the patient to an appropriate clinic. In these situations, the nurses made fewer errors than in situations of moderate urgency, and more errors than in situations requiring immediate response behavior.

Decisions in routine triage are often made with minimal reflection and with the focus on patient symptoms rather than on diagnosis. Patterns of symptoms trigger actions, such as sending an ambulance with a physician to treat a potentially life-threatening condition. Knowledge is tacit and driven by pattern-recognition processes. Decision-making accuracy was significantly higher in nurses with 10 years or more of experience than in nurses with less experience, which is consistent with what we know about acquisition of expertise in other domains. However, the nurses were unable to articulate reasons for their decisions and, when probed to do so, often provided erroneous explanations. The ability to effectively act on knowledge coupled with an inability to articulate an explanation is exemplary of tacit knowledge.

In more complex ambiguous situations, nurses' decisions are more error prone. Under these circumstances, nurses engage in a more elaborate situation assessment, in which contextual knowledge of the situation (e.g., the age of the patient, whether the patient was alone or with others) is considered in order to identify the needs of the client and to negotiate the best plan of action to meet these needs. These situations can result in valuable learning experiences. Eventually, decisions that were once complex and required situation assessment may become routinized, leading to immediate action in more experienced nurses. This is part of a learning process characterized by a tacit-explicit-tacit cycle leading to conceptual change. This is characterized by a reevaluation of one's assumptions underlying action, resulting in tacit knowledge coming into focal awareness and scrutiny. Over time, this now-explicit knowledge can become part of a routine decision-action cycle and therefore tacit once again.

Patel et al. (1996) provided further evidence for the use of implicit knowledge in dynamic decision-making situations in an investigation of group decision making in a medical intensive care unit (ICU). The principal sources of data included audiotaped recordings of medical morning rounds, complete patient charts and records, and interviews with the hospital staff. The rounds are one of the most important activities in any hospital ward. During these sessions, the teams visit and evaluate each patient at the bedside. Various members of the team provide patient reports about the patients' status, retrospectively evaluate each of the decisions and actions, and plan future courses of action. The morning rounds are also used as an instructional forum for resident trainees. The investigators followed one patient from the time he entered the ICU to the time he was transferred to the general medical ward.

The goals of the ICU are: to stabilize the patient and then to identify and treat the underlying problem; and to coordinate collection, analysis, and management of data from the various sources. This involves coordination and distribution of workloads to various participants, namely residents, nurses, laboratory technicians, pharmacists, and nutritionists. The team decision making involves management of multiple streams of information, and communication and coordination between individuals and from different data sources. Most decisions and actions are hierarchically controlled by team leaders, where expertise is distributed among individuals and responsibility is allocated among the team to maximize efficiency. It is apparent that one can learn how to function effectively in an ICU setting only via experience. Effective practice in this context requires considerable coordination with other team members.

The medical team's goals continuously shift as the patient's condition changes and new problems or complications arise. The medical personnel need to be responsive and sometimes reactive to the demands of the changing situations. For example, many ICU patients are put on a mechanical ventilator to assist with their breathing. This can often save a patient's life, but may cause numerous complications. Sometimes, the patient will develop stress ulcers and consequently be given drugs to combat this problem. This, in turn, can change the acid base of the stomach, causing the patient to aspirate bacteria that may result in pneumonia. These complications often will result in rapidly shifting goals and changing priorities.

Team decision making requires skilled communication to coordinate tasks, decisions, and actions. An expert physician and team leader needs to be able to articulate what would ordinarily be tacit knowledge as well as coaxing other team members, when necessary, to make their assumptions as explicit as possible so that they can be considered in the context of treatment and management options. For example, we had observed that a resident made a correct decision not to treat a pneumonia condition because he believed that it was likely caused by medication that the patient had received (chemical pneumonitis). However, when questioned about how one discriminates between a chemical pneumonitis and systemic pneumonia, he had difficulty articulating the reasons. Through a series of questions, the expert physician was able to elicit from the resident the tacit assumptions underlying his decision. The expert challenged his responses until he was able to construct a pattern of findings for discriminating between these two conditions. The team could then evaluate the decision and determine whether the patient's condition was consistent with chemical pneumonitis.

An effective clinical teacher needs to be able to articulate knowledge that would normally be tacit for a practitioner not engaged in instruction. This knowledge can be explicitly verbalized in the form of didactic instruction. Alternatively, the instructor may try to find a clinical situation from which he or she could elicit the conditions of applicability of certain concepts. This is a common exercise in patient rounds, wherein a clinical teacher would engage in a particular problem-solving exercise in the context of a particular patient (Kaufman, Patel, & Poole, 1996). For example, a physician may attempt to focus on specific perceptual cues of a patient in respiratory distress to determine the progress of a patient and the proper course of treatment. Staff in an ICU setting are often provided with detailed guidelines, standards, and protocols that specify appropriate treatment and management strategies. These decision aids are extremely useful in learning to care for critically ill patients. However, the best guidelines are never complete, and rigid adherence to these decision aids can sometimes compromise patient care. A resident needs to pick up on subtle cues to know when to disregard conventional procedure and make alternative judgments. Experienced physicians have evolved specific heuristics that can be conveyed to medical trainees through effective clinical teaching.

Intensive care decision making is characterized by a rapid, serial evaluation of options leading to immediate action. In this real-time decision making, the reasoning is schema-driven in a forward direction toward action with minimal inference or justification. The results of the action, as measured by the patient's response, feed back into the decision-action cycle, and the proper of course of further action is internal. When the circumstance is ambiguous or the patient does not respond in a manner consistent with the original hypothesis, then the original decision comes under scrutiny. This can result in a brainstorming session in which the team retrospectively evaluates and reconsiders the decisions that have been made, and considers several alternative courses of action. We have observed several such distinct patterns of decision making. The goals of these reflective sessions are to critically evaluate decisions that are made, rationalize and debate decisions and actions that are taken, and discuss future plans of action. In this session, the evaluation of action leads to learning. Multiple kinds of reasoning are used to evaluate alternatives in these brainstorming sessions. These include probabilistic reasoning, diagnostic reasoning, and biomedical causal reasoning. An investigation of the cognitive processes involved in these reflective sessions reveals a number of important mechanisms related to coordination of theory and evidence (Patel, Dunbar, & Kaufman, 1995).

This kind of retrospective evaluation is exemplified in a weekly session where all attending physicians and staff meet to discuss various patient problems. The following discussion focused on an ICU patient who had suffered a cardiac arrest. He was treated with streptokinase, a potent blood thinning agent, on his arrival at the emergency room. This treatment was the focal issue of this discussion. Figure 5.3 represents a schematic summary of the dialogue and arguments used by the participants in the evaluation session. These participants included cardiologists, respirologists, residents, and students. We specifically focus on the two respirologists and the two cardiologists who dominated the discussion. The two respirologists argued that the patient had received the appropriate therapy, and the two cardiologists argued to the contrary. The discussion began with a summary of the case by a cardiologist as represented by the box in the top left-hand corner in Fig. 5.3. This led to a discussion concerning an interpretation of the results of the electrocardiogram (ECG), and whether it clearly indicated that the patient had suffered a myocardial infarction (MI). The positive evidence in favor of the use of streptokinase is that it is the usual treatment strategy for patients showing signs of myocardial infarction (abnormal ECG patterns), and it can reduce morbidity and mortality. The critical question was whether the ECG provided conclusive evidence of myocardial infarction. The cardiologists argued that the ECG did not show a pattern consistent with an MI. The diagnosticity of this particular ECG was disputed by Respirologist 1, who argued that delay in testing may have complicated this measure and could be misleading (top right-hand corner of Fig. 5.3). Cardiologist 1 argued (supported by Cardiologist 2, with specific statistics) that only a small percentage of people benefit from this treatment (probabilistic reasoning), and the validity of the decision for this particular patient was in question (second row of Fig. 5.3). The ICU patient was stabilized when he was treated with streptokinase. However, the patient suffered subsequent bleeding, which is a common side effect of this medication. In the ensuing discussion, they collectively constructed the sequence of events (the three boxes on the left-hand side of row 3), debated over the interpretation of specific evidence such as the results of the electrocardiogram

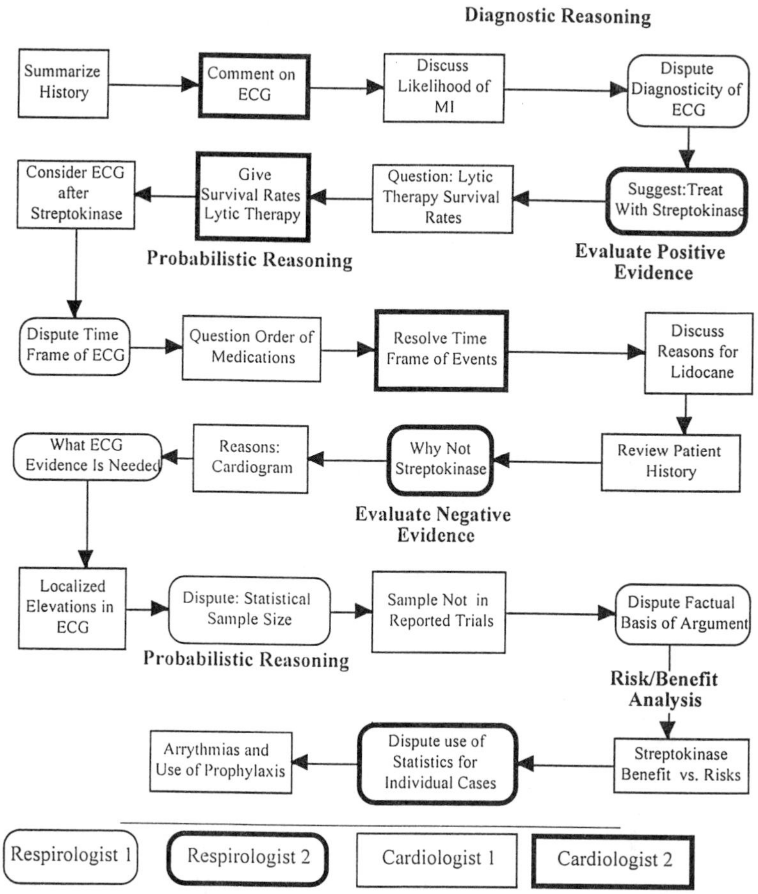

FIG. 5.3. Argument structure in a brainstorming session: Use of streptokinase.

(rows 4 and 5), and discussed the statistical basis of clinical trial research and its interpretation in this therapeutic context (rows 5 and 6).

The discussion was not conclusive, and no specific decisions were made. However, the pros and cons for this treatment regimen were explored in great detail. In this particular discussion, the resident trainees played only a minor role. However, such sessions serve a valuable pedagogical role in that they help to articulate assumptions that would not normally be discussed during clinical rounds. In actual settings, actions may be taken with minimal justification, especially if there is a perceived urgency to act. Justifications are constructed after the fact in deliberations, such as the one shown in this session. Similar patterns of problem solving were observed by scientists during laboratory meetings (Patel, Dunbar, & Kaufman, 1995).

In actual practice, there is little time available for engaging in extended causal reasoning. Nevertheless, the underlying causal models are sometimes critical to support real-time decision making. This type of learning environment helps foster the development of such knowledge. An important question is how would such a learning situation alter the specific practice of trainees. One possibility is that it may provoke them to reconsider and bring into focal awareness some of the (tacit) assumptions that underlie routinized procedures for patient care. This may be more likely to have some impact if the situation violated a previous expectation; that is to say, if it demanded that the learner rethink a seemingly unproblematic application of knowledge. This may, in turn, lead to the formation of new procedures or a change in the conditions of applicability of prior procedures.

ACADEMIC KNOWLEDGE AND THE LEARNING OF PROFESSIONAL PRACTICE

The North American medical education system, prior to the Flexner Report (Flexner, 1910), was a practice-based apprenticeship system in which the arts and crafts of the medical profession were learned, in an implicit way, by following a mentor who was an experienced professional. Flexner, who had been influenced by the educational model in Germany—where medical studies began with a systematic, comprehensive, and in-depth education in the basic sciences followed by clinical practice—believed that the medical curriculum as it existed in North America was not sufficiently grounded in the basic sciences such as biology, anatomy, and physiology. The Flexner Report constituted an argument for a science-based approach to medicine and medical education, in which medicine would move from a craft to a profession to the extent that its techniques would become grounded in basic science theories and methods. The scientific basis of medicine would provide a set of scientifically tested propositions, principles, and methods from which procedures could be derived and explicitly transmitted to the students (Barzansky, 1992). The Flexner Report had a profound impact on medical education in North American medical schools, which almost uniformly adopted a curriculum in which the basic biomedical sciences were taught before the commencement of clinical internships (Hudson, 1992).

In recent years, there has been a movement in the professions to deemphasize academic knowledge and to reemphasize practical knowledge acquired in clinical settings and in simulated clinical settings (e.g., problem-based medical education). This movement has received a great deal of attention recently, and many medical schools are embracing a medical education model based on problems. The new move toward practical learning has been implemented in curricula that emphasize medical learning in a problem-solving context. The new curricula are called problem-based learning curricula (PBL), and they are based on the idea that effective education needs to be situated in the environments where professional practice occurs (Albanese & Mitchell, 1993; Vernon & Blake, 1993). The popularity of PBL reflects an increasing recognition of the role that learning in real-world environments plays in the training of the professional. The basic proposition is that the professional's "true" learning occurs in practice. The benefits of PBL are promulgated on the hypothesis that medical students will acquire necessary knowledge through exposure to clinical practice earlier in their education. Unfortunately, the "clinical training" is most often paper-and-pencil problem solving using clinical scenarios rather than real clinical cases.

Research comparing the outcomes of conventional and problem-based curricula does not give support for the alleged benefits of problem-based education. We may hypothesize that instructional settings that emphasize medical learning in the context of clinical practice impede the development of forward reasoning, a characteristic of expert cognitive performance. Instead, it seems that strong, formal, explicit knowledge instruction in the basic sciences may be necessary for tacit knowledge to develop (Patel, Groen, & Norman, 1993). As stated previously, forward reasoning seems to result from an adequate organization of knowledge, rather than from the deployment of explicitly learned reasoning or problem-solving strategies. Evidence has been provided that this specific pattern of reasoning may be linked to factors related to curriculum and instruction. Patel, Groen, and Norman (1991, 1993) reported two studies that compared the diagnostic reasoning process of students who were trained in two different curricula. One group (the PBL group) was trained in a problem-solving environment, employing written clinical cases. The other group was trained in a conventional medical curriculum, where the students received basic science instruction followed by clinical training. The results of this study showed that the problem-based learning group relied more on backward reasoning, whereas the traditional group relied more on the use of forward reasoning in the explanation of patient problems.

In routine cases of medical diagnosis, forward reasoning is driven by clinical evidence and does not make use of basic science information. Forward reasoning, however, can be disrupted by anomalies (e.g., unaccounted signs or symptoms), which results in backward reasoning, especially in complex clinical cases. Causal reasoning based on biomedical knowledge is not contingent on clinical experience and appears to develop independently of clinical practice. The hypothetico-deductive method involves the development of working hypotheses and the subsequent testing of each hypothesis against every piece of incoming data. This method is explicitly taught in PBL curricula. Patel, Kaufman, and Arocha (in press) presented evidence that learning through this hypothetico-deductive, backward strategy can actually impede the use of forward-driven strategies, even in physicians with considerable clinical experience.

These findings are consistent with evidence in other domains, which suggest that the teaching of goal-directed reasoning strategies—such as the hypothetico-deductive method—and their repeated application to problems prevent learners from acquiring the schemata necessary for comprehending and solving problems (Chandler & Sweller, 1991; Vollmeyer, Holyoak, & Burns, 1994). The evidence shows that when subjects are asked to solve problems by means-ends analysis (a form of hypothetico-deductive method), they fail to understand the structure of the problem. Furthermore, when they are prevented from using a means-ends analysis strategy as a method of learning, students acquire the schemata necessary for solving problems and learning is more efficient and rapid (Sweller & Levine, 1982).

In solving clinical problems in medicine, physicians must attend to the current diagnostic hypothesis, the data in the problem presented to them, and any intermediate hypothesis between the diagnosis and the patient data (e.g., a pathophysiological process underlying the signs and symptoms). If we consider that typically more than one hypothesis is generated, the cognitive resources needed for maintaining this information in working memory must be such that few cognitive resources are left for acquiring the problem schemata (i.e., an abstract representation of the problem), which involves learning and forming generalizations from the case. Although problems can be solved successfully using the hypothetico-deductive method, the scarcity of attentional and memory resources may result in the students having difficulty in learning problem schemata in an adequate manner. It seems, then, that one of the reasons for the failure of students from problem-based learning environments to acquire a forward-directed reasoning style may be the use of problem-solving strategies, such as the hypothetico-deductive method, as a learning strategy. That is, a large part of the training is directed at acquiring strategies for problem solving, whereas learning the underlying biomedical knowledge takes secondary place. Another reason may be that clinical experience based on paper-and-pencil tasks is so unlike the real environment that there is no opportunity to develop forward reasoning. Research results lend support to both of these hypotheses.

ACQUISITION OF TACIT KNOWLEDGE IN MEDICAL PRACTICE: CONCLUDING COMMENTS

Research in medical expertise has offered evidence of the importance of implicit knowledge in various reasoning and problem-solving tasks. This chapter has discussed research findings from both laboratory-based studies and studies in naturalistic, decision-making environments. Implicit knowledge is seen in the expert's ability to solve clinical cases using forward-directed reasoning without seeming to use pathophysiological or biomedical knowledge. Biomedical knowledge supports clinical reasoning, but remains tacit unless the expert encounters loose ends in the data. Only then do expert physicians resort to their underlying medical knowledge to give a coherent explanation of the problem. By contrast, less-than-expert subjects explicitly make use of biomedical knowledge to test hypotheses against data in a typical backward-driven manner. They generate elaborate explanations of the case, showing a backward-directed reasoning pattern. These explanations serve to provide provide feedback from the case constraints, when considering more difficult patient problems. Thus, instruction in real-world problem solving or instruction with classes of problems that are closely related leads to the development of flexibility that one observes in expert performance.

Appropriate actions in practical situations are based on the accurate assessment of the situation, which include selection of relevant cues, evaluation of expectancies, anticipation of urgency, and plans for courses of action to be taken. Adequate knowledge of the domain is a necessary condition for developing the accurate assessment of situations, but because there are a multitude of variables that have to be considered during evaluation of any given situation, these are best manifested in natural practice. Furthermore, knowledge of prototypicality is necessary, because it enables people to detect when expectancies are violated. However, natural practice is usually very messy, and the use of tutors in training is becoming an important option. Computer technology is increasingly able to provide low-cost and high-fidelity simulators for this purpose. Simulated training programs based on real-world practice, where trainees can take risks without adverse effects, are an alternative viable method, given the popularity of technology-based learning. An anesthesia model-based simulator (Gaba, 1992) has been effectively used in training anesthesiologists in the delivery of anesthetic during surgery.

What's Tacit About Medical Practice

So what can we say about the art and science of medicine? Well, first consider the following story. A physician sees a patient and, based on his or her observations, makes a judgment about the diagnosis. Diagnosis is viewed as a theory of a disease. It is most often based on selected findings related to the patient problem. In addition, there are findings that are not easily accountable within the framework of the main diagnosis, which we refer to as *loose ends*. On the basis of the main diagnosis, the physician provides a therapeutic plan and a management plan. If the therapy is effective and the patient recovers, the loose ends are ignored. This is typical of the routine practice of medicine and is analogous to the forward-oriented reasoning that we observe in experts in laboratory tasks. As discussed in the chapter, the knowledge underlying this reasoning pattern is largely inarticulate or tacit in nature, and makes minimal use of biomedical knowledge (Patel & Groen, 1986; Patel & Kaufman, 1995).

What happens when the routine breaks down and the patient returns with unresolved problems? At this point, the unaccountable findings or loose ends come back into the picture, necessitating a reevaluation of the original diagnostic theory. This evaluation involves deliberative causal and backward-directed reasoning, often leading to the generation of alternative diagnostic hypotheses. This kind of reevaluation is very common in real-world medical decision making and is a critical part of the learning process. In this context, what had previously been tacit becomes the focal point of consideration, and is thereby made explicit. This can result in conceptual change and changes in clinical behavior. Eventually, these newly acquired clinical behaviors become routinized and tacit once again. The mechanisms by which these changes occur in practice, and the cognitive and social processes that support these changes, provide us with a better understanding of the role of tacit knowledge in the development of medical expertise.

We consider the art of medicine to be a part of everyday patient care, reflecting the use of tacit knowledge and reflexive reasoning. The science of medicine—and deliberative, reflective causal reasoning—is required when anomalies are generated and need to be explained. This process of explanation often necessitates extensive use of biomedical knowledge. Interestingly, anomalies are often the focal point of scientific inquiry (Dunbar, 1993; Patel, Dunbar, & Kaufman, 1995; Patel, Groen, & Arocha, 1990). Resolving anomalies are essentially creative endeavors shaped by the goals of research. In contrast, practitioners' behavior, shaped by the goals and constraints of clinical settings, are oriented toward treating and alleviating patient problems effectively and expeditiously. As society evolves and the requirements for patient care change, there is a continuous need to reappraise what we mean by *medical expertise,* and the role of tacit knowledge in the development of skilled performance.

ACKNOWLEDGMENTS

The research reported in this chapter was supported in part by a grant from Fonds pour la Formation de Chercheurs et l'Aide à la Recherche (ER1177) and the Social Sciences and Humanities Research Council of Canada (4510-95-1206) to the first author.

REFERENCES

Albanese, M., & Mitchell, S. (1993). Problem-based learning: A review of literature on its outcomes and implementation issues. *Academic Medicine, 68,* 52–81.

Anderson, J. R. (1983). *The architecture of cognition.* Cambridge, MA: Harvard University Press.

Arocha, J. F., & Patel, V. L. (1990). Monitoring knowledge and problem solving performance in medicine. In A. McDougall & C. Dowling (Eds.), *Computers in education. Proceedings of the Fifth World Conference on Computers in Education* (pp. 327–332). Amsterdam: Elsevier.

Barzansky, B. (1992). The growth and divergence of the basic sciences. In B. Barzansky & N. Gevitz (Eds.), *Beyond Flexner: Medical education in the twentieth century* (pp. 1–18). New York: Greenwood.

Broadbent, D. E., Fitzgerald, P., & Broadbent, M. H. P. (1986). Implicit and explicit knowledge in the control of complex systems. *British Journal of Psychology, 77,* 33–50.

Brooks, L. R., Norman, G. R., & Allen, S. W. (1991). The role of similarity in a medical diagnostic task. *Journal of Experimental Psychology: General, 120,* 278–287.

Carraher, T. N., Carraher, D. W., & Schlieman, A. D. (1985). Mathematics in the streets and in the school. *British Journal of Developmental Psychology, 3,* 21–29.

Chandler, P., & Sweller, J. (1991). Cognitive load theory and the format of instruction. *Cognition and Instruction, 8,* 293–332.

Chase, W. G., & Simon, H. A. (1973). Perception in chess. *Cognitive Psychology, 4,* 55–81.

Chi, M. T. H., Feltovich, P. J., & Glaser, R. (1981). Categorization and representation of physics problems by experts and novices. *Cognitive Science, 5,* 121–152.

Chi, M. T. H., Glaser, R., & Farr, M. J. (Eds.). (1988). *The nature of expertise.* Hillsdale, NJ: Lawrence Erlbaum Associates.

deGroot, A. D. (1965). *Thought and choice in chess.* The Hague: Mouton.

Dunbar, K. (1993). How scientists really reason: Scientific reasoning in real-world laboratories. In R. J. Sternberg & J. Davidson (Eds.), *Mechanisms of insight.* Cambridge, MA: MIT Press.

Ericsson, K. A. (Ed.). (1996). *The road to excellence: The acquisition of expert performance in the arts and sciences, sports and games.* Mahwah, NJ: Lawrence Erlbaum Associates.

Ericsson, Y. A., & Smith, J. (Eds.). (1991). *Toward a general theory of expertise: Prospects and limits.* New York: Cambridge University Press.

Flexner, A. (1910). *Medical education in the United States and Canada* (Bulletin No. 4). New York: Carnegie Foundation for the Advancement of Teaching.

Gaba, D. (1992). Dynamic decision-making in anesthesiology: Cognitive models and training approaches. In D. A. Evans & V. L. Patel (Eds.), *Advanced models of cognition for medical training and practice* (pp. 123–148). Heidelberg, Germany: Springer-Verlag.

Hoffman, R. R. (Ed.). (1996). *The psychology of expertise: Cognitive research and empirical AI.* Mahwah, NJ: Lawrence Erlbaum Associates.

Hoffman, R. R., Shadbolt, N. R., Burton, A. M., & Klein, G. (1995). Eliciting knowledge from experts: A methodological analysis. *Organizational Behavior and Human Decision Processes, 62,* 129–158.

Hudson, R. P. (1992). Abraham Flexner in historical perspective. In B. Barzansky & N. Gevitz (Eds.), *Beyond Flexner: Medical education in the twentieth century* (pp. 19–34). New York: Greenwood.

Joseph, G.-M., & Patel, V. L. (1990). Domain knowledge and hypothesis generation in diagnostic reasoning. *Medical Decision Making, 10,* 31–46.

Kaufman, D. R., Patel, V. L., & Poole, E. (1996, April). *Naturalistic decision-making in intensive care medicine: Implications for training.* Paper presented at the American Educational Research Association, New York.

Klein, G. A., & Calderwood, R. (1991). Decision models: Some lessons from the field. *IEEE Transactions on Systems, Man, and Cybernetics, 21,* 1018–1026.

Klein, G. A., & Hoffman, R. R. (1993). Seeing the invisible: Perceptual-cognitive aspects of expertise. In M. Rabinowitz (Ed.), *Cognitive science foundations of instruction* (pp. 203–226). Hillsdale, NJ: Lawrence Erlbaum Associates.

Larkin, J. H., McDermott, J., Simon, D. P., & Simon, H. A. (1980). Expert and novice performance in solving physics problems. *Science, 208,* 1335–1342.

Leprohon, J., & Patel, V. L. (1995). Decision making strategies for telephone triage in emergency medical services. *Medical Decision Making, 15,* 240–253.

Lesgold, A., Rubinson, H., Feltovich, P., Glaser, R., Klopfer, D., & Wang, Y. (1988). Expertise in a complex skill: Diagnosing x-ray pictures. In M. T. H. Chi, R. Glaser, & M. J. Farr (Eds.), *The nature of expertise* (pp. 311–342). Hillsdale, NJ: Lawrence Erlbaum Associates.

Newell, A., & Simon, H. A. (1972). *Human problem solving.* Englewood Cliffs, NJ: Prentice-Hall.

Orasanu, J., & Salas, E. (1993). Team decision making in complex environments. In H. J. Klein, J. Orasanu, R. Calderwood, & C. E. Zsambok (Eds.), *Decision making in action: Models and methods* (pp. 327–345). Norwood, NJ: Ablex.

Patel, V. L., Arocha, J. F., & Kaufman, D. R. (1994). Diagnostic reasoning and expertise. *The Psychology of Learning and Motivation: Advances in Research and Theory, 31,* 137–252.

Patel, V. L., Dunbar, K., & Kaufman, D. R. (1995, November). *Goal-constrained distributed reasoning in medicine and science.* Paper presented at the 36th Annual Meeting of the Psychonomic Society, Los Angeles, CA.

Patel, V. L., & Groen, G. J. (1986). Knowledge-based solution strategies in medical reasoning. *Cognitive Science, 10,* 91–116.

Patel, V. L., & Groen, G. J. (1991). The general and specific nature of medical expertise: A critical look. In A. Ericsson & J. Smith (Eds.), *Toward a general theory of expertise: Prospects and limits* (pp. 93–125). New York: Cambridge University Press.

Patel, V. L., Groen, G. J., & Arocha, J. F. (1990). Medical expertise as a function of task difficulty. *Memory & Cognition, 18,* 394–406.

Patel, V. L., Groen, G. J., & Norman, G. R. (1991). Effects of conventional and problem-based medical curricula. *Academic Medicine, 66,* 380–389.

Patel, V. L., Groen, G. J., & Norman, G. R. (1993). Reasoning and instruction in medical curricula. *Cognition & Instruction, 10,* 335–378.

Patel, V. L., & Kaufman, D. R. (1995). Clinical reasoning and biomedical knowledge: Implications for teaching. In J. Higgs & M. Jones (Eds.), *Clinical reasoning in the health professions* (pp. 117–128). Oxford, England: Butterworth Heinemann.

Patel, V. L., Kaufman, D. R., & Arocha, J. F. (in press). Conceptual change in the biomedical and health sciences domain. In R. Glaser (Ed.), *Advances in instructional psychology.* Mahwah, NJ: Lawrence Erlbaum Associates.

Patel, V. L., Kaufman, D. R., & Magder, S. A. (1996). The acquisition of medical expertise in complex dynamic environments. In K. A. Ericsson (Ed.), *The road to excellence: The acquisition of expert performance in the arts and sciences, sports and games.* Mahwah, NJ: Lawrence Erlbaum Associates.

Peirce, C. S. (1931). *Collected papers of Charles Sanders Peirce: Vol. 1. Principles of philosophy.* Cambridge, MA: Harvard University Press.

Pope, A. (1950). *An essay on man.* London: Methuen.

Reber, A. S. (1989). Implicit learning and tacit knowledge. *Journal of Experimental Psychology: General, 118,* 219–235.

Reber, A. S. (1993). *Implicit learning and tacit knowledge: An essay on the cognitive unconscious.* New York: Oxford University Press.

Ryle, G. (1949). *The concept of mind.* London: Penguin.

Seger, C. A. (1994). Implicit learning. *Psychological Bulletin, 115,* 163–196.

Siegler, R. S. (1989). Mechanisms of cognitive development. *Annual Review of Psychology, 40,* 353–379.

Sloboda, J. A. (1996). The acquisition of musical performance expertise: Deconstructing the "talent" account of individual differences in musical expressivity. In K. A. Ericsson (Ed.), *The road to excellence: The acquisition of expert performance in the arts and sciences, sports and games* (pp. 107–126). Mahwah, NJ: Lawrence Erlbaum Associates.

Starkes, J. L., Deakin, J. M., Allard, F., Hodges, N. J., & Hayes, A. (1996). Deliberate practice in sports: What is it anyway? In K. A. Ericsson (Ed.), *The road to excellence: The acquisition of expert performance in the arts and sciences, sports and games* (pp. 81–106). Mahwah, NJ: Lawrence Erlbaum Associates.

Sternberg, R. J. (1996). Costs of expertise. In K. A. Ericsson (Ed.), *The road to excellence: The acquisition of expert performance in the arts and sciences, sports and games* (pp. 347–354). Mahwah, NJ: Lawrence Erlbaum Associates.

Sternberg, R. J., & Horvath, J. A. (1996). A prototype view of expert teaching. *Educational Researcher, 24,* 9.

Sternberg, R. J., Wagner, R. K., & Okagaki, L. (1993). Practical intelligence: The nature and role of tacit knowledge in work and at school. In H. Reese & J. Puckett (Eds.), *Advances in lifespan development* (pp. 205–227). Hillsdale, NJ: Lawrence Erlbaum Associates.

Sweller, J., & Levine, M. (1982). Effects of goal specificity on means-ends analysis. *Journal of Experimental Psychology: Learning, Memory, and Cognition, 8,* 463–474.

Vernon, D. T. A., & Blake, R. L. (1993). Does problem-based learning work? A meta-analysis of evaluative research. *Academic Medicine, 68,* 550–563.

Vollmeyer, R., Holyoak, K. J., & Burns, B. D. (1994). Goal specificity in hypothesis testing and problem solving. In *Proceedings of the Sixteenth Annual Conference of the Cognitive Science Society* (pp. 916–921). Hillsdale, NJ: Lawrence Erlbaum Associates.

Wagner, R. K. (1987). Tacit knowledge in everyday intelligent behavior. *Journal of Personality & Social Psychology, 52,* 1236–1247.

Wagner, R. K., & Sternberg, R. J. (1987). Tacit knowledge in managerial success. *Journal of Business & Psychology, 1,* 301–312.

CHAPTER SIX

Development of Expertise in Medical Practice

James J. Cimino
Columbia University

The professional expertise of physicians is under closer scrutiny—by the profession, the public, and the government—than is any other profession. In the past, it was our manual competence that drew the most attention: a slip of the knife, a surgical clamp left inside, misapplied obstetric forceps, or a needle pushed someplace it didn't belong. Cognitive expertise was of less importance, at least judging by the relative prices of malpractice insurance for the "procedural" (e.g., surgery and obstetrics) versus "cognitive" (e.g., internal medicine, pediatrics, neurology, and psychiatry) medical specialties. However, the increasing attention on health care costs and outcomes is being manifested as increased interest in the cognitive activities of all physicians. More and more, the decisions that we make are being analyzed in terms of their cost-effectiveness, usefulness, safety, and, of course, appropriateness.

For the most part, this attention to physicians' decision making is focused more on *what* decisions are made and less on *how* and *why* decisions are made. But, after all, at the root of all medical decisions is the expertise of the decision maker. An understanding of this expertise is thus pertinent to understanding how such decisions can be influenced properly. This chapter describes the "what" and "how"—the educational process by which physicians acquire expertise—and shows, by example, the application of the decision-making process as a physician evolves from novice to expert, with particular attention on the activities that lead to acquisition of tacit knowledge by practitioners. Patel, Arocha, and Kaufman, in the accompanying chapter (chap. 5), described the "why." From my practitioner's viewpoint, the mechanisms by which tacit knowledge is acquired are, by definition, obscure. I show by example that expertise develops; perhaps, through these examples, the reader will acquire a tacit understanding of the process. Fortunately, my cognitive science colleagues provided in their chapter some explicit information about the current state of our understanding of this process.

DEFINING MEDICAL EXPERTISE

In order to discuss the acquisition of expertise, we must first be clear on what the expertise is and how we will know it when we see it—that is, how will we measure and judge this expertise. Medical education, like most other educational processes, has many metrics that are set in the path of the student to test factual and procedural knowledge, but top scores do not qualify them as "experts." Even the examinations administered by specialty or licensing boards do not pretend to test expertise. Instead, the label "expert" is conferred on physicians through the subjective judgment of their peers, their patients, and themselves. We therefore look not to their expertise as test takers, nor to their facility with *theory,* but instead to their competence in the *practice* of medicine—that is, are they good practitioners? (Some testing methods have been developed that actually attempt to study such competence, through the use of actors capable of feigning an illness who present themselves as real patients [Barrows, 1993]. Such approaches have many practical limitations, however.)

Physicians perform a variety of tasks but, ultimately, they deal in patient encounters in which the patient has some need and the physician attempts to address that need. The encounter might take place in an office, in an emergency room, at a hospital bed, on an operating table, or even in the patient's home. The need almost always involves some expert assessment of what's going on—what is the diagnosis, what is the progress of a diagnosed disease, or whether there is a response or adverse effect to a prescribed therapy. Addressing the need almost always involves a decision—perform another test, start a therapy, or alter a predetermined therapeutic plan. Therapy can involve advice on lifestyle, writing a prescription, carrying out a procedure, or simply giving comfort.

Being an expert practitioner involves a much larger task than making the right diagnosis or knowing the right treatment. In order to reach the right diagnosis, one must have the right data; obtaining these data may require expert feats. Simply asking the patient the right question is not enough—the question must be asked in a way that the particular patient understands. Furthermore, the physician must observe the patient answering the question to look for evidence that the patient may misunderstand or mislead. When a patient answers "no" to the question "Are you sexually active?" did the patient think the question was about promiscuous activity? Did the patient mumble the answer and look away? Did the patient answer truthfully, but was offended by the question, coloring subsequent responses? Physicians can be taught explicitly to ask the question and can even be tested on their ability to remember to ask the question, but it is when they learn *how* to ask the question that they demonstrate acquisition of expertise. Social skills, notoriously difficult to teach explicitly, are an important factor in the data collection process—the physician must quickly establish trust with the patient. If the data collection goes beyond the interview and requires diagnostic tests, the physician must be able to explain the test to the patient, in order to make the patient a willing participant in the process. Such explanation requires explicit knowledge about the technical details of the test, its justification, and its potential complications. Also required is expertise at communicating this information to the patient. Throughout the process, a kind of negotiation takes place in which the physician convinces the patient to tell his or her story, in a rational manner, and to agree to requisite procedures and treatments.

A strong foundation of explicit medical knowledge is essential for medical practitioners to act in an expert fashion. In many cases, this knowledge can be applied directly to solve clinical problems though a process of evidence-based reasoning (Haynes, 1993). The Clinical Problem Solving series in *Hospital Practice* (later carried on in the *New England Journal of Medicine*) attempts, through case presentation and discussion, to show by example some of the methods for applying medical knowledge through teachable algorithms. These approaches are summarized in *Learning Clinical Reasoning* (Kassirer & Kopelman, 1991), including diagnostic hypothesis generation and refinement, use and interpretation of diagnostic tests, causal reasoning, diagnostic verification, and therapeutic decision making.

Clinical algorithms are explicable and teachable; I leave it to my cognitive science colleagues to determine when experts do and do not actually use them. However, in many cases they *can't* be applied: Their dependency on explicit medical knowledge hinders them when prior medical evidence is insufficient (either because the evidence is weak, conflicting, or nonexistent). Available evidence must often be tailored for use in particular cases in order to account for individual patient differences. Physicians therefore rely on techniques (both conscious and subconscious) called *heuristics* in order to incorporate available evidence into their decision making (McDonald, 1996). For example, through the heuristic of *extrapolation,* physicians determine how strongly they believe evidence for a particular therapy applies to their particular patients, based on differences between their patients and those involved in the published studies.

Besides the inherent susceptibility of such heuristics to the effects of bias (Tversky & Kahneman, 1974), the use of heuristics suffer from a more basic problem: They are difficult to acquire. Some of them can be taught as "tricks of the trade" but, as McDonald (1996) pointed out, we have very little understanding of what most of these heuristics *are*, let alone how and when they should be applied. This means that although experts use them, they can not teach them explicitly. Students observe their teachers and see heuristics in action; however, in order to acquire them, students *must* do so through tacit understanding.

Ultimately, the medical expert becomes capable of applying "book" knowledge to particular cases through some kind of clinical insight, coupled with efficient routines for action (Sternberg & Horvath, 1995). In making a diagnosis, the physician will sometimes apply some causal reasoning in a conscious effort to consider and discard diagnoses based on a sequence of hypotheses and deductions (the hypothetico-deductive approach). Often, however, the physician may instead find himself or herself focusing quickly on a small set of possibilities without being able to explain how or why he or she did so. In choosing therapy, the physician will know the standard medical practice, but he or she will deviate from it as needed to tailor it to the needs of a patient (e.g., will the patient tolerate it, is the patient likely to comply with it, will the patient adopt it for use in a suicide attempt, etc.).

In addition to discrete clinical events (ordering tests, arriving at diagnoses, administering therapy), clinical expertise is demonstrated in the continuous process of care. Physicians must monitor patients as their conditions evolve, worsen, or resolve. The expert will recognize when changes in the patient indicate the need to revise previous diagnoses or plans, and perhaps to detect and correct errors in decision making. The expert will take cultural factors into account when determining patient preferences and priorities. The expert also will have practical knowledge about how to "work the system" (i.e., how to select a pragmatic plan of action that will be the most efficient and effective, given practical constraints). It is in this continuing process that the physician serves as the patient's doctor, acting as a stable point of reference, a counselor, and an advocate.

THE EDUCATIONAL PROCESS

Medical education is founded on the premise, known as *technical rationality* (Schön, 1982), that an understanding of the basic sciences will ultimately serve the practitioner well, both for helping to apply science to medicine and to permit reasoning from first principles when necessary. These basic sciences, in turn, have their own founding principles, which are reflected in medical school admission requirements: biology, chemistry, physics, and mathematics. (Admission requirements also reflect the general notion that physicians will need "humanistic" skills, and use performance in humanities courses as evidence for such skills. There is, however, no clear expectation of which courses are needed for promoting which skills and, in any case, the medical school curriculum itself rarely addresses these issues directly; Levinson & Roter, 1993.)

The medical school curriculum consists of a combination of basic and applied sciences, and a logical progression of these courses is well established (Blois, 1988). Early courses—such as histology, anatomy, physiology, and biochemistry—attempt to teach what is normal. Later courses—such as pathology, microbiology, and pharmacology—deal with deviations from the normal. By the third year, applied medical science is taught in the form of clinical courses that involve combinations of lectures and practical experience in patient care settings. The major clinical courses include internal medicine, surgery, pediatrics, obstetrics and gynecology, neurology, and psychiatry. By the fourth year, the students are given some elective time to pursue other disciplines (e.g., radiology and rehabilitation medicine) and subspecialties (e.g., infectious disease and neurosurgery).

It is in these clinical courses where students are first exposed to the physician's duties and expectations. They are taught how to interview and examine patients, and how to organize their findings and hypotheses into case presentations. They are expected to acquire book knowledge from lectures, textbooks, and the current medical literature, and they are expected to demonstrate an ability to use that knowledge to reason about the patients they are seeing. Their teachers are interns, residents, and attending physicians who demonstrate their own skills for the students and serve as role models.

The teachers attempt to explain their actions to the students, to provide them with a framework for organizing their knowledge and actions. However, much of what the students observe is not explained. They will memorize a list of 100 questions to ask patients, and will then observe their teachers ask one patient only 10 of these questions and another patient a different 10 questions. Sometimes the teacher will explain why certain questions are asked and others omitted. Other times, the teacher will not have the time or will simply be unable to articulate the reasons for the choices, and will expect the student to "Do as I do, not as I say." It is in these situations that tacit knowledge begins to transfer from the expert to the student. However, the student cannot simply record particular actions for particular situations. Instead, the student must reflect on the reasons for the teacher's actions, and develop an internal model that explains these actions. If this model can also be used to predict future actions of the teacher, it can also be used to predict the actions of the student—that is, it can serve as the student's model for action.

To a large extent, the structure of the medical school curriculum has changed little since early in the 20th century, after adoption of the recommendations found in the Flexner Report (Flexner, 1910). Recently, however, medical educators have been adopting a case-based approach. In this method, the information relevant to a particular illustrative patient case, traditionally divided among the basic, applied, and practical parts of the curriculum, are brought together. For example, a patient with heart failure may be described. Information about the case includes anatomy and physiology of the heart, pathophysiology of heart failure, pharmacology of cardiac medications, history-taking to elicit symptoms of failure, and physical examination of the heart. The case-based approach attempts to present basic medical knowledge in clinically relevant ways that will be better understood and retained by the student. In addition, there is an attempt to teach an approach to clinical reasoning. Standardized testing indicates that the case-based approach imparts standard book knowledge in ways similar to the traditional curriculum. Whether or not there is an increase in the development of tacit clinical skills remains a subject for ongoing research (Berkson, 1994).

On completion of medical school, formal education continues with a residency (the first year of which is referred to as *internship*). Medical licensure typically requires at least one such year, but complete training programs, leading to specialty certification, require several years of residency. During residency, the physician is taught in many of the settings familiar from medical school, such as lectures, conferences, and case presentations; however, the focus now is on direct patient care. Residents typically admit patients to the hospital, care for them during their stay, and follow them afterward as outpatients. If the patient has a private attending physician, the resident may be in a secondary role, observing the practice of the attending, with little or no autonomy or decision making. For nonprivate ("public" or "ward") patients, the resident will have a more direct role in decision making, with the attending physician in a supervisory role.

It is this setting where much of the tacit knowledge of medical training is acquired. The resident undergoes a marvelous transformation during this phase, from a novice, loaded with facts, to an organized, efficient expert. Some of the skills are taught directly, but expertise is acquired through practice. The common dictum of "see one, do one, teach one" accurately describes the rapid transition from novice to a level in which competency is sufficient to impart the knowledge to others. Experts are present to guide the resident, but much is learned directly from the patient, as the resident becomes adept at encountering patients and their illnesses, determining what is wrong, and plotting a course of action.

Residency derives its name from the historical role of the physician-in-training to actually reside in the hospital, with the "house staff" being on call at all times. This practice has gradually evolved into a rotating schedule of night call. In the past decade, there has been greater recognition that prolonged work shifts lead to fatigue and attendant lapses in judgment, sometimes with potentially dangerous results (Bell, 1988). Debate continues as to whether reduced hours (now typically fewer than 100 per week, with no more than 16 hours in a shift) lead to improved learning (because of reduced fatigue) or reduced learning (because of interruption in the continuity of patient care; Lane, Goldman, Soukup, & Hayes, 1993).

On completion of residency, the physician may continue in a subspecialty fellowship. In some respects, this is similar to continuation of residency, with direct patient care, on-call hours, case presentations, and conferences. Patient care usually involves much less "scut work" (the menial chores of patient care, e.g., drawing blood and starting intravenous lines) and more opportunity to turn to the medical literature to help answer questions and perhaps to conduct some medical research. Ultimately, the physician will wind up in some private practice setting. Formal learning will be in the form of continuing medical education, which is mandated as part of medical licensure. Tacit knowledge continues to be acquired, often as the result of anecdotal experience.

THE EVOLUTION OF EXPERT BEHAVIOR

The process described previously inundates the physician with knowledge in a variety of modalities, including strict memorization, pattern recognition, and explicit causal reasoning. It remains for the researchers in cognitive science to explain how these experiences produce expertise and which ones work better than others. The fact remains that expertise *does* develop, and the educational experiences are key influences on that development.

I illustrate this expertise with a clinical example of a patient arriving for an office visit. I consider the scenario from the standpoint of three different levels of expertise: *novice, intermediate,* and *expert.* These levels roughly correspond to *student, resident,* and *attending physician,* although there are individual differences. A student may quickly rise to the level of intermediate. A resident might remain stuck in novice mode. An attending, with expertise in one area, might behave as an intermediate or even novice when confronted with a case outside his or her area of expertise.

Let us consider the example of Mr. Case, a new patient who presents to the physician's office with a chief complaint of chest pain. Such a visit involves several different types of clinical activity, including *information gathering, differential diagnosis,* and both *diagnostic* and *therapeutic decision making.* We can observe how different levels of expertise come into play by noting the different actions of three fictional physicians: Drs. Nova, Learner, and Masters.

Information Gathering

Dr. Nova begins by asking Mr. Case some basic questions, and learns that he is a 45-year-old man who generally considers himself healthy, has never been in the hospital, and has not seen a doctor since childhood. He developed pain in the left side of his chest several days ago and it has persisted and today seems worse. She conducts a thorough "review of systems" and learns that Mr. Case has been a smoker for 30 years, that he drinks two to four beers per day, that his father died of a heart problem at age 50, and that he works as a truck driver. The question-and-answer session takes about 20 minutes. Dr. Nova then proceeds to conduct a physical examination. She notes a blood pressure of 145/90 but not much else, although the examination takes another 20 minutes.

Dr. Learner begins with the same basic questions and gets the same answers. Her review of systems is less extensive but yields the same information about smoking, drinking, and family history. She then asks more detailed questions about the chest pain, using the mnemonic PQRST (Position, Quality, things that bring Relief, associated Symptoms, and Time course). She learns that the pain has been more or less continuous, is not worsened by exercise, but is somewhat exacerbated by coughing or deep breathing. She asks about other symptoms, such as fever and respiratory problems, and finds that although Mr. Case has had no substantial cough or sputum and no difficulty breathing, he has noted some chills on and off over the past few months, which he attributes to poor heating in his truck. Dr. Learner then gets negative answers to questions about headaches and exhaust fumes in the truck. This question-and-answer session takes about 10 minutes. Dr. Learner then conducts a physical examination, noting the same blood pressure. On examination of the chest, she notes that there is a faint redness over the anterior aspect of three left ribs and that there is tenderness in this area. She is careful to note that there are no pleural friction rub or other abnormal lung sounds. The remainder of the physical examination, taking a total of 10 minutes, is unrevealing.

Dr. Masters also asks the same basic questions and also gets the same answers. She then asks some questions similar to Dr. Learner's about the time course and factors influencing the pain. She does ask about other general symptoms, as Dr. Learner did, but does not pursue questions about Mr. Case's truck. Like Dr. Learner, she conducts a brief review of symptoms and notes the same personal habits and family history. The interview takes 7 minutes. Dr. Masters' examination initially includes taking the blood pressure and examining the chest. She notes the same rash and also notes that the skin is tender, even on light touch. After looking at the rash and listening to the chest, she examines Mr. Case's throat and neck, where she finds a small white patch next to the right tonsil and several firm, nontender lymph nodes under the jaw. She then examines the axillae (armpits) and groin areas to find several similar lymph nodes in each location. While completing the examination, which takes 10 minutes, she asks some additional questions about personal habits, including sexual practices. She discovers that Mr. Case has had unprotected intercourse with "too many to count" sexual partners over the past few years.

Each of the three physicians has a data collection style that reflects her level of training. Dr. Nova, an intern, is extremely thorough in following a routine process, but at a cost of increased time spent for not a great deal of additional useful information. Some routine questions result in routine answers that she feels obligated to pursue with additional questions, even though they lead her far from the problem at hand. Her physical examination skills are not well organized, and she spends more time trying to focus on what to do and less on what she is observing. Dr. Learner, a resident, is able to conduct both the interview and the examination much more efficiently. She pursues questions with less blind breadth than Dr. Nova, but with more depth. For example, she asks specific questions about the chest pain, which will help her in formulating a diagnosis. One question may lead to another, resulting in deep probing into blind alleys (e.g., asking about other problems related to the truck). Her physical examination shows more efficiency and better powers of observation. Dr. Masters, an attending physician, shows further skill in keeping the interview focused on the basics, with less diversion into unimportant areas. She maintains this focus during the examination, but remains open to changes in her diagnostic reasoning such that as new information is obtained, she can direct her attention to collecting additional verbal and physical information.

Some of the differences we see in our physicians during this information-gathering phase reflect the art of medicine. The more experienced the physician, the more he or she is able to focus on what is important and pursue appropriate actions efficiently. When Dr. Nova hears "chest pain," she recalls a set of serious diagnoses and proceeds to look for confirmatory information. But Dr. Masters notices the rash and is suddenly off in a different direction. What happened? As we see later, the unexpected finding has triggered a reframing of the problem—what Schön (1982) called "reflection in action." In the new framework, physical examination of the heart is no longer central, but Dr. Masters instead directs her attention to other parts of the body, unrelated to Mr. Case's presenting complaint. She even rethinks her approach to the history and proceeds to ask new questions. Her strategy has paid off, because she discovered some abnormal findings. We cannot attribute this to luck, nor can we attribute it to human intuition separable from medical expertise. Instead, we are seeing what is described as art on the surface; beneath this appearance lies a set of very deliberate, rational processes.

Differential Diagnosis

In considering Mr. Case's problems, Dr. Nova considers the chest pain to be of major importance. As she thinks about chest pain, she recognizes that there are some potentially serious causes of chest pain, especially related to the heart. She knows also that high blood pressure, smoking history, and family history of heart disease are all risk factors for heart disease. In listing possible diseases, she considers heart diseases such as myocardial infarction and angina to be at the top of the list, with pulmonary embolism less likely. She also lists hypertension as a diagnosis, based on her measurement of Mr. Case's blood pressure. This finding strengthens her belief in myocardial infarction, because she knows that hypertension is a risk factor for coronary artery disease.

Dr. Learner is not so easily drawn to heart problems as the source of the pain. Because she has obtained more useful information about the pain itself, she knows that it is not typical of pain related to obstruction of coronary arteries, because it is not related to exertion and has been continuous for much longer than would be expected with either myocardial infarction or angina. Because it is related to breathing, it makes her think about problems of the chest wall and lungs. The mention of the truck environment makes her consider possible carbon monoxide poisoning, although this is not typically associated with chest pain, especially noncardiac pain. Her findings on physical examination confirm her hypothesis that the pain is in the chest wall. She thinks primarily of inflammation of the joints in the anterior chest (costochondritis), which she knows can produce continuous chest pain and has characteristic tenderness over the anterior ribs. She attributes the rash to the patient rubbing the sore area. She makes note of the blood pressure as possible evidence of chronic hypertension, but knows that one mildly elevated measurement, found during a first visit to a new doctor during an acute pain episode, is not sufficient for making the diagnosis.

Dr. Masters pursues a line of reasoning similar to Dr. Learner's. She, too, believes that a cardiac cause, particularly infarction or angina, is unlikely, and thinks that a chest wall syndrome is likely. Finding the chest tenderness confirms her reasoning, but the rash gives her pause. To her, the distribution looks similar to that of herpes zoster (shingles) that can often appear as a painful band on the chest that does not cross the midline. The rash does not have the characteristic appearance, but she considers that she may just be seeing it in an early stage. The tenderness to light touch supports the diagnosis of herpes zoster. She favors this diagnosis over other chest wall problems, such as costochondritis, but still considers that there are several possibilities. However, she is not completely satisfied with the diagnosis of herpes zoster for another reason. She has seen similar cases, but always in much older patients. She knows that in older patients, this condition is thought to arise because of deterioration of the immune system. Once she thinks about the immune system, she immediately becomes concerned about other evidence of a faulty immune system that might point to conditions such as diabetes, cancer, and the acquired immunodeficiency syndrome (AIDS). Her further examination of the throat shows a patch that looks like a yeast infection (thrush), which is often seen in AIDS patients. The lymph nodes and the history of sexual activity are less specific, but still raise the suspicion of AIDS. She concludes that the chest pain is caused by the rash, which is most likely early herpes zoster. She considers that AIDS is a possibility that must be considered. Like Dr. Learner, she notes the elevated blood pressure and believes that it may or may not prove to be evidence of chronic hypertension.

All of our physicians began with hypothesis generation. The simple complaint of chest pain was, alone, sufficient to start the process. The subsequent data collection was intended to allow refinement of the hypotheses, but this did not occur in Dr. Nova's case. She tended to look only for confirmatory information, without considering that it might be confirming alternative hypotheses, and she tended not to look for, or ignored, information that might distract her from her diagnosis. Furthermore, her initial set of hypotheses was flawed. Most of her training was in hospital settings and the patients she has seen have been selected precisely because they tend to have more serious disease. Therefore, she is used to seeing patients who, when they have chest pain, will be more likely than average to have some serious underlying cause. As a result, based on her experience, she overestimates the likelihood, or *prior probability,* of conditions such as myocardial infarction. But Dr. Nova doesn't know she is overestimating—she has confidence in her estimate. She now views every piece of information through a lens colored by the belief that myocardial infarction is likely. Supporting evidence sharpens her focus on this diagnosis, whereas conflicting evidence—which should decrease this singular focus—is filtered out.

Dr. Learner begins with a similar hypothesis generation, but is able to use her additional knowledge and experience to generate additional hypotheses. In this case, she generates some extraneous possibilities that temporarily lead her astray (to consider truck exhaust as somehow related). Despite this diversion, she is able to return to the task at hand and refine her hypotheses based on the information she collects. In particular, she considers historical information that lowers her estimation of the likelihood of myocardial infarction (continuous over days, related to breathing). She also attempts to account for the appearance of the rash in the setting of chest pain and brings some "knowledge in action" (Schön, 1982) to bear to help her with causal reasoning. She determines that the chest pain is due to chest wall tenderness, and considers those diagnoses on her list that could explain a rash. She contrives a plausible explanation for the rash, based on causal reasoning (the chest hurts, the patient rubs the sore area, this irritates the skin and produces a rash).

Dr. Masters' hypothesis generation is similar to Dr. Learner's, and the refinement process is also similar except for one point: Dr. Masters has some additional explicit medical knowledge about rashes and chest pain. Dr. Learner does not consider that the rash could be the cause of the pain, whereas Dr. Masters has experience with herpes zoster and knows that it should be included in the differential diagnosis. Both physicians know what it looks like in its typical form, but only Dr. Masters considers the diagnosis at this stage. This consideration is triggered by pattern recognition, which is based on the application of tacit knowledge in action. She does not start out thinking, "Let's see if there is a rash," nor does she discover the rash and consider, "What is the differential diagnosis of this rash?" Instead, she sees the rash and thinks, "This rash is in a pattern that reminds me of herpes zoster, although it is very early in its course, but if this is the case, it could explain the chest pain." To a certain extent, this is a perceptual issue: The rash fits a pattern that triggers a diagnosis. But the rash is not a pattern that explains chest pain directly; the connection between the pattern recognition and the explanatory hypothesis requires a cognitive process.

The consideration of herpes zoster is outside Dr. Masters' initial framing of Mr. Case's problem. But rather than discarding it, she is able to alter her framing. Furthermore, she now reflects on this new framing to ask herself, "Why should this man have herpes zoster?" The new frame is suddenly not so neat and tidy—there is an explanation for the immediate cause of Mr. Case's pain, but not an explanation for the explanation. Dr. Masters does not simply use causal reasoning to work backward, as Dr. Learner does, to explain all observations. She also reasons forward to try to make sense of this new hypothesis. Her framing of the problem has some holes, and she does not hesitate to try filling the holes by redirecting her information gathering to other body regions and even back to history taking.

Conversely, all of our physicians have noted elevated blood pressure, but only Dr. Nova ascribes importance to it. Why? Most likely, it is because the more experienced physicians know that a patient who is seeing a new doctor for the first time may be a bit nervous or tense, with a normal reflex increase in blood pressure. They know that this may simply be a case of "white coat hypertension" and, although noting it carefully, do not attach inordinate importance to it.

Diagnostic Decision Making

Because Dr. Nova finds herself considering some potentially life-threatening conditions, she believes that she needs to gather additional information quickly. She believes that an electrocardiogram and chest x-ray are needed, along with blood tests, including a complete blood count and chemistries for electrolytes and cardiac enzymes (to try to detect damage to heart muscle). As she considers the possibility of pulmonary embolism, she would like to obtain an arterial oxygen level (blood gas) and possibly a (ventilation/perfusion) lung scan. If these tests are performed and the results are normal, she would think about having the patient undergo a treadmill stress test. In considering Mr. Case's hypertension, she entertains the idea of testing for some of the more obscure, correctable causes, such as an adrenalin-secreting tumor, but decides the chest pain needs attention first.

Dr. Learner feels much less urgency in collecting additional information. She is comfortable with her belief that the pain is in the chest wall. She knows that the common conditions producing such pain are not life threatening and often get better on their own. Furthermore, there are no specific tests to help differentiate many of these conditions. She decides that the best course is watchful waiting for the pain as well as the blood pressure.

Dr. Masters shares Dr. Learner's sense that the chest pain does not pose an immediate threat to Mr. Case. She believes that the rash is the cause (not a result of) the pain and that the rash represents early herpes zoster. She knows that there is no good laboratory test to confirm her diagnosis, at least at this stage, but that if she waits and the rash evolves, the diagnosis will become more certain. She is more concerned with the reason for the rash, including evidence she has found supporting an immune deficiency, and chooses a diagnostic workup accordingly. She plans a complete blood count and a blood glucose. She would also like a test for human immunodeficiency virus (HIV, the cause of AIDS), and a chest x-ray to look for tumor and/or lymph nodes. Like Dr. Learner, she is unconcerned by the blood pressure.

Our novice is demonstrating a pattern commonly seen in inexperienced physicians: an overreliance on diagnostic testing. Tests are ordered to help suggest hypotheses, rather than to prove or disprove ones already considered. When used for this reason, tests can often confuse the picture by suggesting many additional possibilities. As a result, the novice can become overwhelmed and disorganized, adding diseases to a patient's problem list simply to explain incidental findings and ordering more tests to confirm the results of previous unnecessary tests, ending up in a vicious cycle of "spiraling empiricism" (Kim & Gallis, 1989). Our more experienced physicians are more careful in their choices—choosing tests only when they believe suspicion of a condition will be pushed beyond a threshold to be "ruled in" or "ruled out." Because they have faith in their physical examination skills, they believe they have localized the presenting complaint in a way that does not require additional tests. Dr. Learner is correct in her assumption that the cause of the pain is not an immediate threat and that expectant observation is a sufficient diagnostic test. It is only because Dr. Masters has revealed some additional findings that she orders tests—not to confirm what she already believes to be true, but to help understand an underlying, related process.

Therapeutic Decision Making

Dr. Nova feels caught in a dilemma. Although Mr. Case looks fairly healthy, she has committed herself to considering some very serious conditions. She feels that if she waits too long to collect more diagnostic information, the condition may worsen and Mr. Case could die. She considers that she could give him some anti-angina medication to try, but decides instead to simply send Mr. Case to the emergency room, where he can get all the tests he needs immediately to rule out life-threatening conditions and also be started on treatment for his hypertension. She therefore tells him she will have someone escort him to the emergency room and that if everything turns out all right, he can come back in 1 week.

Dr. Learner has decided on a course of watchful waiting, treating Mr. Case with "tincture of time." She decides that some symptomatic relief is reasonable, and prescribes an anti-inflammatory agent. Mr. Case is given instructions on taking the medication and told to return in 1 week if he has not improved.

Dr. Masters has a different dilemma from Dr. Nova's: She must consider how much to tell Mr. Case, a person she has just met, about her concerns. She worries that she may cause undue alarm with a premature diagnosis. However, she does not want to defer the diagnosis and, in any event, obtaining an HIV test will be difficult to do without discussing her suspicions. She therefore tells Mr. Case about what she believes is causing his pain and what reasons there might be for this to have occurred. She gives him some pain medication, a course of an antiviral medication for probable herpes zoster, and an appointment to return in 1 week to discuss the results of the tests. She counsels him about the importance of safe sex, regardless of the outcome of the tests, and also discusses the possible conflict between his drinking habits and his occupation.

At this point, all of our physicians have acted appropriately, based on the diagnoses they have entertained. Dr. Nova has forced herself to treat Mr. Case emergently, because she settled onto the consideration of serious conditions. Once she believes that myocardial infarction is likely, she has little choice but to send Mr. Case to the emergency room. Once he is treated there, it is likely that serious conditions will be excluded (at no small expense) and Mr. Case will be sent home to return for his appointment the following week. Dr. Learner has also acted appropriately, based on her beliefs: She is probably correct in her belief that a chest wall syndrome explains the symptoms and needs only symptomatic treatment. She believes that waiting a week may help understand the process better—especially if, in the interim, the symptoms resolve spontaneously. Dr. Masters has arrived at a more complex diagnosis, which calls for a more complex plan. She is required to draw on some very special skills in order to discuss her hypothesis openly and in a caring manner. She is not overwhelmed by the complexity of what began as a simple case of chest pain. She maintains a level of mental organization not evidenced by the others. As she collects her information, she assigns each finding to a problem and then systematically addresses each problem. Even with the unexpected turn of events, she has not lost track of the fact that two items from the history (drinking and driving) suggest a health risk that must be discussed with the patient.

Critiquing the Differences Among Novice, Intermediate, and Expert

There are many individual differences in styles and patterns of medical practice. The thoughts and actions I attribute to my three fictional physicians are, to a large extent, stereotypes. Nevertheless, they are drawn from true-to-life observations made watching my teachers, my students, my colleagues, and myself as we develop our individual expertise. Based on these vignettes, several generalizations can be made about the progression from novice to expert.

The novice physician relies heavily on memorized patterns of behavior, learned explicitly. These patterns can be of great value, especially in emergency situations where panic might preclude reasoned thought. But, in general, they are too generic and are difficult to apply to individual patients without some customization. Often, the result is inefficiency: *Knowing* all the questions that can be asked during an interview is useful knowledge, but actually *asking* them all is rarely practical. Excessive data collection becomes harmful if the physician cannot manage all the information simultaneously and suffers from cognitive overload. This is particularly likely to happen when the previously acquired book knowledge is not yet well organized for appropriate retrieval. Instead, the physician may associate a finding with the most recently learned condition or the most life-threatening condition, rather than the most common condition. Once such an association is established, the physician may proceed down a garden path in which all available data are made to fit the hypothesis and seem to point in an obvious direction. Important data that need to be considered are ignored, and irrelevant data are not recognized as such. Dr. Nova, starting with a complaint of chest pain, doggedly pursues it until arriving at diagnoses in which chest pain is a prominent finding, even if the conditions themselves are somewhat unlikely.

The more experienced physician develops a better sense of how to focus a patient encounter; for example, the questions asked are much more relevant and reveal underlying diagnostic problem solving. Most teachers, when observing a trainee conducting an interview, can watch clearly as the diagnostic wheels turn with recognition, such as "I see why she asked that question—the last answer is making her think about disease X." Sometimes, however, these wheels can turn too much. Whereas the novice can be overwhelmed with data and produce a dearth of hypotheses, the more experienced physician might cope with all the data and then develop a multitude of hypotheses in an attempt to explain them all.

The expert physician has much more of a sense of what is important and what is not. Information gathering becomes much more efficient and automatic, leaving more time for "reflection in action" to consider, rank, and accept or reject additional hypotheses. The expert will feel comfortable discounting some of the patient's complaints, although being careful to acknowledge their presence and being prepared to address the patient's concerns about them. The expert will also know when something is a warning sign that must not be ignored, such as Mr. Case's possible herpes zoster. Dr. Masters did not start out thinking, "Chest pain—I'd better consider HIV disease." Nor did she immediately consider herpes zoster as a proximal cause of chest pain, although she might have in an older patient. But the constellation of pain, chest rash, and skin tenderness triggered retrieval of a diagnosis that fit the pattern. This diagnosis is not in and of itself dangerous—it can be treated to minimize the symptoms and generally resolves without complication—but it was a red flag for Dr. Masters. Her thinking was something along the line of, "Hmm, this looks like herpes zoster, which fits the symptoms and findings, but then why should he get zoster? What else might be going on?" She was not blinded by this red flag, however. Her ability to organize the findings was such that she also kept track of the combination of the patient's occupation (driving) and related risky behavior (drinking), and was able to address it with the patient.

What is it that differentiates these physicians? They all started out with the same set of explicit knowledge. (In fact, those further from their training years might have experienced a decay of the explicit knowledge that they acquired during training.) The experts have two kinds of educational opportunities that the novices don't: continuing medical education (CME) and patient care experience.

As previously noted, physicians are generally required by law to participate in CME if they want to continue in practice. The quantity of material is much less than that taught in medical school, so how can it be effective? The material in CME courseware is often more practical and less esoteric than similar information provided in medical school and residency. In addition, the experienced physician may be much more receptive to learning from such material. The information obtained in CME may make clear how other previously learned information fits together to make sense. It may also provide information that can be related to patient care experiences ("So *that's* why Ms. Jones had that problem").

This brings me to what is ultimately the real learning experience for the expert: patient care. It is only by seeing patient after patient that the recognition patterns develop. From these experiences, the physician can build a set of case prototypes by which to compare future patients. These prototypes can help recognize patterns ("This guy reminds me of Mr. Jones, who had problem X"). They can also help the physician recognize when something is out of place ("I've never seen zoster in a 45-year-old—how do I explain this?").

Prototypes can be misleading. If a physician sees a patient with a common complaint that is ultimately found to be due to a rare condition, the physician may develop a prototype that, when brought to bear in later cases, evokes unusual diagnoses. However, prototypes will not be based on a single case, but instead on common elements drawn from several similar cases. We can presume that explicitly learned knowledge also plays a role in the development of effective prototypes in the thoughtful physician.

For the most part, the learning that goes on during patient encounters is of a tacit nature. We can see that the development of expertise is happening—the physician starts off inexperienced, sees a large number of patients (in which little or no explicit learning is going on), and comes out the other end as an expert. The process itself is something of a mystery that, as I've said, I leave to my cognitive science colleagues to unravel.

CHALLENGES

The process by which medical expertise develops reflects a time-honored tradition of classroom and book learning, apprenticeship, and experience gained in practice. However, the advancement of the field, and changes in the society in which the field is embedded, are placing pressures on the process. These concerns can be seen, for example, in letters written by physicians to medical journals that describe how the changes to the practice of medicine are making it increasingly difficult to perform as an expert.

One tremendous problem is maintaining our fund of knowledge. There is no doubt that just as the tacit knowledge of the physician grows after training, explicit knowledge deteriorates. As soon as we learn something, we begin to forget it; because we are no longer cramming our heads with facts, we enter a state of negative knowledge balance. CME courses and journal reading help refresh our memories, but they can never match the intensity of our period of formal training. We offset this knowledge with the knowledge that we gain through experience, but we are nagged by the concern that this may not compensate fully.

The quality, as well as quantity, of our explicit knowledge is affected. On my first day of medical school, the president of the college told us that half of what we would learn in our 4 years was wrong, but he couldn't tell us which half. This was only mildly pessimistic. As far as I can tell, no new bones have been discovered since then. But many new diseases, drugs, organisms, and physiologic processes have been. More medical knowledge has been accumulated in the last 20 years than in all the years before. To help us counter this problem of information overload, the field of medical information science (medical informatics) has grown during the same period. Medical information systems have been developed to teach us, to provide access to medical literature, to help us organize the ever-increasing body of information we collect about our patients, and even to bring us expert systems (sometimes imbued with tacit knowledge; Nyce & Timpka, 1993) to help us with knotty problems. This increased ability to rely on computer memory may yet help wean us from our reliance on human memory. However, at present, the level of performance of computer-assisted decision making is at a Grade C level (Kassirer, 1994). In addition, it is not clear that internal tacit knowledge can be brought to bear if explicit knowledge resides in some external computer source.

Medical expertise used to refer to the ability to diagnose a patient's problem and effect a cure. Today, however, society demands that physicians add the dimension of cost-effectiveness to their plans. Medical care is recognized as exceedingly expensive, and resources are stretched beyond their limits. It would be a simple matter if all the physician needed to do was to recognize all the alternatives and select the cheapest one that provided the desired outcome. However, we are now faced with choices in which cost must be weighed against benefit. Physicians today face many coercions and incentives meant to influence their decisions in economically favorable directions. In the past, the physician could take the moral high ground as the patient's advocate first and society's advocate second, but with scarce resources comes the obligation to decide responsibly and realistically about how such resources should be expended. Today's successful medical experts are able to include such considerations in their judgments.

Society places a second, opposing pressure on physician decision making in the form of medical malpractice liability. Patients have come to expect miracles from medicine and, when the miraculous does not occur, the issue of malpractice is often raised. When faced with a bad outcome, physicians find themselves better able to defend themselves when they can show in retrospect that they did everything possible (ordered every test, tried every therapy) in an effort to improve that outcome. (Of course, all too often, it is the inappropriate test or treatment that is to *blame* in the first place!) The result is defensive medicine, with decisions made not to help the patient but to protect the decision maker. This clearly leads to increased costs of care, and may lead to decreased quality.

These challenges are being met with an increased recognition that physicians should be practicing "evidence-based medicine" (Haynes, 1993); that is, they should make decisions based not on something they were simply told to do in the past, or on some anecdotal experience, but on results of clinical research that addresses the decision at hand. Such an approach is laudable, because it allows physicians to choose tests and treatments proven to be effective while eschewing those shown not to be so. Knowing what is effective allows one to be cost effective; at the same time, it allows one to practice in a manner that is defensible, without having to resort to defensiveness. There are some drawbacks to attempting to apply the evidence-based approach. Unfortunately, evidence is simply not available for supporting every possible decision. Even when a study has been done to show, for example, that one treatment is better than another for a particular disease, the physician faced with treating a patient with the disease must weigh that evidence to decide if it is applicable in the individual case. There is, of course, no way to teach someone how to carry out this customization process. It is done using heuristics acquired tacitly (McDonald, 1996).

CONCLUSIONS

Expertise in medicine requires mastery of a large body of formal book knowledge to be acquired explicitly before one can begin to apply that knowledge to gain practical experience. Although some tacit knowledge is acquired through observation of our teachers, it is practical experience that turns us into experts.

Expert behavior is easy to detect, if not understand. Next time you see an expert physician in action, if you are not too sick, observe for a moment how he or she collects and organizes information, brings knowledge to bear, and establishes a framework addressing complex issues.

REFERENCES

Barrows, H. S. (1993). An overview of the uses of standardized patients for teaching and evaluating clinical skills. *Academic Medicine, 68*(6), 443–451.

Bell, B. M. (1988). The new hospital code and the supervision of residents. *The New York State Journal of Medicine, 88,* 617–619.

Berkson, L. (1994). Problem-based learning: Have the expectations been met? *Academic Medicine, 68,* S79–S88.

Blois, M. S. (1988). Medicine and the nature of vertical reasoning. *New England Journal of Medicine, 31,* 847–851.

Flexner, A. (1910). *Medical education in the United States and Canada: A report to the Carnegie Foundation for the Advancement of Teaching.* Bethesda, MD: Science and Health Publications.

Haynes, R. B. (1993). Some problems in applying evidence in clinical practice. *Annals of the New York Academy of Sciences, 703,* 224–225.

Kassirer, J. P. (1994). A report card on computer-assisted diagnosis—the grade: C. *New England Journal of Medicine, 331,* 1238.

Kassirer, J. P., & Kopelman, R. I. (1991). *Learning clinical reasoning.* Baltimore: Williams & Wilkins.

Kim, J. H., & Gallis, H. A. (1989). Observations on spiraling empiricism: Its causes, allure, and perils, with particular reference to antibiotic therapy. *American Journal of Medicine, 87,* 201–206.

Lane, C., Goldman, L., Soukup, J. R., & Hayes, J. G. (1993). The impact of a regulation restricting medical house staff working hours on the quality of patient care. *JAMA, 269,* 374–378.

Levinson, W., & Roter, D. (1993). The effects of two continuing medical education programs on communication skills of practicing primary care physicians. *Journal of General Internal Medicine, 8,* 318–324.

McDonald, C. J. (1996). Medial heuristics: The silent adjudicators of clinical practice. *Annals of Internal Medicine, 124,* 56–62.

Nyce, J. M., & Timpka, T. (1993). Work, knowledge and argument in specialist consultations: Incorporating tacit knowledge into system design and development. *Medical and Biological Engineering & Computing, 31,* HTA16–19.

Schön, D. A. (1982). *The reflective practitioner: How professionals think in action.* New York: Basic.

Sternberg, R. J., & Horvath, J. A. (1995). A prototype view of expert teaching. *Educational Researcher, 24,* 9–17.

Tversky, A., & Kahneman, D. (1974). Judgement under uncertainty: Heuristics and biases. *Science, 185,* 1124–1131.

PART FOUR

MANAGEMENT

CHAPTER SEVEN

Tacit Knowledge and Management

Chris Argyris
Harvard University

The argument of this chapter is that tacit knowledge is the primary basis for effective management, and the basis for its deterioration. Stated briefly, the reasoning for this claim is as follows: The primary basis for effective management is to define and transform, as much as possible, the behavior required to achieve the organization's objectives into routines that work (Argyris, 1990, 1993; Argyris & Schön, 1996; Nelson & Winter, 1977). Routines are implemented through skillful actions. Actions that are skillful are based largely on tacit knowledge. Such actions become self-reinforcing of the status quo. The self-reinforcing features tend to reduce inquiry into gaps and inconsistencies in the tacit knowledge. When these surface, they are often embarrassing or threatening. Individuals deal with embarrassment or threat with another set of skillful—hence tacit—actions. These actions are counterproductive to effective management.

EFFECTIVE MANAGEMENT DEPENDS ON TACIT KNOWLEDGE: A SCENARIO

1. All organizations are designed to achieve the objectives intended by the founders. Managing is the crucial process in implementing the design.

2. All designs specify the intended objectives and the actions required to achieve the objectives. Designs are therefore specifications intended to be generalizable and comprehensive.

Designs intended to manage the complexities of everyday life in organizations will always contain two types of gaps. First, no a priori design is likely to cover all the specifics and uniqueness of the concrete case. Managers will always be faced with gap filling. Second, no design is likely to activate all the energies and cognitive capacities of the human beings. Motivating individuals is likely to require that attention be paid to differences in individuals and contexts.

3. In order to minimize the gaps, managers specify ahead of time the jobs and roles of the players as completely as is possible, without the specifications being so complex that they immobilize performance. The rewards and penalties intended to activate the energies and cognitive abilities are also specified ahead of time.

4. The roles are usually specified by reference to the functional managerial disciplines such as human resources, information technology, finance, managerial accounting, marketing, and operations. Each of these disciplines is a theory of action; that is, each specifies the actions required to achieve their particular objectives (which, in turn, are connected to the overall objectives) as well as the conditions under which the specifications hold. Each functional managerial discipline is therefore a causal theory about how to get something done.

5. All designs of managerial theories of action aspire to make their requirements explicit and specific, so that they can be taught to human beings and their causal claims can be tested in the world of practice. For example, activity-based costing is part of the larger discipline of accounting. It specifies, among other things, the importance of diagnosing accurately the cost drivers by focusing on the activities used to produce a product or service. It specifies the sequence of steps to be taken in order to identify the activities that drive the costs. Two individuals using the same numbers and following the activity-based costing specifications should always come up with similar answers. If they do not, they can trace their actions backward and ultimately identify where the discrepancy or error occurred. Such possibilities are tests of the *internal validity* of the causal specifications. Activity-based accounting also specifies the relationship of costs to more comprehensive managerial goals such as profit. These causal claims are part of the *external validity* of activity-based costing.

6. The aspiration of the designers of all managerial functional disciplines is to produce propositions that exhibit high internal and external validity. Such explicitly stated propositions make the discipline transparent and therefore teachable.

7. The objective of teaching the discipline is to make the professionals skillful at carrying out their specifications. Individuals are skillful to the extent that they produce the specifications, automatically and with a low requirement for deliberate thought. Indeed, if they had to focus explicitly on what they were doing, they would likely lose their skill. Individuals do

focus deliberately on their skillful behavior when they produce errors; that is, when they are not behaving skillfully. Skillful actions are automatic and taken for granted.

THE FUNDAMENTAL ASSUMPTIONS MADE BY MANAGERIAL FUNCTIONAL DISCIPLINES ABOUT THEIR IMPLEMENTATION

Embedded in the managerial disciplines is what may be described as a "microcausal theory" of implementation:

> If individuals know the specifications,
> If they have the skills to produce them,
> If they wish to produce them,
> If they are enabled to produce them (e.g., by management, organizational norms, informal employee norms)
> Then they will do so. . . .

The second fundamental assumption is that ineffective performance can be traced to errors or mismatches. Errors can be corrected by acquiring new information and skills, or by reformulating the theory of action of the discipline. Underlying this assumption is a third one: Errors will not be produced knowingly, because to do so is an illegitimate transgression from the specifications (i.e., unprofessional behavior). Individuals will not violate the professional stewardship embedded in their jobs, roles, and other features of their contract with management.

A fourth assumption is that it is management's responsibility to monitor the implementation of the managerial disciplines to ensure the organization that the individuals are not violating the first three assumptions. This monitoring activity is carried out as follows. As many actions as possible are predefined and routinized. Management focuses on identifying any exceptions to the routine in order to correct them (the activity is called *management by exception*).

To summarize: Roles are defined and enablers (such as policies) are created that, if followed, will produce, in theory, the intended consequences. The employees are coached until they perform the role requirements skillfully. Once the appropriate level of skill has been achieved, the actions become automatic, routine, and hence manageable. They also become tacit; hence, the claim that effective management depends on the effective use of tacit knowledge.

ORGANIZATIONAL DEFENSIVE ROUTINES

In real life, most organizations exhibit powerful organizational defensive routines. They are activated when the participants are dealing with any business or human problems that are embarrassing or threatening. A defensive routine is any action or policy intended to prevent the players from experiencing embarrassment or threat, and does so in ways that make it difficult to identify and reduce the causes of the embarrassment or threat. Defensive routines are overprotective and antilearning. Defensive routines are activated under conditions when they are likely to be most counterproductive.

Defensive routines are created because the participants believe that the routines are necessary in order for themselves and the organization to survive. This creates a bind. On the one hand, defensive routines are used to cover up errors that are important to correct if the organization is to perform effectively. Such a cover-up violates formal managerial requirements and stewardship. Participants are not supposed to bypass errors. Moreover, the bypass is undiscussable. And, in order to produce undiscussable behavior that persists, the undiscussability itself must also be undiscussable. On the other hand, if the errors, their undiscussability, and the cover-ups surface, the participants are subject to criticism for acting in these ways.

How does such behavior arise, and how does it become so powerful? There are two fundamental sets of causes: the theories for effective action that individuals learn early in life, and the defensive routines that they create in organizations when the theories are implemented correctly.

DESIGNS FOR ACTION: MODEL I

Human beings have programs in their heads on how to act effectively in any type of interaction, be it as a leader, as a follower, or as a peer. We call these programs their *theories of action*. These theories of action are, in effect, causal theories of how to act effectively.

Human beings hold two types of theories of action. There is the one that they espouse, which is usually expressed in the form of stated beliefs and values. Then there is the theory that they actually use; this can only be inferred from observing their actions, that is, their actual behavior. To date, most human beings studied have the same theory in use. There is diversity in espoused theories, but not in theories in use. A model of the theory in use (that we call Model I) follows. Model I theory in use is the design we found throughout the world. It has four governing values:

1. Achieve your intended purpose.
2. Maximize winning and minimize losing.

3. Suppress negative feelings.
4. Behave according to what you consider rational.

The most prevalent action strategies that arise from Model I are the following:

1. Advocate your position.
2. Evaluate the thoughts and actions of others (and your own thoughts and actions).
3. Attribute causes for whatever you are trying to understand (Argyris, 1982, 1990, 1993; Argyris & Schön, 1996).

These actions must be performed in such a way that satisfies the actors' governing values—that is, they achieve at least their minimum acceptable level of being in control, winning, or bringing about any other result. In other words, Model I tells individuals to craft their positions, evaluations, and attributions in ways that inhibit inquiries into and tests of them with the use of independent logic. The consequences of these Model I strategies are likely to be defensiveness, misunderstanding, and self-fulfilling and self-sealing processes (Argyris, 1982).

Model I theory in use requires defensive reasoning. Individuals keep their premises and inferences tacit, lest they lose control. They create tests of their claims that are self-serving and self-sealing. The likelihood of misunderstanding and mistrust increases. The use of defensive reasoning prohibits questioning the defensive reasoning. We now have self-fueling processes that maintain the status quo, inhibit genuine learning, and reinforce the deception.

For example, a superior believes that the performance of his subordinate is below standard. He also believes that saying so in a forthright manner will lead the subordinate to become defensive and hence close off learning. The superior therefore attempts to ease in and to be diplomatic. He does not say that he [the subordinate] is acting in these ways, because that would upset the subordinate. The subordinate senses the easing in and the diplomacy. He covers up what he is sensing and acts as if he is not doing so.

After the session, the superior and subordinate were interviewed separately to assess how well the session had gone. The superior responded that all went well until the subordinate became defensive. Then the superior backed off in order to be constructive. Similarly, the subordinate responded that all went well until he began to disagree with the superior. At that time, in the eyes of the subordinate, the superior became defensive. The subordinate backed off lest he get into trouble.

When each was asked if he had mentioned his evaluations about the other's actions, the response was, in effect, "Are you kidding? That is a cure that would make the illness worse." The result was that each individual reinforced his attributions about the other. Neither tested the validity of his views, because both believed them to be true and an attempt at a genuine test would only make things worse. Hence, there was a situation of minimal learning, self-sealing positions, and increasing mistrust.

Human beings learn their theories in use early in life, and therefore the actions that they produce are highly skilled. Little conscious attention is paid to producing skilled actions. Indeed, conscious attention could inhibit producing them effectively. This leads to unawareness of what we are doing when we act skillfully. The unawareness due to skill and the unawareness caused by our unilaterally controlling theories in use produce a deeper unawareness; namely, we become unaware of the programs in our heads that keep us unaware. The results are skilled unawareness and skilled incompetence (Argyris, 1980). For example, when individuals have to say something negative to others (e.g., "Your performance is poor") they often ease in, in order not to upset the other. Two of the most frequent easing-in actions that we observe are (a) nondirective questioning and (b) face-saving approaches. In order for these to work, the individuals must cover up that they are acting as they are, in order not to upset the other. In order for a cover-up to work, the cover-up itself must be covered up.

Under these conditions, we find that the recipients are wary of what is happening. They sense that there may be a cover-up. Because they hold the same theory in use, they too cover up their private doubts. The result is counterproductive consequences for genuine problem solving. All of this occurs with the use of skillful behavior; hence, the term *skilled incompetence.*

When organizational worlds become dominated by these consequences, human beings become cynical about changing the self-fueling counterproductive process. Not surprisingly, they learn to distance themselves from taking responsibility, losing, and suppressing negative feelings, especially those associated with embarrassment or threat. Individuals use behavioral strategies consistent with these governing values. For example, they advocate their views, making evaluations and attributions in such a way as to ensure their being in control, winning, and suppressing negative feelings.

In short, individuals learn theories in use that are consistent with producing unilateral control. It is true that organizations are hierarchical and based on unilateral control. It is equally true that individuals are even more so. Place individuals in organizations whose structures are designed to be more egalitarian, and individuals will eventually make them more unilateral and authoritarian. The most massive examples of such situations of which I am aware are the "alternative schools" and communes of the 1970s. Most have failed and slowly have faded away.

For example, in a study of five alternative high schools that I conducted, I found that the schools were (a) given adequate funding, (b) permitted to redesign their curriculum, (c) staffed by teachers who volunteered because they believed in the concept of the school, and (d) attended by students who had the same views. All went well until the teachers began to conclude that academic performance was falling. In several attempts to correct the situation, they were attacked by the students. The students accused them of being traditional, top-down, and authoritarian. The teachers distanced themselves from students, and vice versa. Soon, the teachers requested that the experiments end or, in two cases, the respective school boards did so (Argyris, 1974).

ORGANIZATIONAL DEFENSIVE ROUTINES

Organizational defensive routines are any action, policy, or practice that prevents organizational participants from experiencing embarrassment or threat and, at the same time, prevents them from discovering the causes of the embarrassment or threat. Organizational defensive routines, like Model I theories in use, inhibit genuine learning and overprotect the individuals and the organization (Argyris, 1990).

There is a fundamental logic underlying all organizational defensive routines. It can be illustrated by one of the most frequently observed defenses, namely, sending mixed messages, such as, "Mary, you run the department, but check with Bill," or "John, be innovative but be careful." The logic is as follows:

1. Send a message that is inconsistent.
2. Act as if it is not inconsistent.
3. Make Steps 1 and 2 undiscussable.
4. Make the undiscussability undiscussable.

An illustration of what happens when organizational defensive routines dominate can be seen in this case of cost reduction. Twelve foreman were trying to uncover where cost reductions might be made. In an hour or so, they were able to identify more than 30 areas. Next, they ranked these areas for possible action. Finally, they selected 6 areas on which they promised to take action.

After 3 months, the foremen met to report their accomplishments. Objectives for all 6 areas had been achieved. Management estimated the likely savings to be about $210,000. Everyone was delighted. The mood was understandably festive, and the group turned to the champagne and dinner that top management had provided.

However, a crucial question had not been asked. Indeed, the manager who led the discussion said that he would not have even thought of asking the question. An outside observer studying these cost-reduction meetings asked:

Observer:	Do you remember the list of areas that you identified 3 months ago?
Foremen:	Of course.
Observer:	How long did you know about these lists?
Foremen:	We don't understand. What are you driving at?
Observer:	How long did you know that these problem areas existed?
Foremen:	From 1 to 3 years. It was common knowledge.
Observer:	What led you not to take action until these seminars? What prevented you from taking these actions without the stimulation from the seminar?
Foremen:	Are you kidding? Are you serious?
Observer:	I am not kidding; I am serious. What prevented you from correcting problems that you knew about for years?
Foremen:	Be careful. You're opening up a can of worms! (*Turning to the top management representative*) Do you want us to answer that question? It could spoil the evening.

Reflecting on this story, we see that the criterion for success was a fix that was quick and easily measurable. The cost-reduction program was judged a success. However, the big question was not asked by those who managed it.

Organizational defensive routines are caused by a circular, self-reinforcing process in which individuals' Model I theories in use produce individual strategies of bypass and cover-up, which result in organizational bypass and cover-up, which reinforce the individuals' theories in use. The explanation of organizational defensive routines is therefore individual *and* organizational. This means that it should not be possible to change organizational routines without changing individual routines, and vice versa. Any attempts at doing so should lead to failure or, at best, temporary success.

THE CHALLENGES IN PRODUCING CHANGES IN ORGANIZATIONAL DEFENSES

If this self-reinforcing process is valid, then researcher-interveners face at least two challenges when trying to help both individuals and their organizations deal with these issues. The first challenge is that individuals' senses of competence, self-confidence, and self-esteem are highly dependent on their Model I theories in use and organizational defensive routines. This dependence practically guarantees that when individuals are acting to learn, the consequences will be skillfully counterproductive because the Model I theories in use will not allow Model I governing values to be changed. This illustrates skilled incompetence. This message is not likely to be met with joy by the clients or subjects. Indeed, it is likely to create additional conditions of embarrassment and threat. Thus, one of the first messages required for reeducation will likely trigger the very organizational defensive routines the intervener is asking participants to change. The researcher-intervener does not ignore this dilemma, but instead sees it as an opportunity for learning based on here-and-now data. So far, most of the individuals with whom my colleagues and I have worked have indeed become defensive on hearing this message, but most of them have learned from their defensiveness (Argyris, 1982, 1993; Argyris & Schön, 1996).

The second challenge is that individuals, through acculturation, define social virtues such as caring, support, and integrity as consistent with Model I. For example, to be caring and supportive, say what you believe individuals would like to hear; do not act in ways that make them defensive. This means that they are not likely to recognize the counterproductive consequences of Model I theories in use.

MODEL II: THEORIES IN USE

To help individuals recognize their skillful Model I blindness, the intervener introduces Model II theories in use. Model II theories are, at the outset, espoused theories. The challenge is to help individuals transform their espoused theories into theories in use by learning a "new" set of skills and a "new" set of governing values. Because many individuals espouse Model II values and skills, these traits are not totally new to them. However, the empirical fact to date is that very few individuals can routinely act on their espoused values and scale, yet they are often unaware of this limitation.

The governing values of Model II are valid information, informed choice, and vigilant monitoring of the implementation of the choice in order to detect and correct error. As in the case of Model I, the three most prominent behaviors are advocate, evaluate, and attribute. However, unlike Model I behaviors, Model II behaviors are crafted into action strategies that openly illustrate how the actors reached their evaluations or attributions, and how they crafted them to encourage inquiry and testing by others. Productive reasoning is required to produce such consequences. Productive reasoning means that the premises are explicit, the inferences from the premises are also made explicit, and finally conclusions are crafted in ways that can be tested by logic that is independent of the actor. Unlike the defensive reasoning, the logic used is not self-referenced. As a consequence, defensive routines that are anti-learning are minimized, and genuine learning is facilitated. Embarrassment and threat are not bypassed and covered up; they are engaged (Argyris, 1982; Argyris & Schön, 1974).

To the extent that individuals use Model II theory instead of merely espousing it, they will begin to interrupt organizational defensive routines and begin to create organizational learning processes and systems that encourage double-loop learning in ways that persist. These are called *Model II learning systems* (Argyris & Schön, 1996).

DESIGN OF THE RESEARCH-INTERVENTION ACTIVITIES

There are a few design rules that follow from the theoretical framework described previously that can be used to design the research and the intervention activities:

- Discover the degree to which the clients' theories in use are consistent with Model I.
- Discover the degree to which the clients use defensive reasoning whenever they deal with embarrassing or threatening issues.
- Discover the designs (rules) the clients have in their heads that keep them unaware of the discrepancies among their espoused values, their actions, and their theories in use.
- Discover the degree to which the clients discourage valid reflection on their actions while they are acting. To put this another way: Discover how the clients create designs for action that they do not follow but that they believe they do follow, while they are also being systematically unaware of this discrepancy and are behaving in ways that prevent them from discovering the discrepancy and the causes of their unawareness.
- Discover the defensive routines that exist in the organization and limit learning. Develop maps of these organizational defensive routines, specifying the actions that lead to limited-learning consequences and cause them to persist even though the directors wish to be free of them.

In order to reach these goals, reeducation and change programs should produce relatively directly observable data about these clients' reasoning and actions. The clients must accept responsibility for creating these data, and these data must be in a form from which the clients' theories in use can be inferred (e.g., recorded conversations):

- Encourage the clients to examine inconsistencies and gaps in the reasoning that underlines their actions.

- Surface and make explicit the rules that "must" be in their heads if they maintain there is a connection between their designs for action and the actions themselves.
- View any bewilderment or frustration that results as further directly observable data that can be used to test the validity of what is being learned.
- Produce opportunities to practice Model II ways of crafting actions that will reduce counterproductive consequences.

In principle, the kind of research of which I write can begin with identifying either the theories in use or the organizational defensive routines. It does not matter which, because one will necessarily lead you to the other. I usually make the choice on the basis of which of the two is most likely to generate the participants' internal commitment to the research and to the eventual intervention.

THE LEFT- AND RIGHT-HAND COLUMN CASE METHOD

We often use a case study instrument to get at theories in use and organizational defensive routines. The case method described next is one of several instruments used in our action science research (Argyris, Putnam, & Smith, 1985). The key features of all the research methods and this case method in particular are:

1. It produces relatively directly observable data such as conversation. Such data are the actual productions of action, and therefore can become the basis for inferring theories in use.

2. It produces data in ways that make clear the actors' responsibility for the meanings produced. When used properly, the respondents cannot make the research instrument causally responsible for the data that they produced (e.g., "I didn't *really* mean that"; or "I didn't understand the meaning of that term").

3. It produces data about the respondents' causal theories, especially those that are tacit because they are taken for granted.

4. It provides opportunities for the respondents to change their responses without hindering the validity of the inferences being made. Indeed, the actions around "changing their minds" should also provide data about their causal reasoning processes. It provides opportunities to change their actions as well as actions of groups, intergroups, and organizations over which they have some influence. It provides such knowledge in ways that are economical and do not harm the respondents or the context in which they are working.

The directions to write a case are given to each individual. The directions request:

1. In one paragraph, describe a key organizational problem as you see it.
2. Assume you could talk to whomever you wish in order to begin to solve the problem. Describe, in a paragraph or so, the strategy that you would use in this meeting.
3. Next, split your page into two columns. On the right-hand side write how you would begin the meeting—what you would actually say. Then write what you believe the other(s) would say. Then write your response to their response. Continue writing this scenario for two or so double-spaced typewritten pages.
4. In the left-hand column, write any idea or feeling that you would have that you would not communicate for whatever reason.

In short, the case includes:

- A statement of the problem.
- The intended strategy to begin to solve the problem.
- The actual conversation that would occur as envisioned by the writer.
- The information that the writer would not communicate for whatever reason.

Some of the results can be illustrated by reference to a CEO and his executive group. The executives reported that they became highly involved in writing the cases. Some said that the very writing of the case was an eye-opener. Moreover, once the cases were distributed to each member, the reactions were jocular. The members were enjoying them, as these comments demonstrate:

"That's just like . . ."

"Great, . . . does this all the time."

"Oh, there's a familiar one."

"All salesmen and no listeners."

"Oh my God, this is us."

CASES AS AN INTERVENTION TOOL

What is the advantage of using the cases? The cases, crafted and written by the executives themselves, become vivid examples of "skilled incompetence." They illustrate the skill with which each executive tried not to upset the other

TABLE 7.1
A Collage From Several Cases

Thoughts and Feelings Not Communicated	*Actual Conversation*
He's not going to like this topic, but we had to discuss it. I doubt that he will take a company perspective, but I should be positive.	*I:* Hi, Bill. I appreciate the opportunity to talk with you about this problem of customer service versus product. I am sure that both of us want to resolve it in the best interests of the company.
	Bill: I'm always glad to talk about it, as you well know.
I better go slow. Let me ease in.	*I:* There are an increasing number of situations where our clients are asking for customer service and rejecting the off-the-shelf products. My fear is that your salespeople will play an increasingly peripheral role in the future.
	Bill: I don't understand. Tell me more.
Like hell you don't understand. I wish there was a way I could be more gentle.	*I:* Bill, I'm sure you are aware of the changes (*and explains*).
	Bill: No, I do not see it that way. It's my salespeople that are the key to the future.
There he goes, thinking as a salesman and not as a corporate officer.	*I:* Well, let's explore that a bit. . . .

and to persuade them to change their position. They also illustrate the incompetence component because the results, by their own analysis, were to upset the others and make it less likely that their views would prevail.

The cases are also very important learning devices. It is difficult for anyone to slow down the behavior that they produce in milliseconds during a real meeting in order to reflect on it and change it. The danger is that others will grab the air time and run with it. Moreover, it is difficult for the human mind to pay attention to the interpersonal actions and to the substantive issues at the same time.

Table 7.1 presents a collage from several cases. They were written by individuals who believed the company should place a greater emphasis on customer service.

The dialogue continues with each person stating his views candidly but not being influenced by what the other says. To give you a flavor of what happened, here are some further left-hand column comments:

"He's doing a great job supporting his people. I better be careful."

"This guy is not really listening."

"I wonder if he's influenceable."

"This is beginning to piss me off."

"There he goes getting defensive. I better back off and wait for another day."

If I presented a collage of the cases written by individuals who supported the opposite views, it would not differ significantly. They, too, tried to persuade, sell, and cajole their peer officers. Their left-hand columns would be similar.

REFLECTING ON THE CASES

In analyzing their left-hand columns, the executives found that each side blamed the other side for the difficulties, and they used the same reasons. For example, each side said about the other side:

"You do not *really* understand the issues."

"If you insist on your position, you will harm the morale that I have built."

"Don't hand me that line. You know what I am talking about."

"Why don't you take off your blinders and wear a company hat?"

"It upsets me when I think of how they think."

"I'm really trying hard, but I'm beginning to feel this is hopeless."

These results illustrate once more the features of skilled incompetence. It requires skill to craft the cases with the intention not to upset others while trying to change their minds. Yet, as we have seen, the skilled behavior used in the cases had the opposite effect. The others in the case became upset and dug in their heels about changing their minds.

REDESIGNING THEIR ACTIONS

The next step is to begin to redesign their actions. The executives turned to their cases. Each executive selected an episode that he wished to redesign so that it would not have the negative consequences. As an aid in their redesign, the executives were given some handouts that described Model II set of behaviors. The first thing they realized was that they would have to slow things down. They could not produce a new conversation in the milliseconds that they were accustomed. This troubled them a bit, because they were impatient to learn. They kept reminding themselves that learning new skills does require that they slow down.

One technique they used was that each individual crafted, by himself, a new conversation to help the writer of the episode. After taking 5 or so minutes, the individuals shared their designs with the writer. In the process of discussing these, the writer learned much about how to redesign his words. However, the designers also learned much as they discovered the gaps in their suggestions and the ways in which they made them.

Practice is important. Most people require as much practice to learn Model II as is required to play a not-so-decent game of tennis. However, the practice does not need to occur all at once; it can occur in actual business meetings where people set aside some time to make it possible to reflect on their actions and correct them. An outside facilitator could help them examine and redesign their actions, just as a tennis coach might do. But, as in the case of a good tennis coach, the facilitator should be replaced by the group. He or she might be brought in for periodic boosters or to help when the problem is of a degree of difficulty and intensity not experienced before.

There are several consequences of this type of change program. First, the executives begin to experience each other as more supportive and constructive. People still work very hard during meetings, but their conversation begins to become addictive; it flows to conclusions that they all can own and implement. Crises begin to be reduced. Soon, the behavioral change leads to new values, and then to new structures and policies to mirror the new values.

This, in turn, leads to more effective problem solving and decision making. In the case of this group, they were able to define the questions related to strategy, to conduct their own inquiries, to have staff people conduct some relevant research, and to have three individuals organize it into a presentation that was ultimately approved and owned by the top group. The top group also built in a process of involving their immediate reports so that they too could develop a sense of ownership, thereby increasing the probability that all involved will work at making it successful.

In a recent study (Argyris, 1993) of what is now an 11-year program, the key to change is practice and use of Model II theory in use plus productive reasoning in solving major difficult problems. This means that the participants select key meetings in which to continue their learning. These meetings cannot be scheduled in a lockstep fashion.

It also means that the change program that began at the top is spread to the next levels, as the competence of those above them becomes persistent. This has led not only to changes in the internal management of the firm (which is a managerial consulting firm), but to the development of new services for their clients.

One might ask whether interventions go wrong and, if so, how the errors are corrected. I hope that my previous description illustrates that the participants are made continually responsible for their participation in the program. One of their main responsibilities is to monitor the actions so that if errors occur, they are corrected. Moreover, they are free to stop a program at any time they deem it necessary. To date, no program had been stopped. However, there is variance in the degree of enthusiasm individuals may have for managing through the use of Model II. In a few instances where these differences occur, it would violate the governing values of Model II for one subgroup to require the others to act consistently with Model II. What is required is that the doubters be open about their doubts and that they do not use their power to prevent further dialogue, especially by subordinates or peers.

BASIC CRITERIA FOR SUCCESS IN DIAGNOSING AND CHANGING AT ANY LEVEL OF THE ORGANIZATION

There are four criteria that we found central to design diagnostic instruments *and* interventions in organizations. They are:

1. The criterion for success should not change in behavior or attitudes. We must get at the causes of behavior and attitudes. The criterion should be changes in defensive reasoning and the theories in use that produce skilled unawareness and skilled incompetence and the resulting organizational defensive routines.

2. The changes just described should unambiguously lead to reductions in the self-fulfilling counterproductive activities, at all levels of the organization.

3. It is not possible to achieve Criteria 1 and 2 without focusing on the actual behavior of the participants. The trouble with the old criteria is that they began and ended with behaviors. The new criteria begin with behavior in order to get a window into the mental maps and type of reasoning that the individuals use and the organizational culture that they create.

4. The success of programs is *not* assessed by measuring insight gained or learning reported by the participants. Individuals often report high scores on insight and learning, yet have not changed their defensive reasoning, their theories in use, their skilled unawareness and incompetence, and the organizational defensive routines:

- Most experimental learning, at its best, helps individuals to change their behavior without changing their defensive reasoning or their theory in use. They accomplish this primarily by helping individuals behave in the opposite manner than they presently display. If they dominate, they learn to become more passive. If they talk most of the time, they learn to listen more. Being passive or listening more is not a change to a new theory in use; it occurs by suppressing the old one. Such changes usually wash out the moment the individual is bewildered, threatened, or feels betrayed.

- Most large corporations expose their executives to various kinds of leadership programs where the fundamental criterion is to present knowledge in an interesting manner, in a way that leads to action, and in a way that is not disquieting to the audience. For example, recently I participated in a 1-week program on leadership attended by the top 40 executives of one of America's largest corporations. The presenter, one of the most sought-after speakers, talked about the difference between managing and leading. He advised the top executives to focus more on being leaders and less on being managers. He used cases, videotapes, simulations, and skillful questioning. He generated a great deal of interaction and enthusiasm. The presentation was rated as one of the best.

The next day, I met with the CEO and his immediate reports. They discussed how to become more effective. As the discussion began to get into the undiscussables, the dialogue became cautious—individuals spoke abstractly. They cautioned about changes that were too dramatic and quick. Soon, the group members produced a remarkable example of managing these issues rather than leading. No one appeared to realize the inconsistency they were creating (or, if they did, they were not saying). A month later I had a chance to meet the presenter. We got into a discussion about education for leadership. I then told him the story I just related here. It did not surprise him. After all, he asked, how much can one accomplish in a few hours? How much can one examine senior managers' inconsistencies without getting in trouble? After all, aren't the most effective change attempts incremental? The argument that he was making to defend his own practice was consistent with managing and not leading in his practice.

CONCLUSION

Management of human activities is importantly based on the Model I theories in use and the organizational defenses that the Model I theories in use create. The theories in use and the organizational defensive routines combine to create conditions of limited learning throughout the organization. The actions and the routines are internalized and produced skillfully. Skillful actions are tacit.

It is possible to intervene to help managers learn a Model II theory in use. Once the theories in use are activated, they reduce the organizational defensive routines that, in turn, lead to more effective organizational learning.

REFERENCES

Argyris, C. (1974). Alternative schools: A behavioral analysis. *Teachers College Record, 75*(4), 429–452.

Argyris, C. (1980). Skilled incompetence. *Harvard Business Review, 64*(5), 74–79.

Argyris, C. (1982). *Reasoning, learning, and action*. San Francisco: Jossey-Bass.

Argyris, C. (1990). *Overcoming organizational defenses*. Needham Heights, MA: Allyn & Bacon.

Argyris, C. (1993). *Knowledge for action*. San Francisco: Jossey-Bass.

Argyris, C., Putnam, R., & Smith, D. (1985). *Action science*. San Francisco: Jossey-Bass.

Argyris, C., & Schön, D. (1974). *Theory in practice*. San Francisco: Jossey-Bass.

Argyris, C., & Schön, D. (1996). *Organizational learning II*. Reading, MA: Addison-Wesley.

Nelson, R. R., & Winter, S. G. (1977). *An elementary evolutionary theory of economic change*. Cambridge, MA: Belknap Press of Harvard University Press.

C H A P T E R   E I G H T

The Role of Tacit Knowledge in Management

Nicholas G. Hatsopoulos
Department of Neuroscience, Brown University

George N. Hatsopoulos
Thermo Electron Corporation, Waltham, MA

This chapter is based on three interviews with Dr. George Hatsopoulos, chairman and founder of Thermo Electron Corporation. Throughout this chapter, the pronoun *I* refers to George Hatsopoulos, and the pronoun *we* refers to Thermo Electron Corporation. Because neither author is well versed in the literature concerning tacit and implicit knowledge, the terms used in this chapter—such as *intuition* and *gut feeling*—are colloquial versions that may only partially match the scientifically defined terms used in cognitive science. The thesis described and defended here is that successful managers and executives use a dual-process methodology when faced with a business decision to be made or problem to be solved. The key to successful managerial and entrepreneurial decision making is to come up with solutions in which both the "logical" and the "intuitive" processes agree.

DEFINITIONS

The "logical" process consists of a set of explicit assumptions or propositions that the business community generally agrees to be true. In addition, there is a set of rules by which these assumptions, combined with other sources of knowledge, are transformed into final decisions or solutions to business problems. The important point to remember in regard to the logical process is that the assumptions, the rules, and the other forms of knowledge are explicit; that is, they are conscious. It is this property that provides the logical process with its two major advantages. First, the knowledge can be validated or rejected according to more general assumptions and knowledge. Second, the assumptions, rules, and knowledge can be verbally communicated to others and, therefore, form the basis of formal business education.

In contrast, the "intuitive" process consists of implicit or tacit knowledge from which instincts or feelings are generated. The intuitive process rarely comes up with a detailed set of procedures by which to solve a problem. Rather, it generates a feeling that can be used to either make a simple decision (i.e., yes or no) or to quickly evaluate a more complex solution that has been proposed by the logical process. In either case, its major advantage is its speed and its reliability given incomplete information regarding the situation.

In an ideal situation (i.e., a situation in which all necessary information is available and there is adequate time), both processes should be invoked. If both processes agree on the decision or solution, then the decision is executed or the solution is implemented. On the other hand, if they do not agree, one of two corrective actions is performed.

> The assumptions, rules, and knowledge that comprise the logical process may be reviewed, questioned, and corrected. Alternatively, the knowledge that forms the basis of the intuitive feelings are made explicit or conscious. Once this implicit knowledge is made explicit, it can be evaluated according to logical rules and assumptions.

In practice, managers often do not have enough time to invoke both processes. Instead, tacit knowledge is brought to bear on a problem by generating a gut feeling. Only after a solution or decision has been proposed and executed is the logical process invoked and compared with the intuitive feeling.

TACIT AND EXPLICIT KNOWLEDGE IN MANAGEMENT: AN EXAMPLE

An example of this dual process in action is that of hiring a new employee. Imagine that you are interviewing a man who appears very qualified. He answers all your questions correctly, and his résumé is exceptional. However, your gut tells you that something may be wrong. Your logical and intuitive processes do not agree. This leads you to make corrective actions. First, you talk to his former employers. They give stellar recommendations. You ask him to take an in-house test that you have developed. He does extremely well on the test. At this point, you decide that the logical process is probably not faulty. This motivates you to search for a reason why you don't like him. In other words, you attempt to make explicit your intuitive or gut feelings. You suspect that he may not work well with others at the company, so you have him come in for a couple of days. Everyone seems to like him very much, and he seems to cooperate well with others. Now you are really puzzled. That evening you have a dream of a kid that was a bully in your elementary school. You realize that he looks like your potential employee. The next day you hire the candidate because you realize that your gut feeling was based on a meaningless correlation in the appearance of the employee with a kid you knew in elementary school. This is an example in which your gut feeling was faulty and, therefore, was discounted once the assumptions underlying the feeling were made explicit. However, it could have happened that your logical process was faulty; that is, your suspicion that he might not get along with others was correct. Say that you hire him and, after a couple of miserable days in which he comes into the office and bickers with almost everyone, you realize that your gut feeling was correct because he couldn't communicate well with you during the interview. During the interview, you didn't have the time or mental resources to make explicit the fact that he didn't communicate well with you, which formed the basis of your uneasy feeling. This example brings up a corollary to the thesis being argued in this chapter:

> If your logical and intuitive processes do not agree and the corrective procedures lead you to make explicit an intuitive feeling that turns out be correct, this explicit intuition can be added to your database of knowledge that can be used in the future by your logical process.

In other words, this iterative procedure by which you attempt to make both processes agree can often be creative and leads to learning. A very good example of this occurred for us at Thermo Electron in the 1970s. At that time, we were collaborating with the Ford Motor Company to attempt to make more energy-efficient automobiles. A by-product of this effort was the development of very sensitive instrumentation for the detection of automobile emissions. Quite fortuitously, the government enacted an environmental law that required automobile companies to measure nitrogen oxides with a precision of 1 part per million. Beckman was the leading instruments company at the time, but they didn't have the requisite technology. Mainly because of a strong gut feeling, we decided to get into the instruments business. It turned out that this decision led to one of our most successful businesses at Thermo Electron. Many years after that decision, we tried to analyze it by making our intuitive or instinctual knowledge explicit. After all, we had no name or presence in the instruments market. Moreover, we had no manufacturing plant, no sales force, nor had we analyzed the market thoroughly. In other words, we were missing a number of key ingredients that are generally assumed to be crucial for a successful business. We came up with the following principle: If we have a major advantage in the marketplace (in this case, we had a technological advantage in chemical kinetics), and there is strong need for a product we can provide (the law generated a strong need for a sensitive detector of engine emissions), then we have a good chance of succeeding in this business even if other fundamental ingredients such as name recognition, manufacturing capability, and marketing are missing.

PEOPLE

As the chief executive officer of a company, I am faced with problems to be solved and decisions to be made in two general realms: people and strategy. It is with people where the intuitive process is particularly useful. This is partially true because there are very few explicit principles and pieces of knowledge at one's disposal. I deal with a wide variety of people on a daily basis.

Within the Company

Within the corporation structure, I face three categories of people: employees, the board of directors, and the stockholders. I have already described the benefits and pitfalls of tacit knowledge in the context of hiring a potential employee. However, intuition plays a more important role in managing and motivating people who have already become employees. Very often I need to affect an employee's behavior in a certain way. Suppose a particular employee is not performing his or her job in a manner that I deem suitable. I could reprimand the employee; alternatively, I could try to reward more suitable behavior. The tack I finally decide to use depends on the individual and is determined by trying to imagine how the individual would react to my criticism or my encouragement. Through experience with my different employees, I learn how each individual will react. This empathetic approach has been very successful for me over the years. No one taught me explicitly to use this approach; it was an approach that I discovered to be useful by trial and error, and it is an approach that I implement many times without even being aware that I am doing it.

Another approach that I have developed through experience is to try to fit jobs to particular individuals instead of always trying to fit an individual to a job. For example, as a company reaches a certain size it becomes necessary to hire a treasurer. Some managers use the American Management Association's definition of a treasurer. The problem is that it is rarely possible to find a person who fits the description of an ideal treasurer, which consists of a set of characteristics that no one person possesses. Over the years, I have learned to hire intelligent people who have a strong financial background. The actual position of treasurer changes to match the unique attributes of the individual who is hired. This is an approach that I implement automatically and unconsciously. At some point in my career, I was able to make this intuitive approach explicit.

As the chairman of the board of directors, I also have the responsibility of recruiting the board members. Foremost, I have learned to bring people to the company who believe in what we are doing. This includes believing in the broad goals of the company, the specific technologies that we are developing, and the unique management style we have adopted (i.e., the spin-out strategy). I have also discovered through experience that the board needs to have a diversity of backgrounds. For example, our current board of directors includes two former CEOs, a venture capitalist, a political strategist, an engineer, an oil businessperson, and a former president of a Federal Reserve bank. This diversity has been very beneficial to the company, because it parallels our diverse product line. Again, this principle of diversity was unconsciously and automatically applied for many years. It is only recently that it has been made explicit.

It is the stockholders to whom we, as managers, are ultimately accountable. I have learned that it is important to understand what the stockholders really want. The assumption made by many in the business community is that stockholders are only interested in the bottom line; that is, in making money. However, we have learned that stockholders are also interested in investing in particular technologies, such as environmental or medical technologies. In large part, it is this fact that has made our spin-out strategy at Thermo Electron so successful. By spinning out each new technology as a separate business with publicly sold stock, an investor is able to put his or her money in a technology that suits his or her fancy. We had a hunch that the spin-out strategy would be successful, because it seemed to enable us to retain the advantages of a small business. However, it was only by talking to stockholders and thinking about it for awhile that it was possible to make explicit the idea that investors are interested not only in making money, but also in the technologies and products that we produce.

We have put a lot of effort into cultivating European investors. This has been very important for our success, because we learned early on that they tend to hold stock for a longer time than do their American counterparts. This has been crucial for the development of technologies such as the heart-assist device that has only recently become commercially successful after 30 years of development. This strategy began as a gut or instinctual approach that turned out to be quite useful. Over the years, I have tried to make explicit the reasons why European investors act so differently. One reason is that most American investors put their money into mutual funds, whose goals are inherently short term. In addition, many European countries do not have capital-gains tax but do levy taxes on dividends. This provides an advantage to many high-technology companies that grow fast and pay no dividends.

Outside the Company

There are three classes of people with whom I must deal that are outside of the company: customers, competitors, and business partners. Although I have not dealt with customers directly for many years, I do remember an approach that I often used implicitly. I would make sure to mention to the customer some of the small weaknesses of the product I was selling to them. This is not something that prospective customers are usually accustomed to hear. This would sometimes disarm the customer and result in a role reversal—the customer would begin to defend the product to us.

As for one's competitors, it is not enough to understand their product line and business strategy; it is important that one meet representatives from competing companies at trade shows and meetings. In this manner, one can find out how ambitious, intelligent, and mean they are. One can discover their weaknesses and strengths, not only in the business realm but also on a more general level. Also, one can get a sense of what their long-term goals are for their businesses. A competitor's current products and immediate strategy may change very quickly, but their character, intelligence, and goals will most likely remain constant.

Business partnerships have played a big role in the success of Thermo Electron. Over the years, we participated in a number of joint ventures, with the government as well as with other companies. These ventures have necessitated good negotiation skills. For me, the most successful negotiations have involved imagining how your potential partner might be reacting to or feeling about the negotiations underway. This empathetic response is similar to the one I described earlier in relation to employees. No one ever taught me explicitly to use this empathetic response. Through experience I have discovered that "putting yourself in the other person's shoes" tends to make you a better negotiator. By making this explicit and verbalizing it, it is possible to add it to my database of explicit knowledge that can be used by the logical process. In addition, I have been able to communicate this negotiating strategy to my managers.

Society at Large

As a manager, generally, and as a CEO, more specifically, one expects to interact with people related to the company, such as employees and stockholders. It is also not surprising that one must also interact with people outside the company, such as customers and competitors. However, it may come as a surprise that my interactions with people not directly related to the company have been a key component in my success as an executive. These people fall into two broad classes: the government and the community.

To many managers and businesspeople, the government is an impediment to business. After all, it is the government that levies large corporate taxes and imposes a variety of economic and environmental restrictions that cut into profit margins. However, my approach has been to take advantage of the strengths the government possesses. "Why fight them, if you can join them" has been my credo. Our relationship with the government has occurred in several different forms. Early in the history of Thermo Electron, we used government grants to fund much of our research and development. Unlike many other investors, the government is willing to fund basic research that may not lead to a marketable product for many years. A very good example of this is the funding of the earlier-mentioned heart-assist device, which required several decades of development before a marketable product resulted. I have also had more direct contact with people in government, such as politicians. Successful politicians are often those who can predict what their constituents want before the constituents know it. Therefore, by talking to politicians, one can gain a headstart in developing technologies that will become useful and lucrative in the future. An example of this approach occurred in the early 1970s, before the oil embargo. At that time, there were some politicians who worried that America was importing too much oil. I remember talking to an assistant to H. R. Haldeman, the chief of staff under President Nixon, who expressed his concern regarding this issue. This conversation influenced my decision to pursue the development of energy-efficient devices, such as co-generation, before others in industry. Just as businesspeople can learn from politicians, politicians can learn and be influenced by businesspeople. My interaction with politicians representing the state of Massachusetts has been very useful in this respect. No one ever told me that I should interact with politicians in order to be successful in business. This is certainly not emphasized in business school. However, it is something I learned, by experience, to be important.

Finally, our relationship with the community of which we are a part has been very important. Our community includes not only the people and companies in our immediate neighborhood, but also the citizens and businesses of all of America. The issue of corporate responsibility has become very popular recently in the media. Does a company such as Thermo Electron have any responsibility to the community and society at large, besides its direct responsibility to stockholders? I believe that a successful business does have a responsibility to the community, because it is the community that provides the environment in which it can prosper. In addition, it is the community that we ultimately serve by providing technologies that meet its needs.

STRATEGY

It is often not appreciated how important tacit knowledge and intuition are in corporate strategy. There are two components to strategy that I want to discuss. First, *what* is it that you want to do? You need to decide on your long-term goals. Second, *how* do you want to accomplish your goals? This involves tactical plans.

Goals

The goals that I had set out for Thermo Electron had already begun to form in my mind when I was a young adult. I wanted to use technology to meet society's needs. This goal was based partly on my experience building radios for the underground during World War II (discussed more later in this chapter). I realized the potential for business success when a novel technological device or technique is used to solve a problem that society desperately needs to be solved. The key is that both technology and need come together at the same time. Especially in the high-technology business world, I often see entrepreneurs who are enamored of a novel technology but who don't think about what the technology might be good for. More times than not, this leads to business failure. If anything, the societal need is more important than the technological know-how. In theory, the need is what should drive the search for a technological solution. In practice, I have noticed that the process is actually cyclical: A need leads to a technology that almost always leads to other discoveries or inventions. These ancillary technologies are often modified to meet other societal needs.

Fostering this cyclical process has played an important role in the success of Thermo Electron. The point that I want to stress is that the goals that I set out for Thermo Electron were originally not formed by explicit instruction. Instead, through childhood experiences, I gradually came to possess them tacitly in my mind. Only later did I make them explicit when I founded the company.

Plans

One of the most successful plans (or strategies) that we implemented at Thermo Electron was based partly on tacit knowledge. In the early 1980s, we had a need for capital to fund our research and development. Unlike many other industries, high-technology businesses spend a disproportionately large amount of capital on research and development. At the same time, we understood intuitively as well as logically that we needed to keep our debt-to-equity ratio low because of the inherent risk involved in high-technology ventures. This led us to execute a unique spin-out strategy (in contrast to a spin-off strategy) that has been enormously successful. The idea was to create a new business around each new technology. Each new company would have publicly held stock, but the parent company (i.e., Thermo Electron) would own a controlling share of the stock. For example, we generated a company called Thermo Cardiosystems, based on our left ventricular heart-assist device. We understood intuitively that potential investors might be attracted by the possibility of investing in a particular technology instead of putting their money into a conglomerate. Our hunch was correct, but we were stunned by how successful it was. We soon learned that the strategy had other advantages that we hadn't thought of originally. For example, instead of becoming a large, rigid company, Thermo Electron has become a collection of small, flexible businesses. Each child company has retained the feeling of a small business. With that feeling comes the ability to change quickly if the business environment warrants it. At the same time, each child company can take advantage of many of the services that the large parent can provide, such as legal and marketing assistance. These are advantages that small, stand-alone businesses don't usually have. There are, of course, some disadvantages that have come to light, such as the difficulty of keeping up with all these businesses and the problem of finding qualified CEOs to run each of them. It is an experiment still in progress. The interesting thing is that the creation of the spin-out strategy and decision to implement it was largely based on gut feeling.

WHEN TACIT KNOWLEDGE FAILS

It is important to note that tacit knowledge can fail miserably at times, because it tries to mask itself as being rational or logical. First, it can confuse correlation with causation. Much of our tacit knowledge is acquired by associating one object or event with another. This associative process is very powerful, but can be misleading when the association leads one to make a causal link between the two objects or events.

Second, intuition often makes the mistake of extrapolating from past performance. In mathematics, we are taught that finding a curve to extrapolate outside the range of a given set of points can be dangerous. Only if we understand the mechanism by which the given points were generated can we safely extrapolate beyond them. Intuition is very good at storing large numbers of data points associating a dependent variable with an independent variable. However, by its nature it is not equipped to find and make explicit mechanisms or theories that explain the data. An example of this occurred many years ago, when we had to make a quick decision concerning the acquisition of an electroplating company. We didn't have the time to do an adequate financial and market analysis. We did know that the business was making a lot of profit and had been growing over the past few years. Our intuition led us to believe that the business would continue to grow and make money in the future. The business turned out to be a failure.

SOURCE OF TACIT KNOWLEDGE

It is often a mystery from where the knowledge that forms our intuitions and instincts comes. Are we born with good business instincts, or do we acquire them from experience? I am aware of at least two sources of tacit knowledge that have played a big role in my life as a businessman: experience and analogical reasoning.

Experience

First and foremost, simple trial-and-error experience has been the biggest source of tacit knowledge. This has been particularly true for me, because I never received formal training in business administration. By keeping track of successful as well as failed decisions, one gradually acquires a business intuition. A fine-tuned intuition is based on the accumulation of many associations between attempted decisions and solutions to business situations, and their positive or negative consequences. Just like the chess master who stores a vast number of board configurations, a good businessperson stores a vast number of business contexts along with their attempted actions and consequences. Experience, however, needs to be driven by something. Besides the desire to acquire money, my experience has been fueled by curiosity about how things work and a passion for discovery.

I have gained business experience from other situations besides my 40 years of work at Thermo Electron. As a young child, I engaged in a number of small business enterprises. My father and his friends often wanted something sweet, such as chocolate, after eating their meals. However, for one reason or another, there was never any chocolate in the house. Seeing a strong need (or, more accurately, a desire), I decided to buy chocolates and sell them to my father and his friends. In elementary school, I used to buy leads for mechanical pencils in large volume. This allowed me to buy them for a lower price and sell them to the other students for a profit. During the German occupation of Greece in the 1940s, all radios had been fixed to only one radio station that was controlled by the German army. As a young boy, I had been interested in electronics and used to tinker in a small laboratory I had set up in our garage. I decided to build and sell radios (that were free to pick up any radio station) to our neighbors. This was probably the earliest experience in which I learned about the power of technological know-how combined with a strong societal need.

Analogical Inference

As a mechanical engineer by training, I have used analogies between engineering (and the physical sciences more generally) and business. I have made a number of intuitive decisions in my business by making analogies with thermodynamics, the field in which I did my doctoral dissertation. For example, the concept of equilibrium and the second law of thermodynamics have influenced my thinking with regard to the stock market. The second law states that you can't get work from a closed system in equilibrium. In a similar manner, as a speculator you cannot make money from a stock market that is in equilibrium (i.e., when the stock price accurately reflects the value of the company). Of course, people make (or lose) money from the stock market every day, because the market deviates from equilibrium. That is, if a stock is undervalued for some reason (i.e., the stock price is lower than the per-share value of the business based on careful analysis), the smart investor will make money by buying the stock until the price of the stock increases and matches the value of the company. Likewise, if the company is overvalued, one can make money by selling stock short.

As a child, I remember playing a game with my friends that helped me think about economic issues many years later. We set up a mini-society in which each of my friends and I acted as particular members of the society—one was a butcher, the other was a banker, another was a baker, and so on. We even printed money, so that business transactions could take place between us. I noticed how the printing of more money stimulated more economic growth but also resulted in inflation. As a businessperson and economist, I often make analogies between this mini-society we had created and the actual economic world I was participating in as an adult.

CONCLUSION

In this chapter, an approach to managerial problem solving was described that invokes two processes: a logical process utilizing explicit assumptions and rules, and an intuitive process using tacit knowledge and generating a feeling. If one is lucky enough to have the time, the relevant information, and the necessary theoretical constructs, then both processes should be invoked when a new problem arises. The object of the game is for both processes to agree. If they don't agree, either the explicit knowledge forming the basis of the logical process is questioned, or the tacit knowledge underlying the intuitive process is made explicit and evaluated by the logical process. Unfortunately, most business problems do not arise in ideal conditions. Usually, one of three situations occurs. First, decisions have to be made very quickly. Second, there is not enough explicit knowledge regarding a business problem. Third, there is neither enough time nor enough information. In any case, the logical process is not equipped to make the necessary decision or solve the problem. Therefore, a successful manager needs to rely more often on tacit knowledge to help make decisions and solve problems.

PART FIVE

SALES

CHAPTER NINE

Tacit Knowledge in Sales

Richard K. Wagner
Florida State University

Harish Sujan and Mita Sujan
Pennsylvania State University

Carol A. Rashotte
Florida State University

Robert J. Sternberg
Yale University

Joe Girard can sell anything to anybody. His book, titled, appropriately enough, *How to Sell Anything to Anybody* (Girard & Brown, 1979), was written to teach us his secrets. There certainly are personal reasons for just about anybody to be interested in selling; academic psychologists, for example, are keenly interested in "selling" their manuscripts and grant proposals to journal editors and grant review panels. There also are a number of more scholarly reasons to be interested in selling.

First, selling is an example of persuasion in which almost everyone engages (Cialdini, 1985). Central to selling, in contrast to "order taking" or clerking, is to attempt to persuade through modifying the beliefs, attitudes, and behavior of others (Weitz, 1978). As the rich literature on persuasion shows, attempting to influence others is something almost everyone engages in regularly, in situations ranging from convincing a spouse to accompany you to a favorite restaurant to convincing your department to support you for promotion or tenure (see Petty & Cacioppo, 1981, for a review of this literature). Because much of what we know about persuasion derives from social psychological studies in controlled settings, the validity of the results for explaining persuasion under naturalistic conditions is questionable. Selling provides an important opportunity to examine the interface between social-psychological findings about persuasion on the one hand, and a prevalent form of persuasion as it actually operates in the everyday world on the other. For example, Spiro and Perreault (1979) evaluated influence strategies in the field, and found that aspects of the sales situation (e.g., buyer–seller involvement in the sales call) moderates their use (see also Williams & Spiro, 1985). Cialdini (1985), in an attempt to balance laboratory investigations of persuasion with field investigations, infiltrated organizations that sold encyclopedias, vacuum cleaners, portrait photography, and dance lessons by answering newspaper ads for sales trainees. On the basis of a series of innovative participant-observational studies, Cialdini concluded that individuals in these organizations adopt tactics that are consistent with some social-psychological generalizations about persuasion; for example, the contrast principle that our reaction to say, the price of an item, depends in part on the price of prior items at which we have looked.

Second, success in sales requires the acquisition of a considerable amount of expertise (Weitz, Sujan, & Sujan, 1986). The profession has its acknowledged experts, and much of the sales training that new salespersons undergo is directed toward providing novice salespersons with expert knowledge. Although a large number of studies have now shown that experts differ from novices primarily in the nature of their knowledge and how it is organized, rather than in general or specific aptitudes (see Chi, Glaser, & Rees, 1982, for a comprehensive review of this literature), the domains that have been the focus of study (e.g., chess, computer programming, solving physics problems) are characterized by well-defined problems and tasks, unlike many of the problems and tasks found in the everyday world and in the profession of sales. Selling provides an opportunity to study the nature of complex knowledge in a domain characterized by ill-defined problems. Salesperson research conducted in the field that has examined differences in knowledge organization and content between effective and less effective salespeople has used a variety of theoretical approaches including categorization theory (Rosch, Mervis, Gray, Johnson, & Boyes-Braem, 1976), script theory (Schank & Abelson 1977), and attitude theory (Fishbein & Ajzen, 1975). Illustratively, research has examined differences in declarative and procedural knowledge among field salespeople (Sujan, Sujan, & Bettman, 1988; Szymanksi, 1988). Leong, Busch, and John (1989) and Leigh and McGraw (1989) validated Schank and Abelson's (1977) differences between experts and novices in the use of scripts to guide behavior using real-world salespeople. Interestingly, greater differences were found for less-typical sales situations between expert and novice salespeople (Leong, Busch, & John, 1989). Reliable relations have been found between sales performance and the accuracy of salespersons' knowledge of customers' motives, values, and beliefs (Weitz, 1978).

Third, selling is an endeavor that appears to require considerable intelligence, but intelligence that is more practical than academic in nature. In fact, despite the prevalence of traditional academic intelligence tests in sales selection, the evidence relating scores on these tests to sales success is weak (Weitz, 1981). Obviously, there are multiple determinants of success at selling. Sales success, as suggested by Walker, Churchill, and Ford (1977), depends on a broader set of abilities, as well as motivation and interest (Katerberg & Blau, 1983; Seligman & Schulman, 1986; Sujan, 1986; Tyagi, 1985), and role management (Tyagi, 1985). Practical intelligence, which refers to the intellectual competencies required in the everyday world as opposed to the formal classroom, takes a broad view of intelligence that encompasses an expanded set of abilities, and incorporates motivation and role management (Charlesworth, 1976; Neisser, 1976; Sternberg, 1985; Sternberg & Wagner, 1986; Wagner, 1987). Thus, there is reason to believe that practical intelligence plays an important role in sales success.

Recent models of success in selling suggest that selling requires adaptive behavior (Spiro & Weitz 1990; Sujan, Weitz, & Kumar 1994; Weitz, 1979, 1981; Weitz, Sujan, & Sujan, 1986). Successful salespersons adapt their behavior to different sales situations, and, by observing customer reactions, successful salespersons even are able to adjust their behavior "on the fly." Previously, attempts were made to identify one or more characteristics of successful salespersons. However, over 20 years of research on the characteristics of successful salespersons have yielded contradictory findings (Weitz, 1981). For example, the hard-sell approach appears to work for some salespersons in some situations, but not for the same salespersons in different situations, or different salespersons in the same situation. These contradictory findings, coupled with the observation that there is no one sales situation nor one way to sell (Thompson, 1973), have resulted in models of sales that emphasize adaptive behavior (Grikscheit, 1971; Spiro, Perreault, & Reynolds, 1976; Weitz, 1978, 1981). Successful adaptation requires knowledge to adapt to the customer and the situation. One important aspect of this knowledge is practical know-how that is referred to as *tacit knowledge.*

TACIT KNOWLEDGE ABOUT SELLING: RULES OF THUMB THAT SALESPEOPLE USE

Tacit Knowledge About Selling

In two studies by Wagner, Rashotte, and Sternberg (1994), we sought to determine whether practical intelligence is an important determinant of salespersons' ability to adapt their behavior to sales situations. The particular aspect of practical intelligence that we examined in the present studies is facile acquisition of tacit knowledge (Wagner, 1987; Wagner & Sternberg, 1985, 1986). Tacit knowledge refers to work-related, practical know-how that typically is acquired informally as a result of on-the-job experience, as opposed to formal instruction.

Of particular interest in the present studies is a distinction between two kinds of tacit knowledge (Wagner, 1987). *Local tacit knowledge* refers to practical knowledge that is useful in the short-term accomplishment of the specific task at hand. The aspect of local tacit knowledge that we focused on was knowledge useful in handling face-to-face selling situations. An example of this kind of tacit knowledge is knowing what to do when a customer appears to be stalling. *Global tacit knowledge* refers to practical knowledge that is useful in the attainment of one's long-range objectives, and in placing one's present task in a broader context. The aspect of global tacit knowledge on which we focused was knowledge useful in maximizing the number of high-probability sales situations one will encounter. An example of this kind of tacit knowledge is knowing how to ask customers to provide high-quality leads. We were interested to learn that there are terms in sales parlance to describe individuals who seem to have a mastery of either kind of tacit knowledge: *Great positioners* are individuals who excel at maximizing their number of future sales opportunities; *great closers* are individuals who excel at actually making a sale or closing the deal in a one-on-one sales situation.

It is likely that most kinds of sales require some amounts of local and global tacit knowledge, but we believe that different kinds of sales require more of one kind of tacit knowledge and less of the other. For some kinds of sales (e.g., selling subscriptions to periodicals), the crux of the job is identifying potentially interested buyers, at which point the product either sells itself or it fails to do so. If, for example, you do not care to read *U.S. News & World Report,* it is unlikely that even the slickest sales pitch will work on you. Success at this kind of sales probably depends more on global tacit knowledge about how to identify likely prospects than on local tacit knowledge about how to sell customers in a one-on-one situation. For other kinds of sales (e.g., industrial sales), the identities of the major customers who intend to buy and the competition are already established. Success at this kind of sales probably depends more on local tacit knowledge about how to convince a particular customer to buy from you and not from a competitor, than on global tacit knowledge about how to identify likely prospects. A sales profession we examined in the present study (Study 2) was life-insurance sales. One of our goals was to determine whether success at this kind of sales requires local tacit knowledge, global tacit knowledge, both, or neither.

Expert–Novice Differences in Sales-Related Tacit Knowledge

In the present studies, we examined the local and global tacit knowledge that is acquired and used by successful salespersons. We constructed sales-related scenarios to sample tacit knowledge, and gave them to experienced sales professionals and to undergraduates with no sales experience. Subjects rated the quality of response items associated with each scenario. Half of the scenarios were constructed to sample global tacit knowledge, and half to sample local tacit knowledge. We devised a scoring system that enabled us to determine whether experienced salespersons differed from individuals without sales experience in amount of local tacit knowledge, global tacit knowledge, or both.

Because access to a more detailed description of the nature of expert–novice differences in local and global tacit knowledge might be useful in designing tests to measure tacit knowledge and training programs to facilitate its acquisition, we attempted to determine whether expert–novice differences, if found, could further be specified in terms of a set of salespersons' rules of thumb. According to its dictionary definition, a rule of thumb is "a useful principle with wide application, not intended to be strictly accurate" (Morris, 1978, p. 1134). An example of a rule of thumb for setting sales goals is, "Set goals that are measurable and specific." The salespersons' rules of thumb we evaluated were derived from interviews with successful salespersons and from reading the professional and popular literature on sales.

Individual Difference in Sales-Related Tacit Knowledge

Because individual differences determine who will "make it" in sales, we decided to pay particular attention to them. We looked at two aspects of individual differences in tacit knowledge: their relation to sales, and their relation to psychometrically measured verbal intellectual ability.

If expert–novice differences in tacit knowledge are found, do they matter to sales performance? To answer this question, relations were examined between individual differences in tacit knowledge among sales professionals and measures of their amount of experience and their performance at sales. Amount of experience is an important variable to us, because we suspected that there would be a closer correspondence between experience and success in sales than is typically found for other professions, because only the successful salespeople remain in the business (Beswick & Cravens, 1977; Cravens & Woodruff, 1973).

Verbal ability predicts acquisition of formal knowledge in school with considerable accuracy. However, in previous studies of tacit knowledge, there has been little or no relation between individual differences in tacit knowledge and individual differences in verbal ability. In the present study, we have attempted to explore the relation between verbal ability and tacit knowledge more fully.

To summarize, we set out to answer the following questions: (a) Are there expert–novice differences in local sales-related tacit knowledge and in global sales-related tacit knowledge? (b) If expert–novice differences exist in sales-related tacit knowledge, can such differences be further specified in terms of a set of salespersons' rules of thumb? (c) Are there relations between criterion measures of sales performance and individual differences in local tacit knowledge and in global tacit knowledge? (d) Are there relations between verbal intellectual ability and individual differences in local tacit knowledge and in global tacit knowledge?

In the first study, a tacit-knowledge inventory for sales was given to experienced automobile, furniture, and real-estate salespersons, and to undergraduates with no sales experience. There were two groups of subjects, totaling 80 individuals in all, whose members differed in amounts of sales experience. The salesperson group consisted of 30 individuals whose profession was selling automobiles, furniture, or houses. The average number of years of sales experience for this group was 13.5 ($SD = 11.9$). The undergraduate group consisted of 50 undergraduates who had no sales experience.

Tacit knowledge about sales was assessed by presenting subjects with a series of eight work-related situations, each of which was associated with 8 to 12 response items. Subjects rated the quality of the response items on a 1 (extremely bad) to 9 (extremely good) scale.

The work-related situations were designed to measure either global or local tacit knowledge. Global tacit knowledge—knowledge about longer-range aspects of sales—was assessed by work-related situations that included setting sales goals, getting new accounts, devising strategies for selling a slow-moving product, and devising strategies to improve one's efficiency. Local tacit knowledge—knowledge about handling face-to-face sales situations—was assessed by work-related situations that included handling a customer who backs out of a deal, learning that a customer is about to switch to a competitor, being asked to cut your price, and handling an angry customer.

An example of a work-related situation concerning global tacit knowledge about selling a slow-moving product follows.

> You sell a line of photocopy machines. One of your machines has relatively few features and is inexpensive ($700), although it is not the least expensive model you carry. The $700 photocopy machine is not selling very well, and it is overstocked. There is a shortage of the more elaborate photocopy machines in your line, so you have been asked to do what you can to improve sales of the $700 model. Rate the following strategies for maximizing your sales of the slow-moving photocopy machine.
>
> ______a. Stress to potential customers that although this model lacks some desirable features, the low price more than makes up for it.
>
> ______b. Emphasize that there are relatively few models left at this price.
>
> ______c. Arrange as many demonstrations of the machine as you are able.
>
> ______d. Focus on simplicity of use, because this machine lacks confusing controls that other photocopy machines have.

There were 77 response items. Of these, 72 were used in contrasting pairs to represent 36 salespersons' rules of thumb, and 5 additional response items were added to scenarios for which it seemed especially obvious that the responses consisted of contrasting pairs. The salespersons' rules of thumb are presented in the appendix to this chapter. Of the 36 rules of thumb, 16 concerned aspects of local tacit knowledge, and 20 concerned aspects of global tacit knowledge. We represented the rules of thumb using contrasting pairs of response items, because we were not convinced that simply having subjects rate the quality of a list of rules of thumb would suffice to determine which rules of thumb truly differentiated experts and novices. We therefore employed a less obvious approach in which none of the rules of thumb were actually presented to subjects but, rather, each rule of thumb was represented indirectly by a pair of response items on the tacit-knowledge inventory of sales situations. One item of the pair, the target item, exemplified the rule of thumb; the other item of the pair, the control item, did not. For example, the rule of thumb about setting goals that are measurable and specific was represented by the target response item "Make 10 more sales presentations to potential customers each month," and by the control response item "Increase the number of sales presentations to potential customers." Note that the target and control items are nearly identical sales goals, the primary difference between them being that the target item is more measurable and specific than is the control item.

It was assumed that the extent to which an individual adheres to a given rule of thumb will be indicated by the degree to which the target item of a rule of thumb is more highly rated than its control item. Thus, a simple index of adherence to a rule of thumb is the difference score that results from subtracting the control item rating from the target item rating. The test we used to establish that a given rule of thumb differentiates experienced salespersons from inexperienced individuals was finding a reliably greater difference between target item and control item ratings (in favor of the target item) made by experienced salespersons, compared to the difference in ratings made by undergraduates with no sales experience.

The undergraduate group was given the Verbal Reasoning subtest of the Differential Aptitude Tests (Bennett, Seashore, & Wesman, 1974) to examine relations between tacit knowledge and verbal aptitude.

Tacit Knowledge Scores

Scoring System. Key items—those that reliably differentiated the salesperson and undergraduate groups—were identified by calculating point-biserial correlations between item ratings and a dummy variable that indicated whether the respondent was a member of the salesperson or undergraduate group.

Expert–Novice Differences. With a total of 77 items, 4 significant correlations between item ratings and the group membership variable were expected on the basis of chance alone. In fact, significant correlations were found for 30 of the 77 items. A binomial test of the probability of obtaining 30 significant correlations on the basis of chance yielded $p < .0001$. Thus, the set of response item ratings reliably differentiated members of the salesperson and undergraduate groups.

Tacit-knowledge scores were generated by summing ratings for key items after first reflecting ratings on items the undergraduate group rated more positively than did the salesperson group. These were items that served as distractors, in that they appeared to be better responses to individuals without sales experience than to experienced salespersons. A global tacit-knowledge score was calculated by summing key item ratings from the four work-related situations that were constructed to measure global tacit-knowledge about sales. A local tacit-knowledge score was calculated by summing key item ratings from the four work-related situations that were constructed to measure local tacit-knowledge about sales. A total tacit-knowledge score was calculated by summing the local and global tacit-knowledge scores.

Means and standard deviations of local, global, and total tacit-knowledge scores for the salesperson and undergraduate groups are presented in Table 9.1. The salesperson group outperformed the undergraduate group by a considerable margin, on the order of 2 standard deviation units. Because we only summed items that reliably differentiated the groups in calculating our tacit-knowledge scores, and because a greater than chance number of items did in fact differentiate the groups, it was obvious that the performance of the salesperson group would be reliably better than that of the undergraduate group without additional significance testing. However, to determine whether the performance advantage of the salesperson group over the undergraduate group was the same for local and global tacit knowledge, a Group × Type of Tacit Knowledge analysis of variance with repeated measures on the type variable was carried out. This analysis yielded the expected reliable effect of group, $F(1, 69) = 127.4$, $p < .001$; an effect of type of tacit knowledge, $F(1, 69) = 145.0$, $p < .001$; and a Group × Type of Tacit Knowl-

TABLE 9.1
Means (and Standard Deviations) for the Tacit-Knowledge Scores of the Salesperson and Undergraduate Groups in Study 1

	Group			
Tacit-Knowledge Score	*Salespersons*		*Undergraduates*	
Local	99.1	(9.7)	73.8	(10.1)
Global	109.7	(10.5)	92.3	(7.4)
Total	208.8	(16.2)	166.1	(13.8)

edge interaction, $F(1, 69) = 7.3, p < .01$. There was a reliably greater difference between the salesperson and undergraduate groups in local as opposed to global tacit knowledge. The main effect of type of tacit knowledge is not of theoretical interest.

Individual Differences. Reliabilities (coefficient alpha) were satisfactory, with values of .84, .77, and .68 for the total, local, and global tacit-knowledge scores, respectively.

Individual differences in the two kinds of tacit knowledge were independent, based on the fact that the correlations between the local and global tacit-knowledge scores were not reliably different from 0, with values of .23 ($p > .05$) for the undergraduate group, and .30 ($p > .05$) for the salesperson group. There was a reliable relation between verbal ability as measured by the Verbal Reasoning subtest of the Differential Aptitude Tests and local tacit knowledge, $r(48) = .40$, $p < .01$, but not between verbal aptitude and global tacit knowledge, $r(48) = .05$, $p > .05$.

Salespersons' Rules of Thumb

Prerequisite to examining group differences in their use of individual rules of thumb, a test for group differences on the entire 36 rules of thumb taken at once was carried out. The difference scores associated with each rule of thumb were summed to yield total scores for the salesperson and undergraduate groups that reflected their adherence to the entire set of 36 rules of thumb. The total scores indicated markedly greater adherence to the rules of thumb in making ratings for for the salesperson group ($M = 69.6$, $SD = 22.5$) than for the undergraduate group ($M = 37.4$, $SD = 20.8$), $t(78) = 5.72$, $p < .001$.

Reliable group differences in the expected direction were found for the rules of thumb for (a) setting sales goals: "Set goals that are measurable and specific," and "Commit to reaching your sales goals in writing"; (b) handling the customer who stalls: "Rather than accept the decision, ask why the customer is not ready to buy today," "Keep questions simple and focused," and "Penetrate smoke screens by asking what-if questions"; (c) for attracting new accounts: "Ask your customer to provide leads"; (d) for handling the competition: "Find out what your customer knows and does not know about your competitor's product," "Use the fact that customers associate price with quality to your advantage if your price is higher," and "If you are badly beaten in price, find out what, if anything, your competitor has left out"; (e) for what to do when the customer says the price is too high: "Rather than arguing with a customer, acknowledge the apparent validity of their position and then make your counterpoint"; (f) for managing one's time and tasks: "Make yourself do tasks you dislike"; and (g) for handling an irate customer: "Remember that you represent your company to the customer," and "Find out what the customer wants before making any offers of your own."

Although support was found for more rules of thumb concerning local tacit knowledge than for global tacit knowledge (9 vs. 4), this apparent advantage for rules of thumb concerning local as opposed to global tacit knowledge was not reliable, $\chi^2(1, N = 80) = 3.19$, $p > .05$.

In a second study, the same tacit-knowledge inventory was given to a group of life-insurance salespersons from a large general agency and to another group of undergraduates with no sales experience. The salesperson group consisted of 48 life-insurance salespersons. Their mean years of sales experience was 11.1 ($SD = 10.7$). The undergraduate group consisted of 50 undergraduates who had no sales experience.

Life-insurance salespersons from a large general agency were selected for three reasons. First, to ensure generality of results, it was important to select a group of salespersons that was not represented by the salespersons included in the first study. Second, the confound of having sales territories that differ in sales potential is largely avoided because life-insurance salespersons, unlike salespersons for many other products and services, have no true boundaries on their sales territories (with the possible exception of the immediate family members of another life insurance agent!). Third, the problem of comparing individuals who sell different products that may differ in demand is largely avoided, because agents from the same general agency sell the same line of products.

For purposes of cross-validation, the scoring system derived from the first study was used unchanged in this study, and, once again, salespersons' rules of thumb were evaluated, as was the relation between tacit knowledge and verbal aptitude.

Tacit Knowledge Scores

Expert–Novice Differences. The success of the cross-validation is evidenced by the descriptive statistics for the tacit-knowledge scores of the salesperson and undergraduate groups that are presented in Table 9.2. The performance of the salesperson group was markedly higher than that of the undergraduate group. A group by type of tacit-knowledge analysis of variance with repeated measures on the type factor yielded a reliable effect of group, $F(1, 95) = 241.4$, $p < .001$. The reliable main effect of type of tacit knowledge, $F(1, 95) = 260.2$, $p < .001$, is not of theoretical interest. The Group × Type of Tacit Knowledge interaction was not reliable in this experiment, $F(1, 95) = 0.5$, $p > .05$. Using the local and global scores in a discriminant-function analysis of experts and novices results in correct classification of 96% of the cases and a canonical correlation between the predictor variables and group membership of .83, $p < .001$, and with both local and global tacit knowledge figuring

TABLE 9.2
Means (and Standard Deviations) for the Tacit-Knowledge Scores of the Salesperson and Undergraduate Groups in Study 2

Tacit-Knowledge Score	Group			
	Salespersons		*Undergraduates*	
Local	94.2	(6.8)	73.1	(8.9)
Global	111.6	(7.2)	92.2	(10.4)
Total	205.8	(10.6)	165.3	(14.6)

in prediction (with standardized discriminant function coefficients of .75, $p < .001$, and .57, $p < .001$, respectively) as well as interpretation of the discriminant function (with structure coefficients of .82, $p < .001$, and .67, $p < .001$, respectively).

Individual Differences. Reliabilities (coefficient alpha) for the tacit-knowledge scores were adequate, with values of .82, .71, and .70 for the total, global, and local scores, respectively.

The correlations between local and global tacit-knowledge scores were not reliably different from 0, with values of .14 ($p > .05$) and an identical .14 ($p > .05$) for the undergraduate and salesperson groups, respectively. Correlations between the tacit-knowledge scores and criterion measures of experience and success for the salesperson group are presented in Table 9.3. There were reliable correlations between tacit knowledge and sales experience, both in terms of number of years with the company and number of years of sales experience. There also were reliable correlations between tacit-knowledge scores and several measures of sales performance. Interestingly, there was no relation between tacit knowledge and having attended college. However, having majored in business was reliably related to local tacit knowledge. Although global tacit knowledge was related to sales volume and sales premiums for 2 years, local tacit knowledge was not.

For the undergraduates, verbal ability, as measured by the Verbal Reasoning subtest of the Differential Aptitude Tests, was related to local tacit knowledge, $r(48) = .25$, $p < .05$, but not to global tacit knowledge, $r(48) = -.02$, $p > .05$. To test whether the correlation between verbal aptitude and local tacit knowledge was reliably greater than that for global tacit knowledge, the undergraduate samples from Studies 1 and 2 were combined. Combining samples from the two experiments increased the power of the test of the difference between correlations. For this combined sample, there was a reliably larger correlation between verbal aptitude and local tacit knowledge (.33, $p < .001$) than between verbal aptitude and global tacit knowledge (.01, $p > .05$), $t(97) = 4.31$, $p < .001$.

TABLE 9.3
Correlation Coefficients Between Tacit-Knowledge Scores and Criterion Reference Measures for Salespersons

	Tacit-Knowledge Scores		
Criterion Reference Measures	*Total*	*Local*	*Global*
Number of years with company	.37**	.23*	.32**
Number of years in sales	.31**	.19	.28*
Number of yearly quality awards received	.35**	.28*	.25*
Sales volume (1985)	.22	−.07	.37**
Sales volume (1986)	.15	−.07	.28*
Premiums (1985)	.20	.02	.26*
Premiums (1986)	.17	−.05	.29*
Attended college	−.11	−.01	−.17
Business education	.41**	.35*	.23

Note. The *n*s ranged from 40 to 45 with the following exceptions: sales volume (1985; $n = 31$); sales volume (1986; $n = 39$); premiums (1985; $n = 31$); premiums (1986; $n = 39$); and business education ($n = 33$).

*$p < .05$. **$p < .01$.

Salespersons' Rules of Thumb. As in Study 1, a test for group differences on the entire 36 rules of thumb taken at once (using the sum of the difference scores associated with each rule of thumb) was carried out prior to examining group differences in use of individual rules of thumb. There was markedly greater adherence to the rules of thumb in making ratings for the salesperson group ($M = 70.9$, $SD = 22.9$) than for the undergraduate group ($M = 31.2$, $SD = 18.4$), $t(96) = 9.40$, $p < .001$.

Reliable group differences in the expected direction were found for the rules of thumb for (a) setting sales: "Set goals that are measurable and specific," and "Make a public commitment to reaching one's sales goals"; (b) for handling the customer who stalls: "Rather than accept the decision, ask why the customer is not ready to buy today," "Play your hunches and ask if you suspect another competitor has entered the picture," and "Penetrate smoke screens by asking what-if questions"; (c) for attracting new accounts: "Get satisfied customers to provide testimonials," "Use a bird-dog approach by getting other salespersons to provide leads," "Ask your customers to provide leads," and "Test any changes you make before actually making them"; (d) for handling the competition: "Build up your product and company rather than tear down your competitor's product and company," "Remember that customers buy for their reasons, not yours," "Use the fact that customers associate price with quality to your advantage if your price is higher," and "If you are badly beaten in price, find out what, if anything, your competitor has left out"; (e) for selling a slow-moving product: "Use the contrast effect to your advantage by beginning at the top of the line and moving down"; (f) for what to do when the customer says the price is too high: "Rather than arguing with a customer, acknowledge the apparent validity of their position and then make your counterpoint"; (g) for managing one's time and tasks: "In evaluating your success, think in terms of tasks accomplished rather than hours spent working," "Make yourself do tasks you dislike," "Keep interruptions to a minimum," and "At the end of the day, decide what you want to do tomorrow"; and (h) for handling an irate customer: "Remember that you represent your company to the customer."

There was no reliable difference in support for rules of thumb that concerned local (9) versus global (11) tacit knowledge, $\chi^2(1, N = 98) = .002$, $p > .05$.

Summary

The cross-validation was successful. Using the scoring system derived in Study 1 and the same tacit-knowledge measure on new samples of salespersons and undergraduates without sales experience, we replicated and extended the major findings of Study 1. In this experiment, salespersons markedly outperformed undergraduates with no sales experience on our measure of local and global sales-related tacit knowledge. A substantial portion of expert–novice differences in tacit knowledge were isolated in 20 salespersons' rules of thumb. Individual differences in tacit knowledge, especially global tacit knowledge, were related to criterion measures of sales performance. Individual differences in local tacit knowledge were related to verbal ability, but there was no relation between verbal ability and global tacit knowledge.

We began our chapter by reviewing relevant research in the areas of persuasion, expert–novice differences, and practical intelligence. We return to these topics next to consider implications of our results in the broader context of relevant research.

Selling as an Everyday Example of Persuasion

Our research on selling has not been directed toward resolving current issues in the literature on persuasion. However, selling clearly is an everyday example of persuasion in which most of us engage on some level, and there appear to be some implications of our results for understanding persuasion as it operates in the everyday world.

A number of the salespersons' rules of thumb that we examined correspond to some of the characteristics of successful persuasion. For example, the support found for the rule of thumb "Get satisfied customers to provide testimonials" is evidence for the social validation principle that we are more likely to be persuaded by an individual who is similar (i.e., another customer) rather than dissimilar to us (Cialdini, 1985). Another rule of thumb for which support was found—"Use the contrast effect to your advantage by beginning at the top of the line and moving down"—is consistent with studies of contrast effects in persuasion (Cialdini, 1985).

Surprisingly, no support was found for the rule of thumb "Scarce items are more valued than plentiful items." This rule of thumb exemplifies Cialdini's (1985) scarcity principle, and is consistent with the idea that arousing fear (e.g., if you do not act quickly you will be out of luck) and providing a means for its dissipation (e.g., place your order now) makes for a persuasive message. This rule of thumb also appears to be widely adopted; perhaps that is the reason for its lack of support. Recall that our criterion for validating a rule of thumb was greater adherence by experts as opposed to novices. A rule that is widely adopted by both novices as well as experts may be a useful rule of thumb, but it will not differentiate experts from novices.

An aspect of persuasion that was strongly supported in the present results but that receives little attention in the social-psychological literature is that of taking an active rather than a passive role. The relevant rules of thumb were "Rather than accept the decision, ask why the customer is not ready to buy today," "Play your hunches and ask if you suspect a competitor has entered the picture," and "Penetrate smoke screens by asking what-if questions." Some of the most striking expert–novice differences were found for these rules: Individuals lacking sales experience were easily put off by an unenthusiastic customer, whereas experienced salespersons aggressively fought for the sale. Some additional validation for this finding was provided by Peterson (1993), who examined effective ways to handle objections and found that the direct-answer method (providing a specific response to the exact question raised by the prospect) was the most effective strategy.

Our results demonstrate a correspondence between salespersons' rules of thumb and characteristics of successful persuasion that have emerged from the social-psychological literature, and provide an extension that incorporates additional rules of thumb that are successful in the real world. But how should this correspondence be interpreted? It is possible that this correspondence represents independent confirmation of the ideas of social psychologists in a natural setting. Alternatively, the correspondence between salespersons' rules of thumb and social-psychological findings on persuasion may merely reflect the fact that those who write about selling and train salespersons also comb the social-psychological literature for useful tidbits of information to apply to sales.

Expert–Novice Differences in Selling

Much of the research on expert–novice differences has been carried out using the kinds of tasks that Neisser (1976) characterized as measures of academic intelligence. The present study of expert–novice differences in sales successfully extends the study of such differences to practical as opposed to academic-type tasks, although it is not the first study to do so. There have been several recent studies of expert–novice differences on practical problems. For example, Ceci and Liker (1986) found that expert racehorse handicappers could be differentiated from novices by the experts' use of an interactive model that employed six common race-related variables. Wagner and Sternberg (1985) found that expert academic psychologists and business executives could be differentiated from novices in their respective professions by having acquired certain kinds of practical know-how (see also Streufert & Streufert, 1978; Wagner, 1987). Finally, Scribner's (1986) studies of the practical mental arithmetic of dairy plant workers show that there are useful practical approaches even to what traditionally have been considered academic-type tasks, such as determining the number of cases of milk contained in a space of specified dimensions.

The examination of salespersons' rules of thumb suggest one answer to the difficult question of how to characterize what experts know. There have been a number of attempts to characterize individual differences in knowledge that go beyond mere estimates of its quantity. Perhaps the most common approaches used to characterize differences in the knowledge of novices and experts are to examine differences in how they categorize domain-relevant problems and to create scripts of what experts say they would do (e.g., Brewer, Dull, & Lui, 1981; Lurigio & Carroll, 1985; Murphy & Wright, 1984; Schank & Abelson, 1977). The present results support the notion that rules of thumb are a useful unit of analysis of what experts know. The rules of thumb examined in the present studies appear to be applicable to a variety of sales situations. It may have been possible to generate a set of abstract rules with even more generality, that might apply not only to selling insurance but also to "selling" a spouse on one's vacation plans.

Practical Intelligence in Selling

Consistent with previous studies (Wagner, 1987; Wagner & Sternberg, 1985), reliable differences in tacit knowledge were found between groups of individuals whose members differed in sales experience. These differences were found both for knowledge about longer-range strategies for maximizing the number of future sales opportunities one has (global tacit knowledge), and for knowledge about strategies for actually making the sale in a given selling situation (local tacit knowledge). Also consistent with previous work (Wagner, 1987), the tacit knowledge in sales measured by the scenarios of sales situations appears to be relatively general. In Study 1, the salesperson group was made up of three different kinds of salespersons—automobile, furniture, and real estate—and the cross-validation to life insurance salespersons in Study 2 was successful.

It is likely that the extent to which success at sales depends on local tacit knowledge, global tacit knowledge, both, or neither depends on the kind of sales involved. The relations found between local and global tacit knowledge and the criterion measures available in Study 2 suggest that success at selling life insurance depends in part on local and global tacit knowledge, with global tacit knowledge being perhaps more important.

An important goal for future research is to determine which, if either kind of tacit knowledge, is required for different types of sales. It is likely that some kinds of sales require mostly global tacit knowledge about finding likely prospects (e.g., selling periodical subscriptions), and some require mostly local tacit knowledge about how to convince a customer to buy from you (e.g., industrial sales). It also is likely that some kinds of selling require little, if any, tacit knowledge. For example, some telephone sales require little local tacit knowledge because salespersons work from a branching script that provides the exact response to read for most conceivable responses from the potential customer, and little global tacit knowledge because a computer selects potential customers by dialing the last four numbers of telephone exchanges at random. Finding what characteristics of sales jobs require local or global tacit knowledge would be helpful in determining whether a test of either kind of tacit knowledge is appropriate for personnel selection, and whether training designed to facilitate the acquisition of either kind of tacit knowledge would pay off in higher sales performance.

Perhaps the most important new finding about tacit knowledge is the success of the concept of the rule of thumb in understanding tacit knowledge at a level more specific than that represented by one or more tacit-knowledge scores. The results indicate that part of what experienced salespersons know that inexperienced individuals do not can be expressed as rules of thumb about sales. There are practical consequences of identifying rules of thumb that differentiate individuals on the basis of sales experience and performance. It should be possible to provide more useful feedback to salespeople than is possible by relying on scores alone. For example, one might help a salesperson develop by providing a list of rules of thumb to consider that successful salespersons appear to adhere to that the salesperson does not. It may be necessary to represent each rule of thumb by a variety of response item pairs in different contexts to achieve sufficient reliability for this kind of use of rules of thumb. A validated list of rules of thumb could serve as the basis for a training program designed to convey tacit knowledge about sales.

One issue that relates to training tacit knowledge is that of how "tacit" is such knowledge in the profession of sales. Salespersons often receive considerable training in how to make sales. Is it possible that most of what we have called tacit knowledge is, in fact, explicit knowledge in which salespersons are instructed? Our interviews with salespersons suggest that although sales training accomplishes many important goals, it does not prepare one for the wide variety of sales-related situations one actually will encounter. There are examples from other real-world domains of the incompleteness of formal training. For example, Suchman (1985) found that even with a task as relatively straightforward as learning to use a new photocopy machine, secretaries relied more on collaboratively constructed methods for handling the numerous problems associated with their tasks than they relied on written instructions that came with the machine. Kusterer (1978) discovered that much of the working knowledge of bank tellers consists of what to do in situations that the standard procedures do not cover. Finally, Schön (1983) identified the hallmark of professional expertise to be informal improvising.

RULES OF THUMB: AN ALTERNATIVE PERSPECTIVE

We also examined rules of thumb in selling from an alternative perspective. In a series of studies by Sujan, Sujan, and Bettman (1988, 1991), we assessed rules of thumb using both free elicitation and rating methods. We also examined changes in rules of thumb that accompany the development of expertise through longitudinal studies. We conducted these investigations distinguishing between declarative and procedural knowledge.

Is the Tacit Knowledge of Salespeople Both Procedural and Declarative?

A key characteristic of tacit knowledge is that it is procedural or action related (Sternberg, Wagner, Williams, & Horvath, 1995). More specifically, tacit knowledge is considered to take the form of *if* (antecedent condition) *then* (consequent action) rules. Although "knowing that" or declarative knowledge helps define the antecedent condition, it does not by itself contribute to effectiveness. Knowing an action or procedure that links appropriately with the antecedent condition is the critical issue from the practical standpoint of enabling effectiveness. Consequently, in most empirical studies on tacit knowledge, subjects are provided with the declarative component that defines the antecedent conditions, and their knowledge of consequent actions or procedures is assessed (e.g., Wagner, Rashotte, & Sternberg, 1994). As a result, differences in declarative knowledge between effective and less effective performers are undetected.

Sujan, Sujan, and Bettman (1988, 1991) allowed subjects to generate their own idiosyncratic antecedent conditions and assessed their consequent actions. This more open-ended methodology allowed the assessment of the impact of both declarative and procedural knowledge components on effective performance.

Their subjects were students who worked part time for a telemarketing operation created by a university to raise funds from its alumni. These students were managed by a full-time sales manager and underwent a 1-week training program before they began their sales work. In the first data collection session, subjects were told that the researchers were interested in understanding the kinds of categories or groupings they used to differentiate among the alumni customers they called. They were asked to think about the different types of alumni they encountered on the phone and to jot down these different types on a sheet of paper using short descriptive labels. After this, they were asked to elaborate on their different alumni categories by: describing the characteristic demographics, personality traits, and behavioral patterns of alumni in the category; and describing the strategies and behaviors they used while interacting with alumni in that category. In a second session, subjects were told that the researchers wished to quantify some of their responses. Each subject was given an individualized questionnaire that contained a declarative and a procedural table. The column heads of each table were the idiosyncratic alumni categories that each subjects had reported. The rows were common across subjects. For the declarative table, the rows were a set of the 10 most frequently mentioned characteristics relevant for describing alumni. For the procedural table, the rows were a set of the 10 most frequently mentioned strategies and behaviors used for selling to alumni. Subjects were asked to rate each declarative and procedural descriptor for its appropriateness to the idiosyncratic alumni categories specified in the columns.

Subjects' selling effectiveness was assessed by the sales manager. These data were collected from 41 salespeople. The cross-sectional study was replicated longitudinally with 12 salespeople. Data from these 12 salespeople was collected in the first week of selling, and then 13 weeks later. In the cross-sectional study, based on a median split of the supervisor's performance ratings, there were 21 effective salespeople and 20 less effective salespeople. In the longitudinal study, the supervisor considered all salespeople to be less effective in the first week of their selling and 11 of the 12 to be effective 13 weeks later. Analyses of the longitudinal data were restricted to the 11 salespeople who, as they gained experience, progressed from being less effective to more effective.

Data from both the cross-sectional and the longitudinal studies showed that effective and less effective salespeople do not differ in the number of categories they have for classifying their customers. However, the number of distinct declarative statements that subjects used to describe their customer categories are significantly greater for effective salespeople than for less effective salespeople, on average 4.6 versus 3.7 in the cross-sectional study and 4.4 versus 3.4 in the longitudinal study. Evaluating the content of these statements, effective salespeople use cues to classify their customers that can be characterized as more underlying rather than surface structure and more functional in terms of generating procedures. For example, less effective salespeople use the surface structure and less functional cue of *occupation* to classify their customers, whereas effective salespeople use the underlying and more functional cue of *the alumni's past history of contributions.*

The number of distinct procedural statements that subjects use to describe their behavior with customers are significantly greater for effective salespeople than for less effective salespeople, on average 3.5 versus 2.4 strategies in the cross-sectional study and 3.3 versus 2.5 strategies in the longitudinal study. Evaluating the content of these statements, effective salespeople use strategies and behaviors that can be characterized as more specific rather than general, and more problem solving rather than relationship oriented. For example, less effective salespeople make more *small talk,* a general and relationship-oriented procedure, and effective salespeople give more *concrete examples of the use to which the alumni's donation will be put,* a specific and problem-solving-oriented procedure.

These data indicate that when descriptions of sales situations or the antecedent conditions are permitted to vary idiosyncratically, differences in declarative knowledge between effective and less effective salespeople emerge. The nature of these differences, however, lies in the usefulness of this knowledge in generating appropriate procedures. Effective and less effective salespeople differ in classifying customers on underlying rather than surface structure cues—surface structure cues are more likely to trigger inappropriate sales strategies—and on cues that are clearly more functional for generating appropriate sales strategies and behaviors. Thus, the data strengthen the contention that although "knowing that" might be important, simply "knowing that" without connecting this to "knowing how" is not practical and does not contribute to the tacit knowledge of effective salespeople.

Adaptation and Abstraction: Two Aspects of Tacit Knowledge

Beyond observing that tacit knowledge raises intelligent functioning, it is important to identify why it does. A comparison of the procedural knowledge differences between effective and less effective sales performers found by Wagner, Rashotte, and Sternberg with those found in the Sujan, Sujan, and Bettman data offers some clues. Wagner, Rashotte, and Sternberg (1994) found that knowledge of both local procedures (that relate to the task at hand) and global procedures (that are at a higher level of abstraction and more long term or strategic) contribute to effectiveness; their evidence was stronger for knowledge of global procedures. Sujan, Sujan, and Bettman (1988, 1991) found that knowledge of local procedures (that are specific and relating to the task at hand) contribute to effectiveness. However, they found that knowledge of general procedures (that are widely applicable, thus less contingent on antecedent conditions) negatively impact effectiveness.

One explanation for this difference in findings is that the data collected by Sujan, Sujan, and Bettman did not tap the type of global procedures alluded to by Wagner, Rashotte, and Sternberg. The global strategies as classified by Sujan, Sujan, and Bettman were domain general or noncontingent rather than at a higher level of abstraction. Together, the two sets of data indicate that procedural knowledge that enables both adaptation (based on specific or local tacit knowledge contingent on antecedent conditions) and abstraction (based on overarching or global knowledge) increases effectiveness.

These data also clarify that though global strategies are often both abstract and domain general, their positive effects on performance are likely to be derived from the broader, more abstract perspective they provide on the problem at hand rather than from their domain-general characteristics. This conclusion is consistent with the suggestion made by Sternberg (1985) that intelligent functioning requires not only local planning (the formation of a microstrategy sufficient to solve a particular problem) but also global planning (the formation of a macrostrategy that enables taking a broader and more thematic perspective on the problem). It is also consistent with Sujan, Weitz, and Kumar's (1994) contention that working smart in sales is a combination of adapting to the sales situation at hand and planning ways to achieve sales goals.

The Interconnectedness of Tacit Knowledge

Another way to evaluate adaptation and abstraction is to examine the extent to which salespeople's categories are separate or overlapping. One quality of tacit knowledge is that it might enable salespeople to formulate different contingency rules for their different customer categories. This would be manifested as relatively separate or nonoverlapping categories. This quality of distinctiveness signifies salespeople's ability to adapt. For example, effective salespeople might see rebuy and new-buy customers as distinct, and use different approaches for selling to each customer type. Another quality of tacit knowledge is that it might enable salespeople to formulate rules that embody abstract principles. This would be manifested as overlapping categories interconnected by these abstract principles. Thus, this quality of interconnectedness signifies salespeople's ability to abstract. For example, effective salespeople might uncover an underlying similarity between rebuy and new-buy customers—both are responsive to money-saving deals, although possibly in different ways (add-ons vs. lower price)—so use a common selling procedure (value for money) for both customer types.

Sujan, Sujan, and Bettman (1988) examined, for both declarative and procedural knowledge components, the extent to which salespeople's categories are interconnected or distinct. From the open-ended descriptions they computed the proportion of shared to shared-plus-distinctive features for every pair of customer categories. Averaging this across all category pairs, they computed each salesperson's declarative and procedural knowledge overlap scores. From the ratings' matrices, in the cross-sectional study, they computed first the average variance for each descriptor and then averaged these variances to create a declarative and procedural knowledge variance index for each salesperson.

For declarative knowledge, based on the open-ended responses, the shared-to-distinctive feature indexes revealed an average across-category overlap of 10% for effective salespeople and 8% for less effective salespeople in the cross-sectional study; and an overlap of 14% for effective salespeople and 9% for less effective salespeople in the longitudinal study. These differences between effective and less effective salespeople were statistically significant only in the longitudinal study. For procedural knowledge, these indexes revealed an average across-category overlap of 18% for effective salespeople and 13% for less effective salespeople in the cross-sectional study; and an overlap of 24% for effective salespeople and 14% for less effective salespeople in the longitudinal study. These differences were not significant in the cross-sectional study, and approached significance in the longitudinal study.

For declarative knowledge, the average across-category variance from the ratings matrix indicated lesser variance or greater overlap for effective salespeople than for less effective salespeople (a variance of 6.3 relative to 9.0). For procedural knowledge it indicated, again, lesser variance or greater overlap for effective salespeople than for less effective salespeople (a variance of 3.6 relative to 5.3). Both these differences were statistically significant.

There are two inferences to be drawn from these data. First, the greater overlap (lesser variance) across categories observed for effective sales performers indicates that the tacit knowledge of these salespeople is at a higher or more abstract level than that of less effective sales performers. This suggests, in keeping with Wagner, Rashotte, and Sternberg's (1994) finding, that they can identify globally applicable principles and procedures. Second, it is important to note that this finding does not suggest that effective salespeople do not vary their behavior. Their overlap scores on average were less than 25%. Effective salespeople vary their behavior but do not appear to overadjust to the idiosyncrasies of the situation as less effective salespeople do. This is consistent with the view that adaptation is intelligent variation of behavior that embodies broad principles and situational constraints rather than mere variation.

Building on these data, Sujan (1996) tracked student fundraisers over a 20-week period. At four equally spaced intervals, he evaluated category overlap and obtained the supervisor's evaluation of performance. Separating salespeople whose performance improved during the time intervals from those whose performance did not improve, he found differences in the pattern of overlap change, for both declarative and procedural knowledge.

For declarative knowledge, for improvers, overlap increased for the first two time intervals and stayed steady for the third, whereas for nonimprovers overlap increased for the first time period but steadily decreased thereafter. For procedural knowledge, for improvers, overlap stayed the same in the first two time periods and increased in the third, whereas for nonimprovers overlap increased in the first time period but decreased thereafter. Thus, it appears that differences in the development of abstract tacit knowledge, between salespeople who improve their performance and those who do not, is a result of the former class of salesperson's continuing to search for abstract, underlying principles and the latter class of salesperson's tiring of this search early, seeking instead more local or less abstract principles by which to classify customers and formulate selling procedures.

Teaching Tacit Knowledge

Earlier we suggested that though tacit knowledge is usually acquired from experience with little external prompting, managerial actions and training programs can enhance it. In addition, based on the research of Weitz, Sujan, and Sujan (1986) and Sujan, Weitz, and Kumar (1994), we suggest changes in sales managers' actions and organizational policies as interventions that can enhance salespeople's tacit knowledge.

Compensation Programs. In the development of a compensation plan, a critical issue is the emphasis placed on salary versus incentive compensation (commissions and bonuses). Most sales organizations include, to some extent, incentives in their compensation plan. The use of incentive compensation reduces motivation and impedes knowledge development when it is perceived as controlling and a threat rather than as a symbolic acknowledgment of superior performance. The negative impact of incentive compensation is particularly strong during the initial stages of salespeople's careers, before they have had the opportunity to develop high self-efficacy. Thus, organizational policies that focus on salary compensation and limit the amount and conditions of use of incentive compensation would facilitate the development of tacit knowledge.

Feedback. A key function of sales managers is to provide feedback to their salespeople. A distinction is made between outcome feedback and cognitive feedback. The former is information on whether a desired outcome, such as a quota, is met, whereas the latter is information on how and why the outcome was or was not achieved. Cognitive feedback to salespeople is likely to increase motivation by focusing attention on the content of the selling job. This form of feedback is likely to be particularly helpful in gaining tacit knowledge about strategies and behaviors to use and avoid.

Self-Management. In contrast to directing salespeople toward achieving goals, managers can help salespeople direct themselves. Salespeople can set their own goals, decide how they will achieve these goals, evaluate their performance, and even participate in rewarding themselves. Self-management increases attention to the content of work and thus enhances motivated learning and tacit knowledge.

Salient Attributional Cues. Cues suggesting reasons for why salespeople encounter successes and failures can have a significant impact on how salespeople interpret these outcomes and learn from them. In particular, salespeople often make stable attributions for their failures, such as a lack of aptitude or a tough sales territory, and as a result suffer from demotivation that adversely affects their learning. Sujan (1996) found that luck, mood, and strategy, all unstable attributions for failure, increase category overlap and thus enable salespeople to identify global or abstract principles to guide their behavior. Sales managers can encourage unstable attributions for failure, for example, by using THINK signs, which remind salespeople that poor strategies may have caused their failures and that good strategies are an important ingredient of success.

Learning Orientation. Two categories of goals that motivate salespeople are learning goals (the desire to improve their ability and master the tasks they perform) and performance goals (the desire to demonstrate their current abilities and, as a result, obtain a positive evaluation from their supervisor, customers, and peers). Sujan, Weitz, and Kumar (1994) demonstrated that a learning-goal orientation enables salespeople to work smart, adapt, and abstract (plan). In contrast, a performance-goal orientation does not affect adaptation and abstraction. More important, Sujan et al. showed that the effect of a learning orientation on smart work does not depend on self-efficacy or confidence in one's selling ability; that is, even those who doubt their ability, often termed "losers" in sales organizations, are driven by learning goals to function intelligently. Sujan et al. consequently suggested that sales organizations should create a climate of discovery, not one of identifying winners and losers. In addition to feedback, Sujan et al. suggested that leadership styles of first-level sales supervisors and their vice presidents alter salespeople's learning orientations. A transformational leadership style enhances salespeople's learning orientation, whereas a transactional leadership style harms it. Transformational leaders manage by transmitting a sense of mission and stimulating new ways of thinking, whereas transactional leaders manage by specifying rules and procedures and associated rewards and punishments.

Training Programs. Training programs typically transmit information on the company's products, sales presentation techniques, current and potential markets and customers, and company policies. Although this information is important, it must be *unitized* into sales situations if it is to be used effectively by salespeople. Unitization enables salespeople to recognize standard sales situations and link them with effective selling procedures. Thus, unitization teaches salespeople to connect the declarative and procedural components of tacit knowledge, improving the functionality of their knowledge base.

Training is likely to be most effective when the company's star salespeople become actively involved in developing and teaching in the program. This type of training will cause experts to reflect on and formulate their rules of thumb. Furthermore, exposure to and interaction with these experts will enable less experienced salespeople to learn through the process of contagion.

ACKNOWLEDGMENTS

Support for this research was provided by Contract MDA90385K0305 from the Army Research Institute.

APPENDIX: SALESPERSONS' RULES OF THUMB

Setting Sales Goals

1. Target sales goals in number of units sold, not dollars.
2. Avoid setting goals that are so ambitious they cannot be met.
3. Set goals that are measurable and specific.
4. Commit in writing to reaching your sales goals.
5. Make a public commitment to reaching your sales goals.
6. Set goals that require substantial improvement to reach.

Handling the Customer Who Stalls

7. Rather than accept the decision, ask why the customer is not ready to buy today.
8. Keep questions simple and focused.

9. Play your hunches and ask if you suspect a competitor has entered the picture.
10. Penetrate smoke screens by asking what-if questions.

Attracting New Accounts

11. Be selective in to whom you direct your promotion efforts.
12. Personalize your promotion to individual customers as much as possible.
13. Get satisfied customers to provide testimonials.
14. Use a bird-dog approach by getting other salespersons to provide leads.
15. Ask your customers to provide leads.
16. Test any changes you make before actually making them.

Handling the Competition

17. Build up your product and company, rather than tear down your competitor's product and company.
18. Find out what your customer knows and does not know about your competitor's product.
19. Remember that customers buy for their reasons, not yours.
20. Use the fact that customers associate price with quality to your advantage if your price is higher.
21. If you are badly beaten in price, find out what, if anything, your competitor has left out.

Selling a Slow-Moving Product

22. Dramatize ordinary features and turn liabilities into assets.
23. Remember that scarce items are more valued than are plentiful items.
24. Advertise the price in a way that emphasizes a discount.
25. Use the contrast effect to your advantage by beginning at the top of the line and moving down.

When the Customer Says the Price Is Too High

26. A trivial drop in price may work for buyers who always insist on a price cut before buying.
27. Rather than arguing with customers, acknowledge the apparent validity of their position and then make your counterpoint.

28. If you choose not to drop your price, make follow-up contacts to give customers a chance to change their minds.
29. Never enter a no-profit situation, even if there is promise of future profit.

Managing One's Time and Tasks

30. In evaluating your performance, think in terms of tasks accomplished rather than hours spent working.
31. Make yourself do tasks you dislike.
32. Keep interruptions to a minimum.
33. At the end of the day, decide what you want to do tomorrow.

Handling an Irate Customer

34. Remember that you represent your company to the customer.
35. Find out what the customer wants before making any offers of your own.
36. Get approval from your superiors before making an offer that could cost the company significant amounts of money.

REFERENCES

Bennett, G. K., Seashore, H. G., & Wesman, A. G. (1974). *Differential Aptitude Tests (Form T)*. New York: Psychological Corporation.

Beswick, C., & Cravens, D. W. (1977). A multistate decision model for sales force management. *Journal of Marketing Research, 14,* 135–144.

Brewer, M. B., Dull, V., & Lui, L. (1981). Perception of the elderly: Stereotypes as prototypes. *Journal of Personality and Social and Social Psychology, 41,* 656–670.

Ceci, S. J., & Liker, J. (1986). Academic and nonacademic intelligence: An experimental separation. In R. J. Sternberg & R. K. Wagner (Eds.), *Practical intelligence: Nature and origins of competence in the everyday world* (pp. 119–142). New York: Cambridge University Press.

Charlesworth, W. R. (1976). Intelligence as adaptation: An ethological approach. In L. Resnick (Ed.), *The nature of intelligence* (pp. 147–168). Hillsdale, NJ: Lawrence Erlbaum Associates.

Chi, M. T. H., Glaser, R., & Rees, E. (1982). Expertise in problem solving. In R. Sternberg (Ed.), *Advances in the psychology of human intelligence* (Vol. 1, pp. 7–75). Hillsdale, NJ: Lawrence Erlbaum Associates.

Cialdini, R. B. (1985). *Influence: Science and practice.* Glenview, IL: Scott, Foresman.

Cravens, D. W., & Woodruff, R. B. (1973). An approach for determining criteria of sales performance. *Journal of Applied Psychology, 57,* 240–247.

Fishbein, M., & Ajzen, I. (1975). *Beliefs, attitudes, intentions and behavior: An introduction to theory and research.* Reading, MA: Addison-Wesley.

French, J. R. P., & Raven, B. (1959). The bases of social power. In D. Cartwright (Ed.), *Studies in social power* (pp. 150–167). Ann Arbor: University of Michigan Institute for Social Research.

Girard, J., & Brown, S. H. (1979). *How to sell anything to anybody.* New York: Warner.

Grikscheit, G. G. (1971). *An investigation of the ability of salesman to monitor feedback.* Unpublished doctoral dissertation, Michigan State University, East Lansing.

Katerberg, R., & Blau, G. J. (1983). An examination of level and direction of effort and job performance. *Academy of Management Journal, 26,* 249–257.

Kusterer, K. C. (1978). *Know-how on the job: The important working knowledge of "unskilled" workers.* Boulder, CO: Westview.

Leigh, T., & McGraw, P. F. (1989). Mapping the procedural knowledge of industrial sales personnel: A script-theoretic investigation. *Journal of Marketing, 53,* 16–34.

Leong, S. M., Busch, P. S., & John, D. R. (1989). Knowledge bases and salesperson effectiveness: A script-theoretic analysis. *Journal of Marketing Research, 26,* 164–178.

Lurigio, A. J., & Carroll, J. S. (1985). Probation officers' schemata of offenders: Content, development, and impact on treatment decisions. *Journal of Personality and Social Psychology, 48,* 1112–1126.

Morris, W. (Ed.). (1978). *The American heritage dictionary of the English language.* Boston: Houghton Mifflin.

Murphy, G. L., & Wright, J. C. (1984). Changes in conceptual structure with expertise: Differences between real-world experts and novices. *Journal of Experimental Psychology: Learning, Memory, and Cognition, 10,* 144–154.

Neisser, U. (1976). General, academic, and artificial intelligence. In L. Resnick (Ed.), *The nature of intelligence* (pp. 135–144). Hillsdale, NJ: Lawrence Erlbaum Associates.

Peterson, R. T. (1993). How do you answer objections? *American Salesman, 38,* 9–11.

Petty, R. E., & Cacioppo, J. T. (1981). *Attitudes and persuasion: Classic and contemporary approaches.* Dubuque, IA: Brown.

Rosch, E., Mervis, C. B., Gray, W. D., Johnson, D. M., & Boyes-Braem, P. (1976). Basic objects in natural categories. *Cognitive Psychology, 8,* 382–439.

Schank, R. C., & Abelson, R. P. (1977). *Scripts, plans, goals, and understanding: An inquiry into human knowledge structures.* Hillsdale, NJ: Lawrence Erlbaum Associates.

Schön, D. A. (1983). *The reflective practitioner.* New York: Basic.

Scribner, S. (1986). Thinking in action: Some characteristics of practical thought. In R. J. Sternberg & R. K. Wagner (Eds.), *Practical intelligence: Nature and origins of competence in the everyday world* (pp. 13–30). New York: Cambridge University Press.

Seligman, M. E. P., & Schulman, P. (1986). Explanatory style as a predictor of productivity and quitting among life insurance sales agents. *Journal of Personality and Social Psychology, 50,* 832–838.

Spiro, R. L., & Perreault, W. D. (1979). Influence use by industrial salesmen: Influence strategy mixes and situational determinants. *Journal of Business, 52,* 435–455.

Spiro, R. L., Perreault, W. D., & Reynolds, F. D. (1976). The selling process: A critical review and model. *Industrial Marketing Management, 5,* 351–363.

Spiro, R. L., & Weitz, B. A. (1990). Adaptive selling: Conceptualization, measurement, and nomological validity. *Journal of Marketing Research, 27,* 61–69.

Sternberg, R. J. (1985). *Beyond IQ.* New York: Cambridge University Press.

Sternberg, R. J., & Wagner, R. K. (Eds.). (1986). *Practical intelligence: The origin and nature of competence in the everyday world.* New York: Cambridge University Press.

Sternberg, R. J., Wagner, R. K., Williams, W. M., & Horvath, J. A. (1995). Testing common sense. *American Psychologist, 50,* 912–927.

Streufert, S., & Streufert, S. C. (1978). *Behavior in the complex environment.* Washington, DC: Winston.

Suchman, L. A. (1985). *Plans and situated actions: The problem of human–machine communication.* Palo Alto, CA: Xerox.

Sujan, H. (1986). Smarter versus harder: An exploratory attributional analysis of salespeople's motivation. *Journal of Marketing Research, 23,* 41–49.

Sujan, H. (1996). [Motivation and knowledge development among salespeople]. Unpublished data.

Sujan, H., Sujan, M., & Bettman, J. R. (1988). Knowledge structure differences between more effective and less effective salespeople. *Journal of Marketing Research, 25,* 81–86.

Sujan, H., Sujan, M., & Bettman, J. R. (1991). The practical know-how of selling: Differences in knowledge content between more-effective and less-effective performers. *Marketing Letters, 2,* 367–378.

Sujan H., Weitz, B. A., & Kumar, N. (1994). Learning orientation, working smart, and effective selling. *Journal of Marketing Research, 58,* 39–52.

Szymanski, D. (1988). Determinants of selling effectiveness: The importance of declarative knowledge to the personal selling concept. *Journal of Marketing, 52,* 64–77.

Thompson, J. W. (1973). *Selling: A managerial and behavioral science analysis.* New York: McGraw-Hill.

Tyagi, P. K. (1985). Relative importance of key job dimensions and leadership behaviors in motivating salesperson work performance. *Journal of Marketing, 49,* 76–86.

Wagner, R. K. (1987). Tacit knowledge in everyday intelligent behavior. *Journal of Personality and Social Psychology, 52,* 1236–1247.

Wagner, R. K., Rashotte, C. A., & Sternberg, R. J. (1994, April). *Tacit knowledge in sales: Rules of thumb for selling anything to anyone.* Paper presented at the Annual Meeting of the American Educational Research Association, Washington, DC.

Wagner, R. K., & Sternberg, R. J. (1985). Practical intelligence in real-world pursuits: The role of tacit knowledge. *Journal of Personality and Social Psychology, 48,* 436–458.

Wagner, R. K., & Sternberg, R. J. (1986). Tacit knowledge and intelligence in the everyday world. In R. J. Sternberg & R. K. Wagner (Eds.), *Practical intelligence: Nature and origins of competence in the everyday world* (pp. 51–83). New York: Cambridge University Press.

Walker, O. C., Churchill, G. A., & Ford, N. M. (1977). Motivation and performance in industrial selling: Existing knowledge and needed research. *Journal of Marketing Research, 14,* 156–168.

Weitz, B. A. (1978). The relationship between salesperson performance and understanding of customer decision making. *Journal of Marketing Research, 15,* 501–516.

Weitz, B. A. (1981). Effectiveness in sales interactions: A contingency framework. *Journal of Marketing, 45,* 85–103.

Weitz, B. A., Sujan, H., & Sujan, M. (1986). Knowledge, motivation, and adaptive behavior: A framework for improving selling effectiveness. *Journal of Marketing, 50,* 174–191.

Williams, K. C., & Spiro, R. L. (1985). Communication style in the salesperson-customer dyad. *Journal of Marketing Research, 22,* 434–442.

CHAPTER TEN

Tacit Knowledge in Sales: A Practitioner's Perspective

Scott Gregory
Harcourt Brace

I have been a salesman since I was a kid buying and selling motorcycles. My father used to tell me that I had talent. When I went to college, he told me I could be anything I wanted, but not a salesman. He had been a salesman for many years and didn't want me to have the ups and downs of a commissioned sales job. So I got my degree in psychology. "Great," my father said, "now what are you going to do with a degree in psychology?" I didn't know, but considered going to graduate school and becoming a doctor of psychology. My father thought that was a great idea, so I applied and was accepted into a doctoral program, where I was under the instruction of an old family friend. "What the heck are you doing in here?" he asked. "You made more money in your freshman year than any counselor I know." From the start, he convinced me that although I had the talent to be a psychologist, I would never make the kind of money that I could as a salesman. After visiting with my father, he agreed and was surprised to find that his friend, the doctor, thought of him as an artist.

I am currently a sales representative for Harcourt Brace, a major publisher of college textbooks, but have been selling things all my life, from used cars and motorcycles to stocks and bonds over the phone. My father and grandfather were both in sales, selling cars, trucks, and farm machinery. You could say that the art of selling runs in my family. I use the term *art* of selling in contrast to the *science* of selling, as taught in most books and courses, which consider selling a quantitative activity that anyone can do as long as he or she follows a certain formula or script. On the other hand,

I view sales as an art that, with training and refinement, can be improved on, but, as with musicians or painters, requires talent in order to be successful. As I describe the learning process of selling, I consider the "science of sales"—the outside tools one is taught to sell effectively—as compared to "art of sales"—the inherent traits of a talented salesperson that allow him or her to excel.

My first training as a salesman was from my father, and was short and simple: "Always be honest." He told me, "Nobody will give you awards for always telling your customers the truth, but it only takes one lie or misrepresentation to ruin a good reputation." My father wasn't a college graduate, but he was one of the smartest men I have ever known and was well respected because he was always honest with his customers. His customers invariably became his friends. He also had talent and, as the saying goes, "He could sell ice cubes to Eskimos." I am very grateful to have acquired the talent from him, but the most he ever told me was to be honest and maintain an impeccable reputation for fair dealing. There is one other bit of wisdom I should pass on to those of you who join large companies and sell on commissions: "If the bonus plan is too difficult for a smart person like you to understand, they're screwing you!" This bit of wisdom was as true as his advice on honesty.

Honesty is the base on which I began my own style of selling at age 16, when I opened a used-car lot in Oklahoma City. Over the years, I have been to many seminars and taken several courses on sales. Each of these experiences helped me become a better salesperson, but without talent, I would not have been able to apply these philosophies to my art of selling. This was not always easy, because all those sales classes, books, and seminars present sales as a science, maintaining that anyone who follows their formula can sell and become wealthy. Not to say that these techniques aren't useful; in fact, they are often essential to becoming a good salesperson. But not everyone can master them, just as not every art student can become another Salvador Dali or Andy Warhol.

I don't want to give the impression that there are no rules to selling or that there is no place for academic learning in selling. Quite the contrary, there are many subtle yet essential elements that make a good sales call or presentation. *The 5 Great Rules of Selling* by Percy H. Whiting is an excellent example of what I consider essential elements that the most talented sales artist would be lost without. They are attention, interest, conviction, desire, and close, and are based on sound psychological principles. As Mr. Whiting proclaimed, they work.

Each of us has a unique personality, and how one presents these elements of Mr. Whiting's teaching in practice is largely determined by our perception of the customer, because customers too are unique individuals. The talent or art, therefore, is to be empathetic and flexible enough to read a person and know how and when to utilize these rules. My bachelor of arts in psychology was probably the most useful training of all in preparing me to be a successful salesperson. Everyone who has gotten a bachelor's degree in psychology has asked themselves the same question—"What the heck am I going to do with this?"—but I knew all along that I was honing my listening and counseling skills to improve my success as a salesperson.

Let's walk through the five rules to illustrate the difference between the quantitative approach and the artistic approach to selling by these guidelines.

ATTENTION

You have to get your prospect's attention in order to present your product or service. This might be in the form of advertising, calling on the phone, or knocking on doors. Cold calling, whether by phone or door to door, is probably the most anxiety-provoking method of sales. Calling a stranger to sell something will make most sales rookies run for the nearest employment agency. We've all experienced the unwanted knock at the door or the annoying phone call, usually at the most inconvenient time. The salesperson usually sounds nervous, scared, and almost always canned. A canned presentation is a formal presentation usually memorized or read in a monotonous tone: "Hello, my name is ____, I'm calling because . . . ," usually followed by the prospective customer closing the door or hanging up.

The art of getting someone's attention is in presenting yourself in a manner that gives the prospective customer a reason to listen to what you have to say. The presentation should tell prospects who you are, why you are qualified to be presenting your product or service, and what the most attractive aspects of your product are so that they want to hear more. This takes talent and practice.

When I became a stockbroker, it was very frustrating to phone hundreds of people with a canned sales presentation, getting hung up on, called names, or, even worse, soliciting a bored retiree who wanted to talk to anyone and took up half an hour before telling me he or she had no money. I finally realized that an organized introduction didn't have to sound canned, and that phoning a wealthy part of town beat using the phone book—both good quantitative lessons you can get from any book on sales. I had to get the prospects' attention, and that usually meant getting in touch with their "greed factor." What I came up with sounded something like this: "Hello my name is Scott Gregory with XYZ brokerage and I'm calling today with information on a new issue of tax-free bonds paying 10%. Are you interested in hearing more?" The brokerage firm I worked with was very prestigious, so this introduction validated my credibility. I got the prospects' attention with the greed factor—10% tax-free bonds. I also gave them a polite way out by asking if they wanted to hear more; this put people at ease because they could simply say yes or no. Developing a presentation that is right for the salesperson and delivering it with enthusiasm and conviction takes talent, and is hard to teach.

INTEREST

After getting prospects' attention, a good salesperson gets their interest, like I did with tax-free bonds. The art of getting and keeping a customer's interest is usually much more complex than my phone call example; a truly professional salesperson gets someone's interest most effectively by being honestly interested in the customer's needs and wants. The best way to get sales is to convince people that your product or service best suits their needs, and this can only be done by listening. Listening is an art in itself; it is not just the time between when we stop talking and get to talk again. Whether you are a salesperson, psychologist, doctor, or attorney, listening to the customer will allow you to present your product or service to him or her in a convincing manner.

Many sales courses and books today urge salespeople to ask open-ended questions, like "What is most important to you when choosing a new (car, house, book, computer, etc.)?" These require some thought by the customer, and are designed to elicit a more detailed view of the customer's needs. Others think that closed-ended questions that require a yes or no answer or just a few words work well, such as "How much memory do you think your new computer should have?" Personally, I prefer closed-ended questions as a rule, precisely because they require less thought and keep the customer's mind on the product at hand. They can lead the customer to the conclusion that my product is perfect for his or her needs, which leads nicely to the next rule.

CONVICTION

If the right questions are asked, then convincing the customer that your product is perfect for him or her is easier. In the real world, this is not always so; I have, on occasion, told a client that he or she would be better off with a competitor's product. This may sound like lunacy, but believe me, it pays off in the long run. If you sell an inappropriate product, you will lose a customer forever. But if you are honest and sometimes lose the sale, you will gain the customer's trust, get more sales in the future, and establish a reputation as an honest trader.

As you might have noticed, these rules are not rigid and can be combined and rearranged to suit the situation; that's what an experienced salesperson learns over time from practicing his or her skill. How to improvise, how to read a situation, how to evaluate a prospect, and how to decide when and how to act is not an exact science.

DESIRE

The next step is desire, combining all that has been learned and presented to make your client desire your product or service. The customer might like what you have to sell, but in order to get a sale, this rule states that the customer must desire your product before you can close the sale. I disagree with this entirely. As an investment broker, I often advised my clients to buy life insurance policies, something both necessary for the client and profitable for me. I was quite successful in selling life insurance, but I don't think I ever sold a policy to someone who really "desired" the product—I merely convinced them of the need. They saw the wisdom of the protection and I convinced them to buy by simply going straight to close.

CLOSE

Nowhere in the sales industry is the refinement of the art of selling as finely tuned as in life insurance, which is something virtually everyone admits they need but will not buy unless sold by an excellent closer. I am bringing up the fifth rule, close, and life insurance together for a reason. In all the years I have been selling, I have never made a deal without "closing the sale." This means asking for the order, getting the check, getting the cash, signing on the dotted line, and saying, "Thank you for your business, thank you for your time." It is amazing to me many people barely manage to scrape by as salespeople because they never learned how to close: They *never* ask for the business, but somehow manage to squeak out a living. However, the most important aspect of art of selling is the close. It can happen in the first sentence of a presentation, in the middle, or at the end. The art of the close is refined with practice, and many times the customer finds he or she has committed to a course of action and didn't even realize it.

Let's look back at my cold call example: "The reason I am calling is I have some information on a new tax-free bond issue paying 10%. Would you like to hear more?" That was a close. If the person says yes, then I sold them on listening to more of my pitch. If I ask yes or no questions that are almost certain to elicit a yes, I have made another close and gotten another commitment: "Mr. Jones, do you think $100,000 would take care of your family's needs in the event that something tragic happened to you, or do you think $500,000 would serve their needs better?" These sort of closed-ended questions work better than open-ended ones. Either answer gets me closer to a sale and has the customer committing him- or herself with each answer.

One of the things I have learned that I have not seen in any book is that commitment and nodding yes are contagious. The more you can get a client or even a crowd of people to nod, the more likely they will continue to do so. If you ask the right questions and all the answers are yes, then more times than not, when you ask for the order, the answer will be yes.

As you may have gathered so far, and I will admit freely, I am a professional salesperson, not a writer. I am attempting to put in words something that is as elusive as smoke—what makes the difference between a talented salesperson and one who knows the rules and just can't get it. One cannot know the feeling inside a truly talented speaker feels when he or she has an audience in the palm of his or her hand. That salesperson may have had many courses on public speaking, but it is talent that sets apart great speakers like Martin Luther King, Jr., and President John F. Kennedy. Anyone who had the honor of watching them speak knows that they had something that most public speakers don't.

Once I had a sales manager who talked me into becoming the firm's sales trainer. I was nervous as a cat. I could walk in and sell carpet in the Oval Office and not bat an eye, but the prospect of teaching 10 new rookies how to go out in the city and to sell the way I did scared me to death. It took me awhile to realize that I couldn't do it; I could only teach them the book knowledge ("Do this and this enough times and you will make a sale"). In the sales business, this is known as "Throw enough stuff on the wall and some of it is bound to stick!" After a week or two of frustrating results, I went to my manager and told him about my worries. He said something I will always remember: "Scott, you are an incompetent-competent. You know how to sell better than anyone I have ever known, but you don't know how to teach someone how to do what you do!" Oddly enough, I took this as a compliment. I think that's how he meant it. The short part of this was that he encouraged me to take these rookies, one at a time, out on my sales calls or into my office and show them what I do.

This helped me to become a better salesperson and, even more, to recognize talent. I spent the next 2 weeks letting these rookies watch me make phone calls and ride with me on sales calls. Then I watched them make phone calls and rode with them on sales calls. The one rule I had with them was that they could not talk, other than polite pleasantries, on my sales calls and that I would not talk on their sales calls, even if I could save the sale. Well, I must admit I couldn't shut up and watch a sale go down the drain when I saw a salesman blow his presentation, but we all learned from the experience.

I mentioned earlier that you can learn the rules and techniques of sales just like a would-be artist can learn brush techniques and color patterns but, to make a living, you must have talent and practice. I meant this. What we did in the training experiment was to go to the classroom and practice what we had learned. What frightened the new sales group was that I videotaped our phone calls and practice sales sessions. It was incredible to watch the ones with true talent blossom. I even found mistakes that I was making, and I had been selling for many years.

Let me take the example of two fellows that stood out of the crowd and really set the standard for the two ends of the spectrum (not that there weren't other good salespeople in the group). I'll call them Dave and John (not their real names). Dave had worked for 12 years at a local department store and, even though he had a college degree, he never earned more than $5.00 an hour. He was continually passed over for promotions and decided to try selling stocks and insurance part time to see if he could improve his finances. John, on the other hand, had been selling stocks and bonds as well as insurance for 6 years but was only a marginal producer and barely kept his family fed. Both had read the same books and been on similar sales calls with me. I knew right away that Dave had talent and didn't even know it. John knew what to say but lacked the talent to know how to sell effectively. For example, if a client asked a question out of turn, it totally messed up his presentation.

When we went out in the field, Dave watched my style and saw that I took notes when I was with a client, but that I never took any notes in with me for a sale. On the way back to the car, he commented on this, and I told him, "Dave, I don't use notes because I don't know what I'm going to say until it comes out of my mouth. I don't know what I'm going to sell until I hear what comes out of my client's mouth!" and I laughed. I told Dave that I had learned our products inside and out so I was ready for any question that clients might ask. If I brought notes into the interview, it would give the client the idea I had an agenda other than trying to meet his or her needs. If I walked out with notes, they would feel as though the product I presented was chosen based on their unique circumstances. Dave looked very serious and thought long and hard before saying: "You mean you're the best bull— I've ever known?" and smiled. Of course, he was both right and wrong. I did make up my best sales presentations on the spot, but I was also well prepared and did ask my clients enough questions to know what their needs were. I helped them choose the right product. The difference was that it came naturally to me and Dave was still learning the products and refining his talents.

Unlike Dave, John took meticulous notes when we went into the field together. He wrote down practically every word I said, every question I asked, and everything the client said. Later, John said he didn't know if he could say it like I did. I smiled and told him that was the point; he needed to make it his own—not mine, not some book's, but John's. He never got it.

When we got back to the office, I decided to set up the video camera and have everyone, including me, film our phone calls and practice sales presentations. We had purchased a list of qualified prospects from a local firm, and I passed them out to the group. Dave was the first up and was as nervous as anyone else. All participants had their sales-call sheet, practiced it, and were encouraged to change it to fit their own personality. The call sheet went something like this: "Hello, may I speak to Mr. or Mrs. ____, my name is Dave. I am with the XYZ investment firm here in the city. The reason I'm calling is that I have some important information on a tax-free investment that is currently earning 8%. Are you interested in hearing more about it?"

Well, poor Dave's first card was a foreign name that he couldn't pronounce. Dave didn't notice until the customer answered that the name was Mr. Lang DiQue; you can imagine what happened. The room burst into laughter. Despite his embarrassment, and between laughs, Dave got his message in, got the client interested, and even managed to get an appointment! This is a true story! Later, I went out on the sales call with Dave and his commission was over $3,000 that night. He quit his job at the department store the next day. This was 12 or 14 years ago. I got a phone call from Dave at the end of 1996 and he had won "Salesman of the Year" for the third time. He called to tell me that he wouldn't have made it without my help. It was great to hear, but Dave had talent. Many years and hundreds of thousands of dollars later, he finally believed it. We even had a good long laugh about his first cold call.

Now John, bless him, he did try. John read every book there was on the subject of selling. He even took the Dale Carnegie course twice. John knew it all and didn't mind telling me so. There was nothing about selling I could teach him, yet he still had marginal sales figures. When it was John's turn to get on the phone in front of the camera, he froze. We waited, talked, and finally got him to relax a bit. After all, there were no grades, and the worst that could happen was that the prospect hangs up (and we would just tear up his or her name and throw it in the trash).

Using a video camera in sales practice is as useful as in improving your golf swing. If you can "see" what is wrong, you can fix it. The camera allows you the opportunity to evaluate yourself, make corrections, and even correct the corrections.

Here's how John's call went. He was lucky because he had an easy name like Sam Jones or something. However, what I noticed through the viewfinder and John saw later on the tape was amazing. As John began to speak, his feet began to slide back under his chair, his head and shoulders would begin to hunch down low, and he would pull out his pen from his pocket and begin to play with it subconsciously. As these things happened, John would lose his concentration and misplace his spot on the cold-call sheet. Eventually, he got so flustered that he hung up on the prospect. If you've ever tried cold calling, you know that it's usually the prospect that hangs up first. John was so embarrassed that he left the room. Everyone noticed his body language and posture, and could see how it was affecting his performance. With the encouragement of the other trainees, John returned and watched the tape. He was amazed. He saw how he was moving and the effect it was having on his calls. He immediately wanted to try again and, after four or five tries, he was almost as good as Dave (of course, Dave's calls got easier after Mr. Lang DiQue). We were able to help John with his posture and his confidence, but he always went by the rule book and always sounded "canned," like he was "selling." People don't like to be sold to, they like buying things; a subtle difference, but a huge one in the paychecks of John and Dave. Dave followed the rules but was flexible, used humor when possible, and made his presentations fit his personality. John always sold by rote. If a client ever broke his concentration with a question, it threw him off and he had a hard time getting back on course. But customers don't follow the rule books, and they don't follow a script. That's why a salesperson must have the knack of reading people and changing course in midstream. The last I heard, John had taken a course in heating and air conditioning and was making an excellent living fixing and installing heating and air conditioning systems for people; by the book, I am sure.

The art of selling and the skills learned over years of practicing the trade are changing over time. Consumers are more educated and less likely to be taken in by a pitch than they used to be. Some of the greatest salespeople in the world work in the carnivals at the fair. We've all seen them hawking their T-shirts and games of skill or chance. They live by the timeless saying by P.T. Barnum, "There's a sucker born every minute!" But if you ask these folks, they'll tell you the same thing—people are not as gullible as they once were. Parting people from their money is not as easy as it used to be. They want value for their money, and they expect information, not a sales pitch. They'll go buy a stuffed animal for $5 at the toy store rather than spend $25 trying to win it for their sweetheart. If they're shopping for a new car, they surf the net all night and go into the car dealership knowing more about the product than the salesperson, because they downloaded all the information they needed off the web and even know for how much the manufacturer sold the car to the dealership.

Today's salespersons, if they want to survive, will have to be more like my father—honest and consistent. Honesty, integrity, and longevity will be the foundation of the sales force of the future. People will be buying from you because you stand behind your product, have knowledge, and can be counted on to be there in the future. Whether it's cars, planes, or textbooks, the salespeople of today must rely more and more on product knowledge and the rapidly changing technology of our world, and less and less on sales techniques or pitches. Customers and clients are more likely to call on those salespeople with whom they have dealt in the past—those who know their own products as well as the competition's. Today's customers have the knowledge they need at their fingertips. In order to gain and keep their trust and business, today's salespeople must maintain that knowledge, but also maintain stability.

It used to be said that a good salesperson could sell anything. It was true that most salespeople, including me, had a history of moving from one industry to another, knowing that with talent, we were sure to get by selling anything. Those times are passing. Doctors want to see the same pharmaceutical reps stay with the same firm, so they can be confident in their recommendations and that the reps will be there if they call with questions later. Half of the time car buyers will go back and look for the same salesperson who sold them their last car, if they feel they were dealt with fairly and honestly. College professors want to use a textbook from a publisher whose representative will be there next year to take care of their service needs. It's been a longstanding psychological fact among salespeople the world over that people like to buy from people they know. Thus, new factors are being added to the equation in recent years—stability, product knowledge, and technical expertise.

I still think there will always be a place for talented people in sales, but they will also be technicians, counselors, advisors, and friends to their clientele. They will have to constantly hone their skills and keep up with new technology. My grandfather used to sell Fords, and he used to kid me that, according to Henry Ford, you could get a Model T in any color you wanted as long as it was black! That was in this century but long before television, computers, and fax machines made the consumer a much more knowledgeable prospect. Welcome to the 21st century. It started about 40 years ago!

PART SIX

TEACHING

CHAPTER ELEVEN

Tacit Knowledge in Teaching: Folk Pedagogy and Teacher Education

Bruce Torff
Hofstra University

THE INTUITIVE MIND AND TEACHER EDUCATION

Judith has decided to become a biology teacher, and she knows that she has a lot to learn. After all, an expert teacher draws on a considerable fund of knowledge about teaching, in addition to knowledge of the subject matter (Shulman, 1990). At the same time, Judith does have at least some knowledge about teaching and learning. She has her own ideas about education, ideas that might be called "intuitive" conceptions, to contrast them with the "disciplinary" conceptions to which Judith will be exposed in teacher-education courses. Even people who are untrained in education hold powerful intuitive/tacit conceptions about teaching and learning, and these intuitive conceptions exert a great deal of influence on the way those people think and act with respect to education.

Intuitive conceptions of education often take the form of *tacit knowledge*—knowledge that is rarely openly expressed or stated (Sternberg, Wagner, Williams, & Horvath, 1996). There are many ways to conceptualize the tacit knowledge involved in education, but Judith's case points out an important one, especially for educators charged to teach future generations of teachers. At issue is what happens as Judith learns to become a teacher, as her intuitive/tacit conceptions about education intermingle with the concepts and practices presented in courses in teacher education.

As benefits so fundamental an issue, a large body of literature in teacher education focuses on previously existing ideas that prospective teachers hold about education (e.g., Anderson, 1994; Brookhart & Freeman, 1992;

Bruner, 1996; Hollingsworth, 1989; Kagan, 1992; McLaughlin, 1991; Morine-Dershimer, 1993; Strauss, 1993, 1996; Strauss & Shilony, 1994; Weinstein, 1989; Weinstein, Woolfolk, Dittmeier, & Shanker, 1994; Woolfolk Hoy, 1996; Zeichner & Gore, 1990). Far from being "blank slates" with little knowledge about education, prospective teachers' prior beliefs, expectations, and knowledge influence what they will come to understand, value, and use from courses in teacher education. In essence, there are two pedagogies at hand: a tacit and intuitive one with which students begin, and a disciplinary one provided by the teacher-education curriculum.

Accordingly, effective teacher education depends on a thoughtful understanding of (and response to) the previously existing pedagogical models held by prospective teachers (e.g., Shulman, 1990; Strauss, 1993, 1996; Strauss & Shilony, 1994). However, comparatively little has been written about *how* or *why* prospective teachers come to hold intuitive conceptions about teaching and learning. A theoretical account of the origins and development of these preconceptions may yield insight into the tacit knowledge involved in education. In this chapter, I present such a theoretical account and discuss its implications for teacher education.

The theoretical framework traces teachers' preconceptions about education to cognitive-developmental processes, and in so doing yields a somewhat troubling view of the origins, development, and implications of these preconceptions. At issue is "folk pedagogy"—a set of commonsense ideas about teaching and learning that grows out of our species' "theory of mind" (Astington, 1993; Wellman, 1990) and our culture's "folk psychology" (Bruner, 1990, 1996). On this view, folk pedagogy predisposes individuals to think and teach in particular ways, some of which are inconsistent with the concepts and practices characteristic of expert teaching. As with intuitive conceptions in other domains, folk pedagogy may tend to persist despite successful participation in preservice training programs. Becoming an expert teacher, then, is not simply a matter of gaining new knowledge, nor of replacing inadequate preconceptions in a straightforward manner. Rather, explicit efforts by teachers of educational psychology are needed to counter these uncritically held beliefs, principally by encouraging prospective teachers to engage in activities that facilitate relevant forms of cognitive change. Prospective teachers should be encouraged to confront the scope and import of intuitive conceptions about education, and to experience instructional techniques that fall outside this intuitive understanding.

The following discussion begins with a detailed description of the proposed theoretical framework. I then discuss the educational practices growing out of folk pedagogy, and offer a review of the evidence that folk pedagogy may be persistent despite education and classroom experience. The chapter concludes with a discussion of the implications of the folk pedagogy framework for teacher education.

THEORY OF MIND, FOLK PSYCHOLOGY, AND FOLK PEDAGOGY

Most teachers have had the experience of teaching something to a group of students, only to find that the students' preexisting ideas have interfered with the lesson. These observations are corroborated by a growing body of research in educational psychology. For example, studies in the domain of physics show that students hold fast to misconceived notions about force and agency (notions derivative of "Aristotelian" dynamics), even after successfully passing a course featuring the prevailing "scientific" view of the physical world ("Newtonian" dynamics; diSessa, 1982; McCloskey, Camarazza, & Green, 1980). Even students who perform in an exemplary manner in the course revert to intuitive but inaccurate ideas about physics when tested outside the classroom. In this example, educational outcomes are influenced by intuitive conceptions—preexisting knowledge or knowledge structures that predispose individuals to think in particular ways (and thus constrain behavior). The domain of physics provides the "smoking gun," showing that learning can be impeded, sometimes severely, by intuitive conceptions. Similar phenomena have been noted in a variety of other domains, including biology (e.g., Keil, 1989, 1994), numerical reasoning (e.g., Gelman, 1991; Gelman & Brenneman, 1994), and psychology (or "theory of mind"; e.g., Astington, 1993; Leslie, 1987; Wellman, 1990).

Four themes emerge from this work. First, people employ intuitive conceptions that exert a powerful force on the kind of thinking they do in all sorts of situations, inside and outside the classroom. Second, intuitive conceptions are typically hidden from view and often take the form of assumptions on which patterns of thought are predicated. Third, intuitive conceptions are sometimes (but not always) oversimplified, misleading, or inaccurate. Finally, intuitive conceptions often persist, despite efforts to improve or replace them. For example, Carey and Smith (1993) reported that little success resulted from efforts to initiate conceptual change from misconceived intuitive notions to accurate scientific ones (in terms of epistemological beliefs). Intuitive conceptions are often difficult to dislodge, even by the best of teachers (Gardner, 1991).

At issue in teacher education is "intuitive psychology"—preconceptions about knowledge and learning. What are the origins of these intuitions, and how do they develop? In my view, addressing these questions requires a developmental perspective that encompasses both biological factors (theory of mind) and cultural ones (folk psychology).

In the last two decades, developmental psychologists have focused on the young child's developing understanding of the mind—both his or her own and the minds of others (for a review, see Astington, 1993; Wellman, 1990). To summarize, children benefit from an innate or early-developing theory of mind that predisposes them to particular ideas (or "theoretical beliefs") about knowledge and learning. For example, studies reveal that children as young as 3 years of age are able to determine that another person holds a belief that is false, even when the children have received no environmental input (e.g., instruction or experience) that would equip them with knowledge that such a thing as false belief exists (e.g., Wimmer & Perner, 1983). Similarly, young children come to understand and use such complex mentalistic terms as *think, believe, remember,* and *understand* (Olson, 1997). In essence, the human being is tuned to understand knowledge and learning in particular ways, and cognitive development is guided by these predispositions. Like other people, prospective teachers benefit from an early-developing theory of mind that provides a framework for their understanding of the mind.

Whatever their innate or early-developing intellectual endowment, once children enter the world, they are immersed in a culture. Setting out the program of "cultural psychology" (e.g., Cole, 1971; Rogoff, 1990; Shweder, 1991), Bruner (1990, 1996) argued that the species-specific theory of mind develops in concert with a culturally established folk psychology. Shared among the members of a culture, folk psychology constitutes a set of beliefs about knowledge, learning, thinking, motivation, the "self," and other psychological categories. Folk psychology reflects our commonsense intuitive theories about how minds work—theories that are omnipresent but rarely made explicit in everyday life. Folk psychology concerns how the mind works here and now, and also how the child's mind learns and what makes it grow.

Accordingly, the folk psychology in a society comes equipped with a "folk pedagogy"—a set of ideas concerning what education is and what teachers do. Indeed, people often have strong beliefs concerning how teaching ought to proceed, whether or not they have studied education. Laypersons are typically unable to verbalize their pedagogical beliefs in great detail, but folk pedagogy certainly has a profound effect on behavior. "Watch any mother, any teacher, even any babysitter with a child and you'll be struck by how much of what they do is steered by notions of 'what children's minds are like and how to help them learn,' even if they may not be able to verbalize their pedagogical principles" (Bruner, 1996, p. 46). In a sense, our species' theory of mind and our culture's folk psychology equip us all with intuitive (and often tacit) principles by which to teach. In the following section I describe some of these principles and compare them to the beliefs held by expert teachers.

CHARACTERIZING FOLK PEDAGOGY

Among educational researchers, considerable attention has focused on the preconceptions about education that prospective teachers bring to teacher-education courses (e.g., Anderson, 1994; Brookhart & Freeman, 1992; Bruner,

1996; Hollingsworth, 1989; Kagan, 1992; McLaughlin, 1991; Morine-Dershimer, 1993; Shulman, 1987; Strauss, 1993, 1996; Strauss & Shilony, 1994; Weinstein, 1989; Weinstein et al., 1994; Woolfolk Hoy, 1996; Zeichner & Gore, 1990). An analysis of this literature yields two components of our society's prevailing folk pedagogy, concerning: conceptions of knowledge; and conceptions of education, teaching, and learning.

Folk Conceptions of Knowledge

Folk psychology holds particular views about the nature of knowledge and its source and justification—views that have been described as a "folk" or "commonsense" epistemology (Carey & Smith, 1993; Kuhn, 1989; Olson & Bruner, 1996). On this view, knowledge consists of factual information stored in people's heads or in the tools people employ, such as books and computers. This information is thought to represent objective reality, in the form of facts that reflect "the way things are" in the world (Bruner, 1990, 1996). This objectively held information is "out there" to be known (or not known) by individuals.

Accordingly, studies show that adolescent children often employ a commonsense epistemology in which they see knowledge as a simple collection of many true beliefs that arise unproblematically (and directly) from sensory experiences and inferences (Carey & Smith, 1993). Moreover, there is a growing body of evidence that epistemological views as such often continue into adulthood in all but the most educated persons (Kuhn, 1989). Even the adult participants in Kuhn's studies often failed to distinguish between theory and belief, and to recognize the importance of evidence as a means of providing justification for beliefs. In all, folk epistemology yields a rather simple view of knowledge as a body of objectively held facts, the veracity of which is determined with little regard for supporting evidence.

Folk Conceptions of Teaching and Learning

Emphasis on externally created and objectively held knowledge yields a particular view of the means and ends of education. On this view, what is important about education is the corpus of facts that has been collected about a particular subject. For example, psychology is the body of knowledge that has been collected about human behavior, and a good psychology course is one that brings these facts to the learners' attention. For learning to occur, knowledge has to enter learners' minds, which requires that it be transmitted from the outside world (e.g., from a teacher or book). Effective education, then, results when the teacher explicitly tells or shows learners something about which they presumably know little or nothing (or hold knowledge that is incomplete or incorrect). The term *transmission model* is often used to describe the view of education in which the student's mind is conceived as a vessel to be filled with knowledge that only teachers and texts can provide (e.g., Sternberg & Horvath, 1995; Woolfolk Hoy, 1996).

From the standpoint of folk pedagogy, transmission of content to learners' minds requires that the teacher accomplish three objectives. First, the teacher must present "chunks" of knowledge sized to fit the "opening size" of the student, enabling knowledge to "get through" (Strauss, 1993, 1996; Strauss & Shilony, 1994). The volume of material presented must be matched with what students can manage, and it is important for teachers to regulate the flow of content. Second, for presented content to become new knowledge, the teacher must ensure that it "connects" with existing knowledge (Strauss, 1993, 1996; Strauss & Shilony, 1994). The amount and organization of previous knowledge constrains what (and how much) students can learn, and it is the teacher's job to strive to make explicit the connections between new and previous knowledge. Third, teachers must act in accordance with certain principles of interpersonal interaction. The effective teacher is thought to be fair, kind, flexible, nurturing, knowledgeable, clear, interesting, witty if possible, organized, directive, and eager to boost learners' self-esteem and social skills. On this view, the teacher must strive to engage students—"getting their attention, arousing curiosity, selling ideas, connecting with students' interests, being creative" (Woolfolk Hoy, 1996, p. 42). When learning fails to take place, it is thought to result from difficulties in the students' home background or the teacher's failure to meet one or more of the three objectives. In all, folk pedagogy places much of the burden of education on the teacher.

As for the learner, prospective teachers see children's minds as having doors that open and close, depending on the individual learner's efforts (Strauss, 1993, 1996; Strauss & Shilony, 1994). Learning requires attention and cooperative engagement—if students do with their minds what the teacher requests, then new knowledge will result. For learning to occur, the student must be attentive, follow directions, and practice diligently. Accordingly, folk pedagogy may depict the child as willful and needing correction, or as egocentric and in need of socialization (Bruner, 1996).

These epistemological and educational beliefs outline the folk pedagogy in our culture—the implicit and intuitive basis by which individuals not trained in education make judgments about teaching and learning. The question arises concerning the educational implications of the prevailing folk pedagogy. In what follows I revisit the components of folk pedagogy, with the goal of pointing out the limitations of the educational practices that result from folk pedagogy.

The Limitations of Folk Pedagogy

The distinction is frequently drawn between "externalist" perspectives that emphasize what adults can do for children from outside to foster learning, and "internalist" perspectives emphasizing children's perspectives and capabilities (approaches described variously as constructivist, constructionist, student centered, and child centered). An externalist perspective characterizes the prevailing folk epistemology, which focuses on knowledge that is outside of the learner. As noted, bodies of knowledge are thought to be collected in the mind of educated persons and in tools such as books and computers. On this view, knowledge exists outside the child's mind, in the world; for the child to learn, the knowledge has to get into the child's mind.

A second distinction helps to characterize folk epistemology, and it is that between intersubjectivist and objectivist perspectives of the sources and justification of knowledge. The objectivist perspective holds that knowledge consists of facts that are true because they are consistent with objectively held reality. In this view, objective reality is the source of all knowledge, and all knowledge is justified by its correspondence to this reality. For example, "the Cubs are lousy" is often taken as a fact reflecting the objective reality of the condition of the Cubs, and such an assertion is true or false depending on how accurately it describes the Cubs. In contrast, the intersubjectivist position finds the sources and justification for knowledge in the sociocultural realm. An assertion is accepted as true or false through social interaction—in shared discourses through which members of a culture negotiate the meanings attached to objects, events, and symbols. In this case, the veracity of "the Cubs are lousy" is negotiated by a social group that accepts or rejects it as a true statement.

The folk epistemology, taking the objectivist position, makes no presumption that students should see themselves, or indeed anything, in the same terms in which the teacher does. With emphasis placed on knowledge understood as objective reality, there is no need to formulate a theory of teaching and learning that one can share with learners in order to facilitate their efforts. No special efforts are made to engage learners in a group interaction, except to transmit information from adult to child. And there is no explicit need to have the child think about his or her own thinking and manage "objective" knowledge in relation to negotiated and shared knowledge in a culture. In essence, the folk epistemology portrays schooling as a matter of inculcating objectively held facts.

In folk pedagogy, internalist and objectivist perspectives run parallel—they constitute a commonsense, intuitive epistemology that views knowledge as a collection of externally created, objectively held truths. These beliefs assert themselves in the transmission model of education favored by folk pedagogy. Manifestly external in its focus, the transmission model assumes that the important moment in education occurs when the teacher (or another source) tells or shows the students what they need to know. Moreover, the transmission model rests on the assumption that the knowledge being transmitted is objectively held fact. With no need to involve the learner in the process by which beliefs are justified, truths as such are best transmitted directly. Hence,

TABLE 11.1
Models of Psychology/Pedagogy (Tomasello, Kruger, & Ratner, 1996)

Model of Learner	*Goal of Education*	*Typical Classroom Activities*
1. Child as imitator	Acquisition of know-how	Observation and imitation of a model; drill and practice
2. Child as learner from didactic exposure	Acquisition of propositional knowledge	Lectures; books; worksheets; closed-ended questions; factual-recall activities
3. Child as thinker	Construction of knowledge through critical and reflective thinking	Discovery-learning activities; journals and critique activities; open-ended questions; student-centered assessments
4. Child as collaborator	Participation in intersubjective exchange; self-reflective management of "objective" knowledge	Discussion groups; reciprocal teaching; collaborative-learning activities

a focus on transmission grows out of an externalist and objectivist view of knowledge. In order to see how these views manifest themselves in educational practices, I invoke a taxonomy set out in Table 11.1.

Table 11.1 sets out four ways in which teachers and learners can be viewed, according to a taxonomy presented by Tomasello, Kruger, and Ratner (1993). In Model 1, students are seen as imitative learners and the goal of learning is acquisition of know-how. In a sequence of demonstration and apprenticeship, an adult models a behavior and the learner repeats the behavior until success is achieved. In Model 2, students learn from didactic exposure, based on the notion that students should be presented with facts, principles, and rules that are to be learned, recalled, and applied. Model 2 attributes to children the capacity to acquire new knowledge by employing mental abilities. Model 3 adds reflection, metacognition, and discovery learning to the picture. Students are seen as thinkers, and teachers must therefore concern themselves with what students think and how they arrive at what they know. In Model 4, learners are seen as knowledgeable participants in intersubjective interchanges through which knowledge is created collaboratively. Moreover, they are managers of "objective" knowledge. On this view, learners come to understand that knowledge is not simply *there,* but is humanmade—constructed and negotiated with others, present and past—and students are viewed as participants in the community that undertakes these constructions and negotiations.

Tomasello et al.'s taxonomy helps to characterize the limitations of educational practices resulting from folk pedagogy. In particular, folk pedagogy places a premium on two models (demonstration and didactic exposure), and overlooks the others (reflection and collaboration).

If the goal is transmission of knowledge and acquisition of practical know-how, it follows that demonstration/imitation and didactic exposure would be favored tactics. Because the teacher is viewed as the person with the knowledge, and the goal is for that knowledge to be transmitted, it makes sense to have the teacher serve as a model, and then to have the students imitate the model. For example, when teaching about the quadratic formula, a teacher might complete sample problems on the board, exposing students to the procedures by which these problems are solved, and then give students similar problems to solve on their own. Similarly, folk pedagogy yields a strong focus on didactic exposure. Effective transmission is thought to take place when students listen to lectures and read books that contain the content of the lesson. Overall, folk pedagogy puts the teacher in the roles of demonstrator and instructor, as these are seen as the roles that best facilitate transmission of knowledge from teacher to learner.

Oriented toward imitation and didactic exposure, folk pedagogy largely overlooks the other models of reflection and collaboration. To begin with, folk pedagogy has no truck with reflective thinking or metacognition. If knowledge comes from outside the learner, then his or her thinking processes are virtually irrelevant to learning—the learner's job is to absorb knowledge, not structure things for him- or herself. On this view there is no need for educators to focus on the internal world of the learner, and little reason to organize activities centered on reflection or metacognition, because these tactics entail a higher degree of concern for the individual learner.

It may appear at first blush that two elements of folk pedagogy described previously—regulating the flow and connecting with students' prior knowledge—constitute examples of Model 3, reflection. But on closer analysis, the teacher's role does not extend so far after all. Regulating and connecting do not require that the teacher examine the internal elements of the learner. Rather, the teacher is required only to examine the external element—students' behavior—and use that feedback as a basis for regulating and connecting. Thus, whereas the teacher does focus on the students' responses, there is no impetus for him or her to delve deeper into the learner's intents, theories, and understandings.

There also is little reason for folk pedagogy to involve students in collaboration, as specified in Tomasello et al.'s Model 4. Because knowledge is thought to be objectively held, there is no need to involve the learner in any processes through which knowledge might be collaboratively created, evaluated, and revised. On this view, it can be fun and motivation-boosting to put children in groups, but the real work of schooling takes place when individual students put their minds to the task of learning targeted knowledge. Hence, folk pedagogy does not encourage teachers to use activities in collaborative learning or to encourage students to thoughtfully manage "objective" knowledge presented in texts and other materials. Learners are

TABLE 11.2
Comparison of Folk and Expert Pedagogies

Dimension	*Folk Pedagogy*	*Expert Pedagogy*
Internalist/externalist	Externalist; emphasis on transmission of knowledge and connection to existing knowledge	Internalist/externalist in balance; emphasis on fit of activity to goal, situation, and individual learner
Intersubjectivist/objectivist	Objectivist; emphasis on acquisition of factual knowledge	Intersubjectivist; emphasis on management of "objective" knowledge, collaboration, and metacognition

not asked to participate in discourse processes through which ideas are formulated, discussed, and evaluated. Hence, there is no need to create activities that assemble such groups, or involve students in processes of shared decision making, as is established in Model 4, collaboration.

Taking stock, folk pedagogy is powerful—it gives everyone in our society an intuitive basis by which to make decisions about teaching and learning. Unfortunately, it is limited in significant respects. In particular, it is based on a commonsense epistemology that views knowledge as externally created and objectively held, resulting in educational practices with a strong bias toward imitation and didactic exposure. As such, practices that flow from folk pedagogy are largely inconsistent with those of expert teachers.

There is much debate about what constitutes expert teaching, but Bruner (1996) spoke for many educators by suggesting that expert teaching is characterized by (a) a "constructivist" focus on the internal world of the child, and (b) an "intersubjectivist" perspective in which the child is seen as a knowledgeable collaborator in the community of learners. According to Bruner, the expert teacher functions as instructor and supervisor, but in other ways as well: as facilitator of thought and reflection by individual students, and as collaborator in intersubjective interchanges. Whereas folk pedagogy focuses on bodies of knowledge and gives students a limited role, expert pedagogy focuses on processes of thinking and interaction, and gives students a central role in their own learning (Table 11.2).

Of course, teacher-education courses often focus on the topics of constructivism and collaborative learning—the methods largely overlooked by folk pedagogy. In a sense, these courses facilitate a confrontation (and perhaps a collision) of folk pedagogy stressing imitation and didactic exposure with course content emphasizing constructivism and collaboration. The question is: What happens when prospective teachers' externalist and objectivist perspectives come into contact with the internalist and intersubjectivist ones embodied in much theory and research in education?

PERSISTENCE OF FOLK PEDAGOGY

Adding to the need to take folk pedagogy into account in teacher education, there is the possibility that folk views are persistent despite training and experience, and thus pose a challenge to teacher educators. At issue is the extent to which educational practices are "premised on a set of folk beliefs about learners' minds, some of which may have worked advertently or inadvertently against the child's welfare" (Bruner, 1996, pp. 49–50).

Strauss and colleagues provided evidence that teachers' "pedagogical content knowledge" tends to remain unchanged despite preservice training and years of experience in the classroom (Strauss, 1993, 1996). Characterizing teachers' naive views as a mechanistic approach to learning, Strauss and colleagues reported that both espoused and in-use pedagogical content knowledge are similar in teachers with 1 and 10 years of experience. Pedagogical content knowledge, Strauss and colleagues concluded, can be quite persistent.

The findings reported by Strauss and colleagues are consistent with the folk pedagogies framework, which predicts that teachers' preconceptions stem not from inadequate knowledge, but at a deeper level—from deeply rooted biological and cultural forces guiding the development of thought. As such, the framework predicts that folk pedagogies are likely to be robust and resistant to change due to preservice/inservice training or classroom experience.

First, it is not the case that teacher education replaces, for once and for all, the folk view with the disciplinary one. In theory, folk psychology/pedagogy is pervasive—it is infused into our thinking about education and professional training. After all, people remain members of their culture, even after training that counters certain beliefs held by laypersons in that culture. Folk pedagogy is strongly enculturated before teacher training begins, and its logic and practices remain in the background, even among the most educated and experienced teachers. As such, folk conceptions function as a largely tacit "default mode" for teachers' reasoning about education.

Second, as a practical matter, competition between folk and expert pedagogies emerges, and temporary or permanent shifts to the default mode seem difficult to resist. To begin with, nobody is perfect; under conditions of stress, teachers tend to shift toward the transmission of knowledge. Moreover, all manner of environmental conditions push toward the default mode. For example, when an introductory psychology course is enrolled with 500 students, the teacher's options are severely limited. In general, educational practices stemming from folk pedagogy are often deeply embedded in institutional structures. Only an institution that accepts (if tacitly) the folk model would put 500 students in a room.

Activities that draw on folk pedagogy are often easier to pull together than are activities stressing intersubjective and internalist viewpoints. Doyle and Carter (1996) noted that the topics in educational psychology often comprise abstractions that are framed in terms of principles and strategies, whereas teacher knowledge is typically framed in terms of specifics such as events and stories. Folk pedagogies seem grounded and concrete, as if to speak with the voice of common sense. Applying folk pedagogy (e.g., in lesson planning) is rarely difficult, at least by comparison with the abstractions and formalisms of disciplinary approaches. For a variety of reasons, folk pedagogy tends to remain in place even after preservice and inservice training, and as such it merits the full attention of teacher educators. The following section considers the implications of the folk pedagogies framework for teacher education.

FOLK PEDAGOGY AND TEACHER EDUCATION

The theoretical position taken in this chapter echoes Anderson et al. (1995) and others, who suggested that prospective teachers' conceptions about education be taken into account in teacher education. What the folk pedagogy framework adds is the insight that these preconceptions are rooted in biological and cultural processes that guide the development of thought. As such, folk pedagogy constitutes a deep background to the everyday practices of the teacher; it likely never disappears, even in the most expert practitioners. Unfortunately, folk pedagogy provides an inadequate basis for educational practices. From this perspective, teacher educators should take steps explicitly to address the enduring problems caused by intuitive conceptions.

In particular, what's needed are interventions that address the root causes. Interventions that simply encourage teachers to use Models 3 and 4 of Tomasello et al.'s taxonomy (reflection and collaboration) may not have lasting effects, because they do not address the underlying epistemological beliefs that drive the intuitive pedagogy. Prospective teachers may *appear* to learn to value reflection and collaboration, and they may even believe that they have achieved a better understanding, but in actuality be inclined to revert later on. What's needed is to encourage prospective teachers' epistemological development.

Promising initiatives have been put forth by Strauss (1993), Blumenfeld, Hicks, and Krajcik (1996), and Renninger (1996). These projects may not have been designed with the notion of folk pedagogy in mind, but they nonetheless employ strategies that seem likely to encourage prospective teachers to confront and critique folk pedagogy and to integrate it with the content of courses in teacher education. Strauss (1993) and colleagues developed methods for encouraging prospective teachers to examine their own ideas about children's minds and learning. Similarly, Blumenfeld et al. (1996) employed specially designed activities in instructional planning: "Making explicit what often remains implicit, preservice teachers can confront and reexamine their assumptions and understandings about educational psychology" (p. 51). Finally, Renninger (1996) described assignments that encourage students to engage in self-reflection about the principles that govern their thinking about teaching.

According to the folk pedagogies view, a key factor in the success of these initiatives is students' reflection on and questioning of folk epistemology/pedagogy, and the externalist and objectivist perspectives that these entail. In what follows I describe three steps that can be taken to encourage prospective teachers to engage in the reflection and questioning needed to move beyond folk pedagogy.

Confronting Folk Pedagogy. From the perspective of the folk pedagogy framework, a key goal in teacher education is to put teachers into close contact with their own intuitive conceptions about education. In particular, there is a need to have prospective teachers (a) encounter, reflect on, critique, and evaluate the folk pedagogy; and (b) maintain awareness of folk pedagogy as the backdrop against which educational decisions are made, even by expert teachers.

Of course, it is not going to help to provide prospective teachers with formal instruction in epistemology, and it would be ironic indeed to teach about this topic only through demonstration and didactic exposure. Rather, it makes sense to start with the learners' perspective—the transmission-style educational practices that grow out of folk pedagogy. Teacher-education programs should help prospective teachers to see for themselves what is and is not gained from transmission-style instruction.

These objectives can be accomplished by encouraging prospective teachers to engage in reflective thinking in relation to closely observed incidents of learning. Engaging prospective teachers in preservice fieldwork is a common and useful strategy that can be adapted to address the problems caused by folk pedagogy in the classroom. In this instance, it can be beneficial to charge prospective teachers to teach a body of content, ask a set of questions, and write a report about the lesson. The goal is to involve teachers in activities that reveal how little is learned, and how shallow and inert the learning may be, when learners are simply told or shown. Procedures such as these work to put teachers into direct contact with the shortcomings of transmission-style instruction.

Another way to foster awareness of folk pedagogy is to make it an explicit focus in the teacher-education classroom. To help students develop a sense of the pervasive nature of folk pedagogy, students can be asked to keep a journal in which they articulate and analyze their intuitive responses. The result of these efforts to shine the spotlight on folk pedagogy is the development of self-reflective teachers who are aware of their own patterns of thinking and who are inclined to question the assumptions underlying their intuitive judgments about teaching and learning.

Experiencing the Utility of Alternative Instructional Modes. As proponents of constructivism have been arguing for decades, prospective teachers need to recognize that internalist and externalist perspectives must come into balance. This insight does not require a broad shift from an externalist perspective to an internalist one; instead, it requires prospective teachers to gain an awareness of the need to focus on the learner's thoughts and intentions, although not to the exclusion of the curriculum at hand.

From the standpoint of the folk pedagogies framework, a laudable goal is to have teachers experience the instructional uses of reflective thinking and metacognition. In terms of fieldwork, it is useful to ask prospective teachers to teach through reflection and write a field report, encouraging them to consider the diagnostic power of focusing on the students' intentions. Engaging students with alternative assessments (such as portfolios) can also help to enhance prospective teachers' understanding of reflection and metacognition. Portfolios are student-selected collections of classroom work that serve as a celebration of growth and a vehicle for reflection. Often, students collect three or four pieces of work into a portfolio, which they review with teachers, parents, and peers. Portfolios have the added benefit of helping prospective teachers to understand the implications of constructivism, as they focus on individual construction of meaning/knowledge and promote questioning and listening skills. Overall, fieldwork and alternative assessment activities can help prospective teachers to learn firsthand how reflection and metacognition work, and to develop the skills necessary to foster reflective thinking in their students.

Similar tactics can be used to help prospective teachers understand the instructional value of collaborative learning and the processes of intersubjective exchange. Here the goal is to have the teacher engage in fieldwork to experience the group processes through which people teach each other and themselves. Teachers need to learn that collaborative learning is not simply a vehicle for teaching social skills, but also a vital process through which knowledge is constructed collectively. In so doing, teachers will recognize that knowledge is humanmade, socially negotiated, and revisable. A key goal in the classroom, then, is to involve students in the intersubjective interchanges through which ideas are posited and evaluated. Moreover, teachers need to examine the processes through which students manage objective knowledge (i.e., information regarded as fact in a community) facts shared in relation to their own (personal) knowledge (Bruner, 1996). fieldwork in collaborative learning often involves assigning prospective teachers to teach a set of lessons to a group, and to engage in close observation of collaborative problem finding, problem solving, and reflective thinking. Activities such as these help teachers to see their role as one of facilitation.

Matching the Curriculum Objective and Instructional Mode. The first two steps described previously aim to give teachers a strong sense of the nature and limitations of folk pedagogy, and of the benefits of instructional modes that transcend these limits. The final step involves helping teachers to learn how to deploy the four different instructional styles as they are matched appropriately to the curriculum objective at hand. At issue is the correspondence between the "what" and the "how" of teaching, which has been widely recognized as a hallmark of expert teaching (Bruner, 1996). Such an objective involves creating teacher-education activities that encourage prospective teachers to analyze curriculum goals (the "what" of teaching). This analysis results in the selection of an instructional mode (or set of modes), with the goal of employing the modes that best suit the subject matter.

Different topics require different instructional modes, and all four modes play a useful role. If one is teaching how to make a layup in basketball, for example, an activity stressing demonstration and imitation might be very effective, given the exigencies of teaching about complex physical movements such as those pressed into service in basketball. If one is teaching about the stars that are nearest the Earth, however, the strategy of didactic exposure seems promising. How far are these stars? What are their names? How long would it take to get there at 55 mph? A well-written newspaper article answering these questions might be used by a teacher employing didactic exposure to teach effectively about the subject at hand.

In other cases, the strategy of reflection may be the wiser choice. For example, the teacher might be required to teach a unit in a social studies class on the Civil War. Why did the war last so long? Students exposed to the military movements and decisions made on both sides might well be engaged in critical thinking about those movements and decisions, reaching conclusions of their own (e.g., military ineptitude prolonged the war). Moreover, students may well learn about their own learning (e.g., "I learn a lot when I get to study a map"). Nowhere in the learning environment are these conclusions drawn explicitly, yet the students put the pieces together themselves and build new knowledge through reflective thinking.

Finally, there are instances in which activities stressing collaboration constitute an appropriate instructional regime. An example is a language arts class on the symbols and messages in Hemingway's novel *For Whom the Bell Tolls*. Many expert teachers would opt not to provide students with the opinions of literary critics, but instead to involve the group in a discussion in which the students put forth and debate their own ideas. What is the significance of Hemingway's decision to have the narrative begin and end with the protagonist hiding on the forest floor, with the enemy approaching? Answers to such questions are developed through intersubjective exchanges in which students pose ideas, evaluate their merit, and move ahead with socially shared judgments.

By examining curriculum objectives and matching them to instructional modes, prospective teachers learn how the folk and expert pedagogies diverge in the context of everyday classroom activities. In essence, this step helps teachers to develop the classroom skills that grow out of the educational practices of expert educators, rather than the practices of folk pedagogy.

In sum, I have proposed three steps toward making teacher education more responsive to prospective teachers' folk conceptions about education. In essence, the plan works in a bottom-up fashion, by addressing first the transmission view of education set out by the folk view, and then considering its underlying epistemological beliefs. In so doing, the folk pedagogy in our culture becomes an explicit focus in courses in teacher education. To that end, a key aspect of the tacit knowledge that operates in education is brought to light and examined, for the betterment of teaching and learning.

CONCLUSION

Judith, the biology teacher in training, enters her teacher-education program with plenty of ideas of her own about teaching and learning. When prospective teachers study education, their learning is guided not just by topics presented in teacher-education courses, but also by tacit knowledge about the mind and about education—intuitive conceptions inherent in our species' theory of mind and our society's folk psychology. The resulting folk pedagogy is not simply a set of wrongheaded ideas that can be disabused easily through direct instruction. Indeed, intuitive conceptions as such can be enduring. Prospective teachers ought to be encouraged to encounter and evaluate these uncritically held beliefs, and to develop a greater understanding of the limitations and pervasiveness of folk pedagogy. Moreover, they can be encouraged to adopt at least two new perspectives: an internalist (constructivist) approach, focusing on the student's thoughts and intents; and an intersubjectivist perspective, focusing on collaborative processes through which knowledge is created and negotiated.

Thoughtful teacher education thus strives to accomplish the same goals that it requires prospective teachers to pursue. In teacher-education courses, we teach prospective teachers to adopt internalist and intersubjectivist perspectives; effectively the same is done by teacher educators who remain aware of (and responsive to) the intuitive conceptions held by prospective teachers. Whatever the subject matter, a key objective is to understand the student's mind and move ahead with instruction that is based on that understanding. "Once we recognize that a teacher's conception of the learner shapes the instruction he or she employs, then equipping teachers (or parents) with the best available theory of the child's mind becomes crucial. And in the process of doing that, we also need to provide teachers with some insight about their own folk pedagogies that guide their teaching" (Bruner, 1996, p. 49). In the end, Judith is best served by teacher-education practices that strive to understand and teach the intuitive mind.

ACKNOWLEDGMENTS

The work reported herein was supported under the Educational Research and Development Centers Program, PR/Award R206R50001, as administered by the Office of Educational Research and Improvement, U.S. Department of Education. The author wishes to thank Talia Ben-Zeev, Howard Gardner, Joseph Horvath, Robert J. Sternberg, and Sidney Strauss for their comments.

REFERENCES

Anderson, L. (1994, October). *Reforming our courses and rethinking our roles.* Paper presented at the meeting of the Midwestern Association for the Teaching of Educational Psychology, Chicago.

Anderson, L., Blumenfeld, P., Pintrich, P., Clark, C., Marx, R., & Peterson, P. (1995). Educational psychology for teachers: Reforming our courses, and rethinking our roles. *Educational Psychologist, 30*(3), 143–158.

Astington, J. (1993). *The child's discovery of the mind.* Cambridge, MA: Harvard University Press.

Blumenfeld, P., & Anderson, L. (Eds.). (1996). Teaching developmental psychology [Special issue]. *Educational Psychologist, 31*(1).

Blumenfeld, P., Hicks, L., & Krajcik, J. (1996). Teaching educational psychology through instructional planning. *Educational Psychologist, 31*(1), 51–62.

Brookhart, S., & Freeman, D. (1992). Characteristics of entering teacher candidates. *Review of Educational Research, 62,* 37–60.

Brown, A. (1994). The advancement of learning. *Educational Researcher, 23*(8), 4–12.

Brown, A., & Campione, J. (1990). Communities of learning and thinking, or a context by any other name. In D. Kuhn (Ed.), *Developmental perspectives on teaching and learning thinking skills* (pp. 108–126). Basel, Switzerland: Karger.

Bruner, J. (1990). *Acts of meaning.* Cambridge, MA: Harvard University Press.

Bruner, J. (1996). *The culture of education.* Cambridge, MA: Harvard University Press.

Carey, C. (1985). *Conceptual change in childhood.* Cambridge, MA: Bradford/MIT.

Carey, S., & Smith, C. (1993). On understanding the nature of scientific knowledge. *Educational Psychologist, 28*(3), 235–251.

Cole, M. (1971). *The cultural context of learning and thinking.* New York: Basic.

diSessa, A. (1982). Unlearning Aristotelian physics: A study of knowledge-based learning. *Cognitive Science, 6*(1), 37–75.

Doyle, W., & Carter, K. (1996). Educational psychology and the education of teachers: A reaction. *Educational Psychologist, 31*(1), 51–62.

Gardner, H. (1991). *The unschooled mind.* New York: Basic.

Gelman, R. (1991). First principles organize attention to and learning about relevant data: Number and animate-inanimate distinction as examples. *Cognitive Science, 14,* 79–106.

Gelman, R., & Brenneman, K. (1994). First principles can support both universal and culture-specific learning about number and music. In E. Hirschfeld & S. Gelman (Eds.), *Mapping the mind: Domain specificity in cognition and culture* (pp. 369–390). New York: Cambridge University Press.

Greeno, J. (1989). A perspective on thinking. *American Psychologist, 44*(2), 134–141.

Hollingsworth, S. (1989). Prior beliefs and cognitive change in learning to teach. *American Educational Research Journal, 26,* 160–189.

Kagan, D. (1992). Implications of research on teacher belief. *Educational Psychologist, 27,* 65–90.

Keil, F. (1989). *Concepts, kinds, and cognitive development.* Cambridge, MA: MIT Press.

Keil, F. (1994). The birth and nurturance of concepts by domains: The origins of living things. In E. Hirschfeld & S. Gelman (Eds.), *Mapping the mind: Domain specificity in cognition and culture* (pp. 234–254). New York: Cambridge University Press.

Kuhn, D. (1989). Children and adults as intuitive scientists. *Psychological Review, 96*(4), 674–689.

Leslie, A. (1987). Pretense and representation: The origins of "theory of mind." *Psychological Review, 94,* 412–426.

McCloskey, M., Camarazza, A., & Green, B. (1980). Curvilinear motion in the absence of external forces: Naive beliefs about the motion of objects. *Science, 210,* 1141–1149.

McLaughlin, J. (1991). Reconciling care and control: Authority in classroom relationships. *Journal of Teacher Education, 40*(3), 182–195.

Morine-Dershimer, G. (1993). Tracing conceptual change in preservice teachers. *Teaching and Teacher Education, 9,* 15–26.

Newman, D., Griffin, M., & Cole, M. (1989). *The construction zone.* New York: Cambridge University Press.

Olson, D., & Bruner, J. (1996). Folk psychology and folk pedagogy. In D. Olson & N. Torrance (Eds.), *Handbook of education in human development* (pp. 9–27). Oxford, England: Blackwell.

Renninger, K. (1996). Learning as the focus of the educational psychology course. *Educational Psychologist, 31*(1), 35–40.

Rocklin, T. (1996). Variations in excellence: Context matters in reforming our courses and rethinking our roles. *Educational Psychologist, 31*(1), 35–40.

Rogoff, B. (1990). *Apprenticeship in thinking.* Cambridge, MA: Harvard University Press.

Shuell, T. (1996). The role of educational psychology in the preparation of teachers. *Educational Psychologist, 31*(1), 5–14.

Shulman, L. (1990). Reconnecting foundations to the substance of teacher education. *Teachers College Record, 91*(3), 300–310.

Shweder, R. (1991). *Thinking through culture.* Cambridge, MA: Harvard University Press.

Sternberg, R., & Horvath, J. (1995). A prototype view of expert teaching. *Educational Researcher, 24*(6), 9–17.

Sternberg, R., Wagner, R., Williams, W., & Horvath, J. (1996). Testing common sense. *American Psychologist, 50*(11), 912–927.

Strauss, S. (1993). Teachers' pedagogical content knowledge about children's minds and learning: Implications for teacher education. *Educational Psychologist, 28*(3), 279–290.

Strauss, S. (1996). Confessions of a born-again constructivist. *Educational Psychologist, 31*(1), 15–22.

Strauss, S., & Shilony, T. (1994). Teachers' models of children's minds and learning. In E. Hirschfeld & S. Gelman (Eds.), *Mapping the mind: Domain specificity in cognition and culture* (pp. 455–473). New York: Cambridge University Press.

Taylor, C., & Nolen, S. (1996). A contextualized approach the teaching teachers about classroom-based assessment. *Educational Psychologist, 31*(1), 77–88.

Tomasello, M., Kruger, A., & Ratner, H. (1993). Cultural learning. *Behavioral and Brain Sciences, 16*(3), 495–511.

Weinstein, C. (1989). Teacher education students' perceptions of teaching. *Journal of Teacher Education, 40*(2), 53–60.

Weinstein, C., Woolfolk, A., Dittmeier, L., & Shanker, U. (1994). Protector or prison guard: Using metaphors and media to explore student teachers' thinking about classroom management. *Action in Teacher Education, 16*(1), 41–54.

Wellman, H. (1990). *The child's theory of mind.* Cambridge, MA: Bradford/MIT.

Wimmer, H., & Perner, J. (1983). Beliefs about beliefs: Representation and constraining function of wrong beliefs in young children's understanding of deception. *Cognition, 13,* 103–128.

Woolfolk Hoy, A. (1996). Teaching educational psychology: Texts in context. *Educational Psychologist, 31*(1), 35–40.

Zeichner, K., & Gore, J. (1990). Teacher socialization. In W. Houston (Ed.), *Handbook of research on teacher education* (pp. 329–349). New York: Macmillan.

CHAPTER TWELVE

Expertise in Teaching

Jim Minstrell
Mercer Island School District
Mercer Island, WA
(former teacher)

On the surface, nearly everyone knows what goes into good teaching: knowing the subject matter, knowing and relating to the students, appropriately implementing a good curriculum, and knowing how to manage the classroom and students. Most citizens believe they know a lot about teaching, having spent 8 or 12 or many more years in classrooms with teachers. Then, if they get a chance to be a "teacher," especially in the precollege classroom, they find the situation to be a whole lot more complicated than they expected. So, what makes good teaching so difficult? What are the elements of professional expertise in teaching, and how can that expertise be engendered in preservice and inservice teachers?

THE PROBLEM

Teaching is an ill-defined problem where "every student–teacher interaction can change the teacher's goals and choice of operators" (Bruer, 1993, p. 32). There are multiple solutions that depend on the prior experiences, knowledge, interests, and motivation of the students who are present. The solutions also depend on the teacher's background, knowledge of subject matter, understanding of learning, knowledge of the curriculum activities available, and prior experiences in the learning and teaching of the subject matter. These factors are changing from moment to moment. Expert teaching requires seeing these apparently messy situations as problems. However, the problems of real-world practice, including teaching, do not present themselves as well-formed structures to which people can apply a ready set of technical procedures. Essentially, teachers have to construct the problem out of the particulars of the situation and from familiar theoretical ideas and techniques (Schön, 1987). As conditions of the situation change, then other theoretical assumptions and practical techniques are brought into the construction of the problem. Teachers need to become aware of the evolution of the problem. Expert teachers, like expert problem solvers in any discipline, need to think of "problem solving itself as consisting of successive reformulations of an initial problem" (Kilpatrick, 1987, p. 125).

The simple model of problem solving as initial state, goal state, and intervention to move from initial to goal state is too simplistic to be an adequate model of a solution for teaching problems. The teaching-learning process is too complex to completely specify in advance. Most significant changes in instruction will occur by helping teachers learn to address and reconstruct teaching problems and to make decisions informed by past experience and by research (e.g., analyses of children's knowledge). The expert teacher can think flexibly about problems in teaching. Attempting to program teachers to perform in a particular way based on preset problems is not productive (Carpenter, 1988).

MOVING TOWARD SOLUTION: NEED FOR A COHERENT THEORETICAL VIEW OF TEACHING AND LEARNING

There are too many different teaching situations for us to regard teaching as situation specific. In addition to learning procedural solutions to teaching problems, teachers need to know and recognize the conditions under which the technical procedures apply.

This suggests a need for teachers to have and operate under a coherent vision of the nature of teaching and learning; to have a theoretical view of teaching and learning in a particular discipline. The theoretical view may be implicit within the teacher's mind, but without that coherent view, teachers present an inconsistent picture of learning to students. If students are to learn one thing but be assessed on another—or hear the teacher say one thing is important but see the teacher do something inconsistent—then the lack of coherence is a source of conflicts with students and therefore an impediment to learning (Tobin & LeMaster, 1992).

What is the tacit component to a coherent set of beliefs and knowledge about teaching and learning, and how might that tacit knowledge be developed in the professional teacher? First, I discuss the tacit knowledge in each of the following: knowledge of the nature of the subject matter, knowledge of the nature of learning, knowledge about learning and teaching the subject matter to children, and knowledge about managing the learning environment.

Finally, I discuss the development of professional expertise through personal reflection, relationship with a mentor, participation in a professional network, and the adoption of a personal inquiry perspective on practice of teaching.

The discussion to follow is grounded in over 30 years of teaching, mostly of science and mathematics. Although I have taught for short periods from preschool through graduate school and beyond, most of my experience has been at the high school level. In spite of these limitations to my experience, I am encouraged by other teachers in other disciplines and at other levels who suggest that most of what is written here applies in their classrooms as well. With that caution, I offer my own view in what follows.

TACIT KNOWLEDGE IN TEACHING

Understanding the Nature of the Discipline

As a teacher, I need to have *command of the nature of the discipline* as well as knowing its products. What is the discipline about? What are its central questions? What are the processes and the ideational products? What does it mean to come to know something in that discipline (McDiarmid, Ball, & Anderson, 1989)?

When I am developing a curriculum unit, I identify the central ideas that I want to address in order to create a complete story line. Having a story line—a possible route through the "territory" of the subject matter—provides some focus and rationale for what we are doing and where it will lead us. There can be lots of opportunities for wandering in and out of related ideas and processes along the way—for being responsive to students' particular interests and discoveries—but we need to know the territory of the discipline well enough so we don't get lost in the quagmire of just doing a collection of fun activities. Teachers often get stuck with the focus on memorizing the products and procedures without making explicit the nature of the discipline that produces them.

I also map out the territory of related ideas. That will give me some ideas of how far to allow my co-travelers to wander without losing a main trail of experience and understanding. Later, as I give students some freedom to explore additional aspects of the territory, I need to distinguish between the critical issues they must definitely visit and explore and the additional ideas that are all right for us to spend time visiting (ideas that are somewhat related to the central ideas), but that won't take us too far afield from the main story line. Novice teachers, in an effort to allow students freedom to explore, may miss the core ideas that all students are supposed to have sufficient opportunity to learn.

I want students to know how *pervasively the ideas of the discipline apply* to the world around us, real and imagined. What are the typical applications for these aspects of the discipline? How does one know or decide when these ideas and reasonings apply? What are the characteristics of relevant situations? The discipline is not simply a set of principles and procedures that get applied when we are told to apply them; knowing the nature of the discipline implies that we know and can recognize the conditions under which the ideas apply. What is the extent to which the ideas and processes will generalize? How broadly? A large proportion of beginning and experienced teachers I have met do not have this sort of understanding of the nature of the discipline. This is true in spite of the fact that they got A's in their major courses.

Great teaching requires the expertise of the subject matter specialist. On the other hand, there are those (in the general public, including academic professionals) who believe deep knowledge of the subject matter is the only thing necessary to be a great teacher. It is not.

Understanding the Nature of Learning

Early in my career, I focused on what *I* did as a teacher. I could have done what I did regardless of which students were in the class, or even whether there were any students in the class. I taught "the course." Now, I focus on the learners and their learning. Expertise in teaching requires knowing a lot about learning, and that knowledge about learning needs to be part of the coherent view of teaching and learning that is a characteristic of expertise in teaching.

Students come to my classes with experiences from which they have constructed an understanding. They come with *preconceptions*—conceptual understandings and reasoning strategies that have served them well so far. Yet much or their thinking is problematic. If these initial understandings are not addressed, there may be little change in their understanding and little residual learning. If I simply set aside their initial thinking and just teach the formal ideas, students may exit my class with two sets of ideas: their personal understanding of science and their school science—which to their view doesn't apply to the real world. As a teacher I need to know what preconceptions about the subject matter my students have, and I need to possess techniques for determining them. The identification, engagement, and management of students' preconceptions are discussed in the section on pedagogical knowledge.

When presented with a novel problematic situation, students tend to look to the *surface features* for cues as to what learned ideas and procedures to apply: "What other problem have I done that has the features of this one?" In physics, students look for features like inclined planes or pulleys rather than for possibly relevant principles such as forces or energy conservation (Chi, Feltovich, & Glaser, 1981). For example, when two bodies interact, as in a collision, students tend to attend to features such as which one is moving faster, which is bigger, and which will sustain the greater damage, rather than considering equal and opposite action and reaction forces (Camp & Clement, 1994; Minstrell, 1992; Minstrell & Matteson, 1991).

Learning is an active process. Confronted with the phenomena around them, students will learn. But left on their own, much of the learning will be situation specific. It takes guidance and a "minds-on" approach to come away with the abstract principles that can generalize across situations. Although active, the learning system is basically conservative. That is, learners exhibit "confirmation bias," wherein they will observe the least they need to and focus on the aspects that are consistent with present beliefs and ideas, typically dismissing the rest. If learners believe that the object that inflicts the greater amount of damage exerts the larger force, then they will see the greater damage and infer the greater force, thus comfirming their expectations. Reflection on phenomena and experiences needs to be fostered.

Although parsimony is valued in science, learners tend to be overly parsimonious in their thinking. They typically reason on the basis of a single factor related to an effect, rather than isolate and accumulate the effects of multiple factors. For example, they may know both of the following principles: (a) "the greater the force (for a given time period) on a given object, the greater the resulting motion"; and (b) "the greater the mass of an object (for a given force applied for a given time period), the less the resulting motion." Yet, for problems involving heavier and lighter falling bodies, they will typically apply one or the other principle (usually the first), concluding that the heavy and light objects will get to the floor in substantially different amounts of time. Thus, they conclude that "heavier falls faster" on the basis of the single principle "a bigger force will produce a bigger motion" (Minstrell, 1982, 1992). The appropriate application of scientific principles requires that both be considered at the same time, with each compensating for the effects of the other, and yielding the result that the bodies fall together (assuming air resistance is not a significant factor).

When assisting learners it is also helpful to note that they have *limited working-memory capacity*. To allow learners to cope with capacity limitations, they will need opportunities and representational formalisms to "off-load" details of a problematic situation. Pictures, words, graphs, tables, equations, and the like can capture a lot of detail, but the learner needs to know how to construct and interpret these representations, which become "objects" to learn about in their own right. Some physics teachers will shortcut learning by having students memorize, for example, that the slope of a position-versus-time graph is the velocity. Students may learn to "play the game" of using the representation of slope to get the velocity, but they may not understand velocity or the mathematical idea of slope and how these concepts relate to each other. Expert teachers are careful not to concentrate on the learning of representations so much that they forget why the representation can help learners make sense of the situation. The representation, if understood, can become a method of "chunking" detail and reducing load on working memory. For example, graphs, if developed for understanding, can be used to summarize a lot of situational information in a way that makes that information easy to remember.

To be a great teacher takes more than discipline knowledge and knowledge of learning. The teacher also needs practical and technical knowledge related to effects of the interaction between students and specific curriculum activities in the discipline.

Pedagogical Knowledge in Teaching the Discipline

How do expert teachers decide what activity to do when, and how do they know what effects it might or might not have on students? What teaching strategies will be implemented, why, and to what expected effects? How will diagnostic assessment be incorporated, and what effects will it have on choosing or adapting instruction? Shulman (1987) referred to these sorts of questions and issues, and the associated expertise, as "pedagogical content knowledge."

This pedagogical expertise in teaching, and the acquisition of pedagogical knowledge related to the teaching of the particular discipline at an appropriate level for the given class of learners, generally requires teaching experience. More specifically, this expertise involves choosing appropriate, achievable learning goals, implementing curriculum activities that address those goals, questioning and discussing techniques to foster student thinking, implementing assessments that guide learning and inform instruction, and managing the environment to foster learning.

The classrooms of expert teachers are complex environments of emergent goals and decisions. These teachers integrate what they know about their students' thinking with goals for their understanding of the content and skills of the discipline. As particular learning needs are identified, these teachers choose or adapt lessons known from their past experiences to address these needs and promote the desired understanding. Then, expert teachers assess for appropriate learning, identify the next goal, design the next instruction, and so on.

In the section to follow, I first discuss issues of curriculum design, and then consider creating and maintaining an environment for inquiry.

Curriculum Design

Although many teachers allow the textbook to dictate the design of their curriculum, expert teachers typically have a story line that is consistent with their purposes. In my own work, these purposes include implementing a curriculum to foster development of students' conceptual understanding and reasoning (Minstrell, 1989). I need to be able to monitor my students' initial and developing understanding and choose or design activities that perturb problematic understanding and build more powerful understanding. All of these goals require a recognizable intellectual story line for building students' understanding.

Diagnosing Students' Thinking. At the beginning of units of study, I attempt to elicit students' thinking with one or more questions particularly designed to address the issues and ideas of the coming unit. Based on research on students' naive conceptions, I have collected and grouped students' responses and associated them with apparent understanding and reasoning. Each particular characterization of students' understanding I call a *facet of students' thinking,* and these facets then are grouped in clusters around particular conceptual ideas or particularly significant physical situations (Minstrell, 1992). If I am clever in my choice or design of questions, they will elicit student thinking about some of the major issues for the unit, and the resulting facet coding of students' responses will allow me to diagnose what the students appear to be thinking about those issues.

Instruction to Address Students' Thinking. By using the diagnostic information, I can more effectively choose or design experiences that engage students' thinking and foster deeper understanding. I try to create situations in which students hear and consider each other's ideas and then have a chance to test those ideas against experimental results, modifying their ideas as needed (diSessa & Minstrell, in press). Because transfer of understanding generally requires that learners see and apply the ideas in several diverse contexts, my students participate in several (usually five or more) problem tasks or lessons designed to develop understanding of these and related ideas.

Frequently, students' attention is drawn to the surface features of situations from which they infer solutions. For example, during an interaction (e.g., a collision) between two objects, if one object is larger, heavier, stronger, or more energetic, then typically beginning physics students will infer the one with "more" will exert the larger force. In science, one usually has to look beyond the surface features to more abstract principles. Thus, when I am teaching about forces during interactions, I create situations in which students can investigate and judge the extent to which surface features affect the observed outcome. For example, I create situations in which students can see that the relative size, strength, activity of the interacting objects, and so on have no bearing on which exerts the larger force on the other during an interaction. In general, I want students to move from explanations based on surface features to explanations based on principles—a hallmark of expertise in many disciplines (Chi et al., 1981).

Activities With Purpose. Many teachers choose activities simply on the basis of what is in the next section of the text, but frequently the student perceives that the sequence is arbitrary, and that the activities are "strung together" without connected purposes. All teachers have heard the question, "Why do we have to do this?" The answer, of course, should *not* be, "Because you are going to need this for the next chapter/course." That may be part of the reason, but it disregards their "why" question, and in so doing, diminishes their motivation.

Frequently, there are multiple curricular purposes for what is happening in class at any particular time. At a surface level, the class is trying to answer the question or solve the problem before them. But, at a deeper level, they are trying to understand a class of situations related to content goals for the discipline. And, at a still deeper level, they are trying to understand the epistemology of the particular discipline. The epistemological question relates not only to understanding the discipline, but also to what it means to learn. So, at any given moment, the class may be learning how to solve a particular problem, how to approach a class of problems, how to know when to apply particular ideas or procedures, how one comes to know something in this discipline, and the general nature of learning. Of course, for the student there are more extrinsic purposes like having fun with friends, getting a good grade, or finishing the task. Managing these multiple purposes is part of gaining expertise in teaching.

To achieve my purposes, I need to help students to balance freedom to explore and the constraint necessary to carefully control experimentation in their approach to learning; when to hypothesize and to gather rough data, and when one needs to measure and observe carefully. For example, in order to determine whether one quantity or quality is a factor in determining an outcome, one may need to manipulate a variable with rather rough, gross changes while carefully controlling other variables. By contrast, in order to determine the specific, functional relation between variables, one must carefully measure the various values of the manipulated variable and then carefully measure the associated values of the dependent variable, as well as carefully controlling all other variables.

Cycles of Diagnosis and Relevant Instruction. Within the unit of study, I and the students want to know how their learning is progressing. One approach that my colleagues at the University of Washington and I have designed to address this has been to develop a computerized Diagnoser that incorporates pairs of questions (Hunt & Minstrell, 1994; Levidow, Hunt, & McKee, 1991). The first question is phenomenological; that is, it asks "What would happen if . . . ?" after which the system makes a preliminary diagnosis on the basis of the facets of students' thinking discussed earlier. The second question that the Diagnoser presents is about associated reasoning—"What reasoning best justifies the answer you chose?" On the basis of the students' response to this question, the system makes a secondary diagnosis. Because a necessary aspect of science is that there is reasoning associated with answers, the system looks for a match between the two diagnoses and reports on apparent consistency or lack thereof. The system then prescribes relevant prior class experiences to be considered or simple new experiences to be conducted. Each prescription is associated with a particular facet diagnosis. Thus, I try to tie my instruction to the conceptual needs of students as evidenced by the diagnostic assessment.

Through class discussions, laboratory activities, and group problem solving, I try to know and understand what students are thinking and adjust my instruction accordingly in order to foster more effective learning. Part of the tacit knowledge accompanying expertise in teaching is this knowledge of what the students are thinking, how they will respond when confronted with a particular problem situation, and what one might do to stimulate them to rethink their understanding. With the facet clusters and technology like the Diagnoser, I hope to be able to make more explicit some of these tacit instructional decisions that I and my teacher colleagues make as a result of years of experience in the classroom.

Maintaining an Inquiry Environment to Foster Learning

Understanding a discipline involves asking, and attempting to answer, questions that will deepen the understanding of the community of learners. Therefore, the learning environment should support the asking and answering of questions.

Questions and Questioning. The expert teachers whom I've observed ask questions that require their students to think, and encourage their students to ask thinking questions as well (Minstrell, 1978; vanZee & Minstrell, 1997a). Although expert teachers ask questions to help students clarify their observations, they seldom bother with questions requiring simple rote learning of facts or procedures. These teachers ask for predictions, interpretations, and explanations, and they ask for justifications (e.g., "How do you know what you know?" "Why do you think that will happen?"; Arons, 1983).

In contrast, the questioning of inexpert teachers "fishes" for a particular, acceptable answer—usually rotely determined and memorized. Such questions are unlikely to get students thinking in the best ways. Rather, they suggest that the teacher (or the text) is the authority and that the students should guess the accepted answer. Expert teachers also foster the asking of questions by their students. They want students to ask each other questions that will stimulate reflection about critical ideas or events in the natural world. They model asking and responding to questions in an open, respectful manner. To get students to respond to their own community of learners when they ask me a question, I reflect their questions back to the class. This method has value for their later intellectual development and professional practice. They will not always have some authority who knows the answer, but all their lives they will have colleagues who are likely interested in investigating the same questions. Thus, I reflect their questions back out to the community of inquiry in order to teach them to rely on each other rather than relying on the teacher in the construction of their understanding (vanZee & Minstrell, 1997a, 1997b).

After asking questions, I try to model listening—to hear the meaning behind what students are saying. Many teachers ask a question and listen for what they want to hear, take that as confirmation that the thinking is representative of the class, and then move on. Expert teachers are able to keep the inquiry open. Opening my mind to listen for the meaning from some of the more disparate voices in my classes has yielded interesting information that has caused me to change substantially what I do during instruction. For example, once, when I was idealizing situations (a common practice of physics teachers), I "waved away" friction. The students were still concerned about air resistance, so I waved that away as well. "Assume there is no friction, assume there is no air in the room. Now what would happen in the situation?" At that point I wanted to hear them talk about the "idealized" motion that would ensue. I did hear some of that, but I heard other things from quiet voices off to the side of the conversation. "Then, everything would just drift off the table and float around the room," someone said. I was tempted to hear only the motion answer I wanted to hear, but I didn't. I probed further. "So, what would actually happen with no air?" Several more students joined the argument. "With no air, there would be no gravity and everything in the room would just drift around." What they were telling me was that air pressure is what causes objects to weigh something—that downward push by air is the mechanism of gravity. Without air, things wouldn't weigh anything. This has had profound effects on the way I now teach about the nature of gravity and its effects (Minstrell, 1982).

Although it might seem that listening to, and hearing, what students are saying is part of what all teachers do, that isn't the case. There is a tendency for a listener only to hear that the student doesn't have the idea or procedure he or she wants the learner to have. Then, typically, the listener tells or shows the student the "right" way to answer the question. This is likely another of those tacit pieces of knowledge in teaching. When I am in a classroom with another teacher, I frequently feel the need to call attention to what I believe to be the meaning behind the words or actions just exhibited by a student. Then, I test my inference by asking the student another question that would be sensitive to my inferred idea about the students' thinking.

The tacit knowledge here is to be able to think like a novice—to hear the ideas of the beginning learner. I now do this fairly naturally, but it took a few years of practice to get into the habit of always asking, "What is the learner really saying here? How might that make sense to him or her?" If, after listening to the student, I can't answer these questions, I now take the time to probe for that understanding with additional questions. In some cases I probe with the entire class with oral or written questions. In situations where the idea seems to be coming from one or only a few students, I take up this line of questioning with them separately.

Teachers can effect better learning if they exhibit wait time after asking thinking questions and after a student has presented his or her answer. Wait time is the time a teacher waits after asking a question and before interjecting a comment or calling on another student. Pause time is the time a teacher waits after the student responds and before the teacher evaluates or otherwise speaks (Rowe, 1974). Rowe found that if teachers could increase their wait time and pause time to something above 3 seconds (the average is about 1 second), students' answers were longer, more thoughtful, and more on target. Also, students who hadn't kept up with fast-paced questioning were now responding in constructive ways.

Appropriate questioning and listening are not easily learned by most new teachers. It typically takes substantial coaching during their initial teaching experiences and periodic "reminders" throughout their career. This is especially difficult for prospective teachers who are predisposed to listen without hearing, who talk a lot, or who talk quickly. If all students are to have an opportunity to think, they need time and silence during which to gather and process their thoughts.

Conducting Discussions. In large or small group discussions undertaken for the purpose of generating understanding, expert discussion leaders do two things that may to be at cross purposes. They guide students to be *critical of ideas* suggested by anyone, but at the same time they guide students to be *respectful and supportive of people* as they take the risk to share their ideas. After asking the student for an answer or for their sense of the situation, I ask why that makes sense (e.g., "What experience leads you to say that makes sense?"). After hearing the student, I try to remain neutral with respect to evaluating the statement, paraphrasing it in a tone and words that support the student's contribution and acknowledge the aspects of what was said that makes the statement seem plausible. "OK, what you are saying is ____, and that seems plausible because of your experience with ____. Others have had this experience as well, and it seems that it might be relevant. Let's hear what others have to say about it." Frequently I have students share their ideas with one other student and then in small groups before requesting ideas from the class as a whole. To free students to be critical of ideas, I may divest any particular student of the idea by writing out students' ideas and offering them as coming from the class rather than coming from particular individuals. Then I might ask how a reasonable person might come to this conclusion.

One tacit aspect of expertise associated with discussions is knowing "when to hold 'em and when to fold 'em." Expert teachers encourage students to voice their questions, but they don't let the class discussion get so far afield that the class loses the story line of the inquiry. Those teachers have sufficient command of the subject matter that they know what questions, issues, and ideas to allow the discussion to follow and which lines of inquiry will pull the class too far afield. I begin a unit with my own handwritten map of the territory and ideas I want to visit. Then, in each of my classes, I check off which ideas we've visited and whether the ideas were simply mentioned, initially developed, or fully developed during the preceding discussion. In this way I will know, during later discussions or other lessons, where in the territory a particular class has been. If some issue or idea gets introduced that is not on my original list, I need to decide on the spot whether it is worth following in this discussion. Keeping the map helps to reduce the number of decisions that I need to make "on the fly."

DEVELOPMENT OF PROFESSIONAL EXPERTISE

How is professional expertise in teaching developed? Expert teachers whom I have known do not acquire expertise simply by listening to lectures about content, about learning, or about pedagogy. Although I have seen gifted beginning teachers, the sort of expertise I have described typically requires guided practical experience and ongoing professional development throughout a career. In addition to having resources and opportunities available to them, it requires significant desire and time investment on the part of the developing teacher. The development of what expertise I have as a teacher has paralleled my development as a learner. I have experienced and observed the world of the classroom, enjoyed the guidance of a mentor, interacted within a community of colleagues, and taken on my own investigations into the nature of teaching and learning. The benefits I enjoyed as a developing learner about teaching are similar to those that I attempt to create in the environment for learning for my precollege students.

Informal Observation and Reflection on Experience

My early teaching experiences offered opportunities to explore environments for teaching and learning. When I used a traditional style of teaching, in spite of the fact that my students and administrators thought I was a good teacher, I knew that the learning product fell short of what I desired and expected. I then explored other approaches incorporating more or less structure, more or less multimedia, more or less student autonomy, and so on. With each approach, I observed what happened with my students and what aspects of the approach seemed to foster what attitudes and learning by my students. These experiences were important to my development of a coherent personal view of teaching and learning.

As I was gathering my own personal experience, I also observed other teachers. I considered what aspects of their models of teaching made sense to me—which were coherent with my developing "theory" of teaching and learning.

Relationship With a Mentor

Extremely important to my development was having a personal mentor. Mine was Arnold Arons, who at the time was a physics professor at the University of Washington. He helped me become more aware of what I could do as a teacher to affect the cognition of my students. While we taught, side by side, within physics programs for teachers, there were occasions when he looked on as I interacted with these "students." The feedback he gave me was practical and yet fit my developing coherent view. When he saw me showing students what to do, he would coach me to make them more responsible for their learning: "Keep your hands in your pockets and make the students show you what they would do to answer the question." "You have two ears and one mouth, use them in that proportion," he would say when he saw me telling the students what to do or how to think.

Also, he modeled these aspects when I asked him a question about physics. He made me do the thinking about the subject, about the question I asked, and about how I might construct a sensible answer to the question. He was a good role model for productive tutorial interaction. As his student, I felt more responsible for my own learning, and I learned more about my own capabilities as a learner. I felt more empowered and wanted my own students to feel this empowerment. I adopted and adapted many of his methods of teaching interaction.

Active Participation in a Professional Network

Many teachers, especially physics teachers, experience isolation. They go into their classroom, close the door, and they are pretty much on their own with the exception of a rare day of observation by an evaluator. This limits their opportunities for growth. Early in my career, I had the opportunity to participate in the development of the Project Physics curriculum (Holton, Rutherford, & Watson, 1970). As a field consultant teacher, I met other teachers and discussed the effects of our lessons. We compared results on assessment items and shared different approaches to improving our curriculum and instruction. Later, as a result of working on an advanced degree, I met and had the opportunity to consult with experts in mathematics, physics, psychology, and educational measurement. I also helped to coordinate local area physics teachers' meetings in which we shared expertise from the disciplines and from the classroom. These activities provided me with a social and professional network that expanded on my personal knowledge and experience. My interactions with Arons, Hunt, and other teachers improved my understanding of science, of learning, and of teaching. In turn, I felt that I contributed to their understanding of the practical issues of the classroom.

Because these experiences had been important to my development, I and my colleague Earl Hunt are now creating networks, both face to face and electronic, in which classroom teachers and discipline specialists can share their expertise. By teachers having access to expertise in other classrooms and in other scientific disciplines, it should be easier for them to take on professional inquiry within their classes. At the same time, discipline specialists may gain a better understanding of the nature of the classroom and the dynamics of teaching and learning.

My Own Classroom Inquiry

The development of professional expertise in teaching also requires the opportunity and support for pursuing one's own line of inquiry. I have benefited from having the freedom to ask and attempt to answer questions about my students' learning and to design and test instructional interventions for effecting better learning (Minstrell, 1984). That freedom required support from my school community, especially students, parents, and administrators. I have also enjoyed the benefit of access to resources in and out of school. Without these opportunities and resources, I likely would not have been motivated to strive for excellence. I am still, and suspect I will always be, striving to better understand the nature of learning and teaching. Having that freedom has kept me from stagnating as a professional.

SUMMARY

Teaching is a complex, ill-structured problem. Expertise in teaching requires a theoretically coherent view of teaching and learning. Although expertise in teaching requires depth of understanding of content knowledge, it also requires an understanding of the nature of learning and pedagogical knowledge specifically related to the learning and teaching of the particular discipline. A significant aspect of this pedagogical knowledge involves knowing how to create and maintain an environment of inquiry for learners.

Development of expertise in teaching goes beyond what can be learned in classes; it takes a predisposition for observation and reflection on one's experiences as a teacher and learner. A mentor can help stimulate the reflection and can model expertise in teaching and learning. Because teaching expertise involves accumulation of experience, it is useful for teachers to participate in networks of professionals. New teachers can learn from the experiences of other new teachers as well as from more experienced teachers. Finally, expert teachers tend to adopt an attitude of personal and professional inquiry about what happens in their classes.

ACKNOWLEDGMENTS

Preparation of this chapter was supported in part by a grant from the James S. McDonnell Foundation Program of Cognitive Studies for Educational Practice. The ideas in this chapter are those of the author and do not necessarily represent the ideas of the foundation.

REFERENCES

Arons, A. (1983). Achieving wider scientific literacy. *Daedalus, 112*(2), 91–122.

Bruer, J. (1993). *Schools for thought: A science of learning in the classroom.* Cambridge, MA: MIT Press.

Camp, C., & Clement, J. (1994). *Preconceptions in mechanics: Lessons dealing with students' conceptual difficulties.* Dubuque, IA: Kendall Hunt.

Carpenter, T. (1988). Teaching as problem solving. In R. Charles & E. Silver (Eds.), *The teaching and assessing of mathematical problem solving* (pp. 187–202). Reston, VA: The National Council of Teachers of Mathematics.

Chi, M., Feltovich, P., & Glaser, R. (1981). Categorization and representation of physics problems by experts and novices. *Cognitive Science, 5,* 121–152.

diSessa, A., & Minstrell, J. (in press). Cultivating conceptual change with benchmark lessons. In J. Greeno & S. Goldman (Eds.), *Thinking practices.* Mahwah, NJ: Lawrence Erlbaum Associates.

Holton, G., Rutherford, J., & Watson, F. (1970). *The Project Physics course.* New York: Holt, Rinehart & Winston.

Hunt, E., & Minstrell, J. (1994). A cognitive approach to the teaching of physics. In K. McGilly (Ed.), *Classroom lessons* (pp. 51–74). Cambridge, MA: MIT Press.

Kilpatrick, J. (1987). Problem formulating: Where do good problems come from? In A. Schoenfeld (Ed.), *Cognitive science and mathematics education* (pp. 123–147). Hillsdale, NJ: Lawrence Erlbaum Associates.

Levidow, B., Hunt, E., & McKee, C. (1991). The Diagnoser: A HyperCard tool for building theoretically based tutorials. *Behavior Research Methods, Instruments, and Computers, 23*(2), 249–252.

McDiarmid, G. W., Ball, D. L., & Anderson, C. W. (1989). Why staying one chapter ahead doesn't really work: Subject-specific knowledge. In M. Reynolds (Ed.), *The knowledge base for the beginning teacher* (pp. 193–205). Elmsford, NY: Pergamon.

Minstrell, J. (1978). *An evaluation of the University of Washington program in physical science and science teaching for the elementary school teachers.* Unpublished doctoral dissertation, University of Washington, Seattle.

Minstrell, J. (1982). Conceptual development research in the natural setting of the classroom. In M. B. Rowe (Ed.), *Education for the 80's: Science* (pp. 129–143). Washington, DC: NEA.

Minstrell, J. (1984). Teaching for the development of understanding of ideas: Forces on moving objects. In C. Anderson (Ed.), *Observing science classrooms: Observing science perspectives from research and practice. 1984 AETS yearbook* (pp. 53–73). Columbus: Ohio State University.

Minstrell, J. (1989). Teaching science for understanding. In L. Resnick & L. Klopfer (Eds.), *Toward the thinking curriculum: Current cognitive research. 1989 Yearbook of the Association for Supervision and Curriculum Development* (pp. 129–149). Alexandria, VA:

Minstrell, J. (1992). Facets of students' knowledge and relevant instruction. In R. Duit, F. Goldberg, & H. Niedderer (Eds.), *Proceedings of the international workshop: Research in physics learning—Theoretical issues and empirical studies* (pp. 110–128). Kiel, Germany: The Institute for Science Education, University of Kiel (IPN).

Minstrell, J., & Matteson, R. (1991). *Engaging students' thinking* [Video recording]. Mercer Island, WA: Mercer Island School District.

Rowe, M. (1974). Wait-time and rewards as instructional variables: Their influence on language, logic and fate control. *Journal of Research in Science Teaching, 11,* 81–94.

Schön, D. (1987). *Educating the reflective practitioner: Toward a new design for teaching and learning in the professions.* San Francisco: Jossey-Bass.

Shulman, L. (1987). Knowledge and teaching: Foundations of the new reform. *Harvard Education Review, 57,* 1–22.

Tobin, K., & LeMaster, S. (1992). An interpretation of high school science teaching based on metaphors and beliefs for specific roles. In E. Ross, J. Cornett, & G. McCutcheon (Eds.), *Teacher personal theorizing: Connecting curriculum practice, theory, and practice* (pp. 115–136). Albany: State University of New York Press.

vanZee, E., & Minstrell, J. (1997a). Using questioning to guide student thinking. *The Journal of the Learning Sciences, 6*(2), 229–271.

vanZee, E., & Minstrell, J. (1997b). Reflective discourse: Developing shared understanding in a physics classroom. *International Journal for Science Education, 19*(2), 209–228.

EPILOGUE

What Do We Know About Tacit Knowledge? Making the Tacit Become Explicit

Robert J. Sternberg
Yale University

The chapters of this book have in common the authors' attempts to make the tacit become explicit: to open up the inquiry into a kind of knowledge that usually remains buried beneath the surface, both individually and organizationally. What conclusions can we draw about tacit knowledge that cross across the six different fields of professional practice considered in this book?

In order to give order and structure to the answer to this question about general conclusions, the answer is divided into three parts: (1) Nature of Tacit Knowledge, (2) Acquisition of Tacit Knowledge, and (3) Utilization of Tacit Knowledge. In order to maintain the flow of this final chapter, contributors of points regarding tacit knowledge are noted parenthetically after their points are made.

THE NATURE OF TACIT KNOWLEDGE

Tacit knowledge is procedural knowledge that guides behavior but that is not readily available for introspection. Tacit knowledge is intimately related to action and relevant to the attainment of goals that people value (Horvath et al., chap. 3). Often, the knowledge takes the form of rules of thumb for what to do under what circumstances (Wagner, Sujan, Sujan, Rashotte, & Sternberg, chap. 9). Moreover, tacit knowledge is important to success in a field, no matter how much codification of "rules for success" there may be

(Marchant & Robinson, chap. 1). The reason for this state of affairs is simple: As soon as knowledge is made explicit and even codified, it simply ceases to serve as an equally important source of individual differences. Thereafter, other knowledge that has not yet been made explicit or codified takes its place as an important source of individual differences. For example, if, in the past, knowledge about the importance of buying the boss a gift for his or her birthday was tacit, those who possessed this knowledge were at a distinct advantage. But if now everyone knows and uses this piece of knowledge, it will no longer serve to differentiate employees, in the boss' eyes, and most likely some other as-yet tacit knowledge will take its place.

As this example points out, tacit knowledge can become explicit. Moreover, tacit knowledge and explicit formal knowledge interact. For example, knowing whether a particular explicit rule applies in a situation represents such an interaction. It is also often important to ascertain whether there is a useful analogy between a past case or experience and a present case or experience, and determining whether there is such an analogy may depend on tacit knowledge (Marchant & Robinson). If the analogy is only superficial and does not apply in actual context, more harm than good may be done by applying the analogy and overextrapolating from past experience (Hatsopoulos & Hatsopoulos, chap. 8).

Although tacit knowledge is important to success, organizations often give no recognition to it. There are a number of reasons for this fact (Spaeth, chap. 2). One is that tacit knowledge may conflict with codes of ethics or action, with the organization not wanting to acknowledge this conflict (Spaeth). For example, payoffs may be required to get a contract, but payoffs may be against company policy and even against the law. A second reason is that whereas tacit knowledge should foster both self-awareness and contextual sensitivity, it can turn into self-serving deviousness, and thus thwart rather than help a company (Ulmer, chap. 4). For example, an employee may see how to use the system in a company to advance his or her personal interests, even if it is at the expense of the company. A third reason is that tacit knowledge is so situated by nature that it may resist any kind of useful codification that actually could be recognized (Patel, Arocha, & Kaufman, chap. 5). A fourth reason is that technical knowledge is often essential for the use of tacit knowledge, and so the organization may not see the tacit knowledge as really distinct from the technical knowledge (Gregory, chap. 10). A fifth reason is that it may sound like knowledge that is learned only by chance, and organizations may not want to believe, or want others to believe, that workers (or students) would acquire what they need to know only by mere accident (Spaeth).

People at different levels of a hierarchy of expertise or of a hierarchy of an organization may have different tacit knowledge, and use the tacit knowledge they have differently. For example, novices tend to rely too heavily on standard kinds of operating procedures and, worse, to overestimate the validity of their tacit knowledge (Cimino, chap. 6). Often, they do not know which questions could be asked, or they know those questions but also know many others not worth asking as well, and they just don't know which ones are actually worth asking (Cimino). Or they may ask the right questions but then follow through incorrectly on the answers they receive (Cimino).

Tacit knowledge at the upper levels of an organizational hierarchy often emphasizes organizational values. At the lower levels of the hierarchy, tacit knowledge may emphasize personal values. People in the middle management of an organization may get caught in the middle trying to satisfy both organizational and personal constraints (Horvath et al.). Unfortunately, people at the bottom of a hierarchy, for all their concerns with persons, may not have adequate tacit knowledge about developing subordinates and, thus, in attempting to give advice, may give some that is not very good (Horvath et al.). Tacit knowledge for leadership is also different from tacit knowledge for followership, so that as people rise in a hierarchy, they need to learn new kinds of tacit knowledge that reflect their changing role in the organizational hierarchy (Horvath et al.).

THE ACQUISITION OF TACIT KNOWLEDGE

Tacit knowledge is acquired largely from experience, preferably from experience in the environment where the tacit knowledge later will be needed (Patel, Arocha, & Kaufman). Sometimes it is hard to know whether tacit knowledge is relevant to a situation because the user of the knowledge no longer remembers the environment in which the knowledge was acquired (Spaeth). Moreover, relevant tacit knowledge can change over time, and if the individual does not remember when the tacit knowledge was acquired, he or she may apply knowledge that has become out of date and even potentially harmful (Cimino).

Tacit knowledge is best acquired in an environment that fosters inquiry and that encourages criticism of ideas but respect for the people who have proposed the ideas (Minstrell, chap. 12). The individual also needs a personal predisposition for observation and learning (Minstrell), because it is not experience per se that matters to acquisition of tacit knowledge, but instead how well one utilizes that experience in order to acquire the knowledge that can be extracted from the environment. Professionals who work in isolation may have only limited opportunities to acquire tacit knowledge, and thus may become poorly adapted to their work environments (Minstrell). In any environment, an important element of acquiring tacit knowledge is knowledge of the right person or people from whom to acquire it (Hatsopoulos & Hatsopoulos), because poor models can be worse than no models at all.

Unfortunately, the environment often makes acquisition of tacit knowledge difficult (Horvath et al.; Marchant & Robinson). Organizations may actually have incentives for not wanting to disseminate this knowledge. For example, if tacit knowledge leaks to competitors, it may be used against the original organization, and if this knowledge is disseminated to employees, the employees may learn things about the organization that the organization does not want them to learn. Hence, tacit knowledge may be hidden.

Unusual situations are often better opportunities for acquiring tacit knowledge than are common situations (Marchant & Robinson). If acquisition of tacit knowledge is via some kind of problem-based curriculum, then the problems and the attendant situations need to be as much like real ones as possible (Patel et al.). The danger of abstracting prototypes for action from such situations is that the situations may not apply equally well in other situations, leading to possible misuse of the tacit knowledge (Cimino).

UTILIZATION OF TACIT KNOWLEDGE

Often, people have a wealth of tacit knowledge they can apply to a given situation, and the hard part of problem solving is deciding what tacit knowledge to apply in a given situation (Marchant & Robinson). Understanding what tacit knowledge to apply in a given situation can spell the difference between success and failure in that situation (Spaeth). Sometimes codified principles can serve as a basis for deciding what tacit knowledge to apply (e.g., knowledge about promotions, discipline, or whatever), but even codified principles can be subject to alternative interpretations, making it difficult to know how to use these principles in an actual problem-solving situation (Marchant & Robinson).

Utilization of tacit knowledge can be highly pattern driven, meaning that given a certain pattern of circumstances in the environment, one deploys certain tacit knowledge to deal with those circumstances (Patel et al.). But patterns and situations can be ambiguous, and the more ambiguous they are, the more likely the use of tacit knowledge will be incorrect or at least less than optimal (Patel et al.). Experts tend to have a better sense of what information fits a pattern better than do novices, and also will be more likely to encode the patterns than will novices (Cimino). Ironically, one can have excessive tacit knowledge that might seem applicable in a situation, so that one becomes confused as to exactly what tacit knowledge to apply (Cimino).

Utilization of tacit knowledge often needs to take into account the roles of other people. Sometimes an extremely important part of tacit knowledge is anticipating how others will react in the face of one's actions (Hatsopoulos & Hatsopoulos). In competitive situations, it may be important to be aware of the tacit knowledge available to competitors, and to anticipate and counter their actions by anticipating their reactions, based on the tacit knowledge they are anticipated to have (Marchant & Robinson).

Almost all work in organizations, or even individually, occasionally involves selling, whether of products or ideas. Thus, utilization of tacit knowledge for sales is important in virtually all occupations (Wagner, H. Sujan, M. Sujan, Rashotte, & Sternberg). Part of this knowledge is that of how to read other people, and either figure out their wants or create in them a want they do not yet have but are ready to have (Gregory). In sales situations, an individual may have to convince potential clients that a competitor's tacit knowledge is wrong (Marchant & Robinson), for example, regarding the usefulness of a product or service the competitor offers.

There are many forces in the environment that render the utilization of tacit knowledge difficult. These forces result in even adequately acquired tacit knowledge being improperly rendered when it is needed for problem solving and decision making.

First, tacit knowledge can lead to deteriorating performance as actions become self-reinforcing of the status quo (Argyris, chap. 7). In such cases, tacit knowledge can be a conservative force when there is a need for change (Ulmer). People and organizations exhibit powerful defensive routines that are activated when situations arise that present a potential embarrassment or threat to them (Argyris). Although the people and organizations believe that these defensive routines are necessary for their survival, the routines may in fact jeopardize their survival (Argyris). Ironically, the more the need to break the status quo, the more the pressure may end up being to leave it exactly in place. Often, tacit knowledge seems to be rational or logical not because it is, but because we so desperately want it to be (Hatsopoulos & Hatsopoulos), resulting in our taking action that seems logical but really is not.

Second, people and organizations often believe they are following designs for action that they are not actually following (Argyris). In other words, they may believe they are acting in ways to guarantee the future, when in fact they are acting in precisely the opposite way. Worse, their defensive reasoning leaves them unable to see that what they are doing is hampering the attainment of their own goals (Argyris).

Third, preconceptions of various kinds—what may be called *folk conceptions*—can interfere with our use of tacit knowledge (Torff, chap. 11). For example, we may have tacit knowledge as to what to do in a given situation, but bring into that situation prior beliefs that actually go against the tacit knowledge we have (Torff), resulting in our acting less than optimally. It is difficult to fight these folk conceptions, because most people are unaware they even have them. For example, if a teacher has been brought up with a certain negative stereotype about an ethnic group, this stereotype may interfere with the teacher's doing the best for the student because of the prior belief that the student is hopeless in any case.

Finally, we may find ourselves in situations in which our codes of ethics or societal codes of ethics conflict with tacit knowledge about what to do in a given situation—in essence, creating opposing motives (Cimino). For example, what a doctor or lawyer or business executive believes he or she needs to do to serve a client best may leave the individual open to exposure to a lawsuit. As a result, the professional or business executive may end up acting in a way that he or she actually knows does not optimally serve the client, but rather serves the individual's own need for self-protection in a litigious environment.

To summarize, tacit knowledge can be a source of highly effective performance in the workplace. It can also be a source of decline and ultimately of failure. The efficacy of tacit knowledge depends on its being acquired and then being effectively used. We hope that this book has been helpful in suggesting effective strategies for the acquisition and use of this important kind of knowledge.

Author Index

Subject Index

D

Great , sales, 158

M

N

O